Changing Minds

Changing Minds

How Aging Affects Language and
How Language Affects Aging

Roger Kreuz and Richard Roberts

illustrations by Enkhtur Bayarsaikhan

The MIT Press
Cambridge, Massachusetts
London, England

This book was set in Stone Serif by Westchester Publishing Services. Printed and bound in the United States of America.

Library of Congress Cataloging-in-Publication Data

Names: Kreuz, Roger J., author. | Roberts, Richard (Richard Miller), 1959– author.
Title: Changing minds : how aging affects language and how language affects aging / Roger Kreuz and Richard Roberts.
Description: Cambridge, MA : MIT Press, [2019] | Includes bibliographical references and index.
Identifiers: LCCN 2018046136 | ISBN 9780262042598 (hardcover : alk. paper)
Subjects: LCSH: Older people—Communication. | Language and languages—Age differences. | Language disorders in old age. | Psycholinguistics.
Classification: LCC BF724.85.I57 K74 2019 | DDC 401/.9—dc23
LC record available at https://lccn.loc.gov/2018046136

10 9 8 7 6 5 4 3 2 1

Siblings are the only relatives, and perhaps the only people you'll ever know, who are with you through the entire arc of your life.
—Jeffrey Kluger, *Salon* (2011)

This book is dedicated to our brothers and sisters.

Contents

Acknowledgments

Roger would like to thank Tori Tardugno, whose efficiency and professionalism provided him with the time he needed for working on this project. He is also grateful to Tom Nenon for his support and encouragement.

Richard would like to thank Jennifer Berne, who brought his understanding of the topics we discuss to a new level by pointing out the symmetry between the influences of aging on language and language on aging. This insight is reflected in the subtitle of the book. Jeff Newbern and Mark Seaman graciously opened up their homes, hearts, and minds. Richard always appreciates Greg Morgan's ability and willingness to explain complex concepts in terms even Richard can understand. And to Joyce Bender and Mary Brougher, who bring hope and joy wherever they go—lead on!

On Okinawa, Richard would like to thank Joel Ehrendreich, Aya Toyama, Makiko Tasato, and Shina Miyagi for their willingness to give him the time needed to complete this book. They keep work from feeling like work. And thanks also go to Anup Patel and the team at the Fogelman Executive Center for their hospitality.

Both Roger and Richard thank Phil Laughlin for his faith in this project and his continued support. We appreciate the hard work of everyone at the MIT Press, including Judy Feldmann, Molly Seamans, Susan Clark, and Stephanie Cohen. Thanks also to copy editor Bill Henry. Special thanks go to the Benjamin L. Hooks Institute for Social Change, which generously provided space for us to work. Three anonymous reviewers provided helpful comments at the beginning of the project. We are particularly thankful to Susan Fitzgerald, Gina Caucci, and Alex Johnson, whose keen eyes kept a number of infelicities from finding their way into the finished work.

Because Richard works for the US Department of State, he would like to make clear that the contents of the book are his opinions and not those of the US government.

Roger Kreuz and Richard Roberts
Memphis, Tennessee
July 2018

Prologue

A common metaphor for thinking about one's life is to conceptualize it as a journey.[1] One of the companions we have on this journey is our native language. We acquire it, seemingly without effort, in infancy and early childhood. And in some sense, we acquire it a second time during formal education as we learn to read and to write. During these years of schooling, though we already possess the body, we learn about our language's skeleton and its connective tissue—its grammar and rhetorical styles. Our vocabularies become larger. We discover the great heights to which language can soar in the prose, poetry, and plays of our native tongue.

And then what? For most people, that seems to be end of the story. We may choose to study other languages, but we typically do so in ways that are fundamentally different from how we acquired our native language. And our native tongue itself may seem like a finished product once our schooling ends. Over time, we will learn additional vocabulary and strive to become better writers, but we typically don't spend a lot of time thinking about it. Language is simply one of many skills that we might possess, like being able to juggle or to play the piano. But most jugglers don't move on to study Newton's laws of motion, and most pianists don't feel compelled to study compositional counterpoint or the history of piano building. For most, juggling, playing music, or using language is simply a means to an end and not an end in itself.

Contrary to popular belief, the consensus of researchers who study cognitive aging is that "language systems remain largely stable across the lifespan."[2] But does this mean that language is unaffected by aging? Language is a complex phenomenon that relies on other cognitive processes, such as perception and memory. Anyone who struggles to recall someone's name is reminded of language's dependence on memory. Furthermore, as we strain to hear our partner in a noisy restaurant or to read the menu, language's dependence on perception becomes clear as well.

It may be helpful to introduce an analogy at this point. Imagine that someone has built an elaborate sand castle on the beach. The castle itself might be impressive, but sand castles are only as strong as their base. And as the tide begins to roll in, the foundations of the castle are threatened. The lapping waves will hollow out its underpinnings, and after a time, the elaborate towers and arches may perch precariously on an increasingly eroding base. Nevertheless, the castle may still stand, even though part of its sandy foundation has been washed away.

So how does language hold up as the tide of aging wears away at the foundation of perception and memory? Does a changing mind foreshadow the decline of our linguistic abilities? As it turns out, language, like a well-built sand castle, can display surprising resilience in the face of cognitive disruption. The complete story of language change in adulthood is one of decline, adaptation, resilience, and even enhancement.

These seemingly contradictory outcomes are easier to understand if we conceptualize language not as a unitary phenomenon but as a set of interacting components. Viewed broadly, language consists of four major domains: listening, speaking, reading, and writing. Keep in mind that each domain is part of one integrated, multicomponent system. The underdevelopment of one domain for any individual does not mean that he or she lacks linguistic ability. For example, throughout the world, many people never learn to read or write, but we wouldn't characterize those individuals as not having language. In fact, on the evolutionary timescale, the entire human species was illiterate until relatively recently. In addition, blind and low-vision individuals experience the written word but do so through other senses, like touch and hearing. Likewise, Sign languages are as expressive and as rich as any spoken language.

Researchers who explore the relation between language and aging do so using a variety of perspectives. In an admittedly simplistic way, we can subdivide the principal approaches into four broad perspectives: developmental, physiological, social, and cognitive. Obviously, these ways of studying language are not mutually exclusive, and many topics that we discuss draw on the contributions of all four.

From a developmental perspective, researchers focus on how the four domains are acquired and change over time. For example, when we are born, we are predisposed to identify the sounds of our native language and go on to master the rudiments of speaking in our second year. Reading and writing formally begin with preschool and kindergarten, with reading largely mastered by middle school and writing in high school. Of course, few would claim that they ever totally master writing.

From a physiological perspective, research on language and the brain suggests that the four domains are capable of functioning somewhat independently. This is perhaps most apparent when we consider the effects of brain injury. The disruptions caused by stroke or head injury can be surprisingly selective. A person who suffers a stroke might lose the ability to read, for example, but may have little or no impairment in the ability to speak and understand language, and even the ability to write may be preserved.

From a social perspective, researchers take into account the roles of society and culture to study language use. For example, they look at the effects of stereotypes on aging and the social consequences of ageism. These researchers also study the ways in which the demographics of aging are changing societies around the world.

From a cognitive perspective, researchers may zero in on specific constituent processes of language, such as word finding. At the other end of the cognitive spectrum, researchers also explore how the domains operate more broadly, such as in writing about trauma. Because we are cognitive scientists, we draw primarily on research from this field.

In the early chapters, we focus on how aging affects the four domains of language. We begin by discussing some of the methodological issues that confront researchers who study aging across the life span. We then consider some of the cognitive processes that underlie language ability. It's interesting to note that the number one fear of people in their sixties, seventies, and beyond is the loss of memory.[3] For this reason, we explore memory's role in listening, speaking, reading, and writing. For example, is the word-finding difficulty that many older adults complain about an issue of memory, language, or some combination of both?

In the later chapters, we examine the profound impact of language on aging. The development of more nuanced and insightful ways of communicating allows individuals to achieve a heightened self-awareness. It increases our skill in understanding not just our own experiences and motivations but those of others as well. The maintenance and even improvement of some linguistic abilities serve as a counterweight to offset declines in cognitive processes like perception and memory.

Harnessing our linguistic abilities to enhance the quality of our lives seems to have no upper limit. Among other topics, we look at the benefits conferred by reading, reflective reminiscing, and conversation. Bottom line up front: it behooves us all to use language in the service of healthy aging.

1 Setting the Stage

One of the most famous journeys in US history was made by the Corps of Discovery under the command of Meriwether Lewis and William Clark. But before their expedition to the Pacific Northwest could begin, they had to make a great many preparations. The explorers had to secure supplies to meet every conceivable need, such as food, tents, clothing, and medicine. In addition, Lewis, as the group's leader, had to familiarize himself with a wide range of subjects such as astronomy, botany, navigation, and surveying. His mastery of these disciplines helped to ensure the expedition's success when facing the unknown.

In a similar way, in this first chapter, we review a variety of topics that are important to keep in mind when thinking about language and adult development. These topics, while diverse, are of fundamental importance and will set the stage for discussing the interaction between language and aging in later chapters.

Language by Design

Psychologists seem to be stagestruck. In fact, stage theories of development have so permeated our culture that it may seem natural to believe that people pass through different stages as a normal part of getting older. But whether or not such an assessment is accurate has a great deal to do with how we study changes across the life span.

In stage theories, certain identifiable characteristics describe the passage from one stage to another. Consider the work of the developmental psychologist Jean Piaget. He was interested in how children's thought processes changed as they grew. For Piaget, children in the first stage of his cognitive theory do not understand that objects exist in the world when the object is out of sight.

Here's an example of how the presence or absence of object permanence could be measured. Imagine a young child sitting in front of a circular train set. A train is running on the track, and in one of the cars is a large plastic dinosaur. At one point the train enters a tunnel. When the train exits the tunnel, the dinosaur has been replaced by a teddy bear. This would surprise those of us who possess a sense of object permanence. If a train enters a tunnel carrying a dinosaur, then we expect it to exit the tunnel with the same dinosaur. Therefore children who show surprise at this strange turn of events could be said to have achieved object permanence.

If we compare a group of younger children to a group of older children within Piaget's first stage, we would expect to find that the younger children are not consistently surprised by the switch from a dinosaur and teddy bear, whereas the older ones are. This kind of comparison is an example of a cross-sectional study. Cross-sectional studies compare people at different ages performing a particular task. When people at different ages show differences in a task, we can reasonably assume that those differences reflect different points of development. Many studies that compare younger and older adults are cross-sectional in design.

The methodology of such studies naturally leads to results that emphasize discontinuity and abrupt transitions. In other words, conclusions drawn from cross-sectional designs can offer support for the idea of discrete stages in development.

Instead of recruiting groups of different ages, however, one could simply track the performance of the same individuals over time. Such longitudinal studies are more likely to show gradual changes and continuity. However, these types of studies are difficult to conduct. For one thing, they require the ongoing participation of the subjects, who may move away or decide not to continue their involvement. These studies are also expensive and, most significantly, can take years or decades to complete. For all these reasons, researchers use longitudinal studies less commonly than cross-sectional studies.

Here's an example of why this matters. If we went to an elementary school and measured the heights of children in kindergarten through grade five, we would find that children in different grades have different average heights. A graph of these differences might look like a set of steps. But if we measured the heights of children consistently every few months over the six-year span, we'd see a gradual change in their heights. A graph of these results would look more like a gently upward-sloping line.

Researchers can make use of a techinque that fuses these two approaches. It is called a cross-sequential design. In cross-sequential designs, different people at different ages are measured (as in a cross-sectional study), but the same people are also tracked for a short period (as in a longitudinal study). Studies that use cross-sequential designs are not as common as longitudinal and cross-sectional studies. However, they illustrate the importance of thinking about distinct stages of development as likely resulting from more gradual processes.

Comparing Apples to Oranges

Just as we saw in the last section, researchers can also use cross-sectional studies to compare the abilities of younger and older adults. At first blush, it seems like this should be a straightforward enterprise. Younger and older adults could be recruited and given a battery of tests to complete under controlled laboratory conditions. The performance of the two groups could then be compared to see if any statistically significant (i.e., reliable) differences exist in the cognitive abilities of the two groups. And while this procedure does seem straightforward, the reality is more complex. It turns out that younger and older adults differ on a variety of dimensions, not just their age. As a result, determining which factors are responsible for any differences in performance is often difficult.

Imagine a cognitive aging study conducted in the United States in the year 2015. Researchers recruited participants who were about age twenty-five (the younger group) and about seventy-five (the older group). The groups thus had a fifty-year difference in age, but did they vary systematically in other ways?

To begin with, it is likely that they differed in the number of years of formal education they had attained. Participants in the younger group would be more likely to have had at least some higher education under their collective belts, whereas the older group were of college age in the early 1960s—a time when fewer people attended college. In 2015, 65 percent of adults aged 25 to 34 had attended at least some college, whereas only 50 percent of adults age 65 and over had done so.[1] Therefore, if our sample of younger and older adults was typical, then the participants varied by educational attainment as well as by age.

The type of education was probably quite different as well. Our younger group would have started elementary school in the mid-1990s, just as the internet was taking the world by storm. As a result, they are "digital natives" for whom the internet has always been part of their lives. For the older group, the online world didn't exist until they were in their mid-fifties. They are "digital immigrants" who may use the internet and all that it offers, but the web hasn't always been a pervasive part of their lives.[2]

And younger people are simply smarter than older people—at least if we equate intelligence with performance on an IQ test. It's important to realize that intelligence is a relative attribute, since we have no absolute measure of a person's intellect. When we say that someone has "average" intelligence, we mean that their measured IQ is about 100. Intelligence tests are carefully constructed and standardized so that the median performance ends up at that nice, even number. The problem is that people have been getting better on such tests over time. For example, the

Wechsler Intelligence Scale for Children (WISC) has been res-
tandardized four times since it was developed in 1949. This has
been necessary because average performance kept improving, at
a rate of about three IQ points per decade in the United States.[3]
Therefore revisions of the test have been designed to be a bit
more difficult so as to maintain the average score at 100.

This phenomenon is called the Flynn effect, after James
Flynn, who documented large gains in IQ over a forty-five-year
period in the United States,[4] and then in more than a dozen
other countries.[5] Although the Flynn effect seems quite real,
researchers have put forth varied explanations for what might
be causing it. As we have already seen, younger people tend to
have more education than their elders. However, research has
also suggested that parental literacy, changes in family structure,
and improvement in nutrition and health may all play a role.[6]
Researchers also debate whether the Flynn effect is continuing[7]
or even reversing.[8] For our purposes, it's enough to note that it
represents yet another way that younger and older adults may
differ besides chronological age.

Older adults also differ from younger adults in that they
are ... well, older! Although aging does not cause cancer or car-
diovascular disease, declines in a person's health can also lead to
cognitive decline. But this would not mean that the cause of the
decline was age per se. Rather, the cause would be the underlying disease state. Although researchers may want to recruit only
older adults without any known cognitive impairment, they
cannot always be sure. For example, although most people never
develop dementia, the longer one lives, the more likely it is to
occur. For people who do develop dementia, the cognitive consequences may show up years before a diagnosis is made. And

the procedures that researchers use to screen for dementia may not be sensitive enough to pick up these early declines. As a result, studies that purportedly consist of older participants without cognitive problems may actually contain individuals who are in the early stages of cognitive decline.[9]

Let's consider another issue. If you are an older adult who is completing a battery of cognitive tests in a lab, you might well be worried about your performance in a way that simply isn't comparable to younger adults. You are well aware of the negative stereotypes regarding the memory abilities of older adults. You may recall recent occasions when you weren't able to think of a word you were searching for. You might begin to worry that the tests you are taking will objectively document your cognitive decline. These concerns may increase your anxiety and cause you to perform poorly. For younger adults, however, the memory and perceptual tasks might seem more like a video game and arouse no anxiety.

This example illustrates a general phenomenon called stereotype threat, which was first documented by the social psychologists Claude Steele and Joshua Aronson. They gave black and white participants a difficult test of verbal ability. One condition emphasized that the test results would reflect one's intellectual ability. In other conditions, the test was described as either not diagnostic of ability or simply a challenging exercise. Steele and Aronson predicted that believing the test measured intellect would activate negative stereotypes for the black, but not the white, subjects. The results were consistent with that hypothesis. Black participants performed worse than white participants in the stereotype threat condition, but about the same as the white participants in the nonthreatening conditions.[10]

Researchers have observed stereotype threat in older adults as well. When a task was described as requiring memorization, older adults displayed higher levels of stereotype threat than younger participants.[11] Stereotype threat in older adults may be moderated by a variety of factors. Thomas Hess and his colleagues found that participants in their sixties were more affected by stereotype threat than those in their seventies. In addition, stereotype threat was also higher for participants who had more education.[12] Presumably, adults in their sixties are just beginning to confront memory decline, and because educational attainment depends on memorization, any perceived decline would be more concerning.

Education, intelligence, and stereotype threat are just three of the ways, besides chronological age, that younger and older people differ. We should keep such confounding factors in mind when interpreting the results of cross-sectional research studies on language and aging.

Components of Cognition

After reaching a certain point in life, we all begin to experience the effects of aging on our bodies. Joint and muscle stiffness, a slower metabolism, and declines in endurance are all too common as we get older. But the brain undergoes changes as well, and this affects a number of cognitive systems. Let's begin by reviewing some of the cognitive processes that are affected by aging.

At a general level, evidence points to a decline in how quickly our cognitive processes operate. This is referred to as a decline in processing speed.[13] This slowing has a detrimental effect on functioning for a wide variety of cognitive tasks, such as visual matching (identifying similar objects) and visual search (comparing two pictures for differences),[14] to name just two.

Memory also seems to change over time. But different types of memory change differently. For example, let's compare short-term memory and working memory, which share similarities but are in fact different. Short-term memory can be thought of as the ability to maintain items in conscious awareness, such as a telephone number, a list of words, or a set of directions. The size of short-term memory doesn't change greatly with age. However, this is not true for working memory, which involves transforming the information in some way, such as recalling a list of words in reverse order. The ability of working memory to perform such transformations shows age-related declines.[15]

Another aspect of cognitive processing is called executive function, which coordinates a range of cognitive activities such as memory, perception, attention, decision making, and language. If cognitive processes are likened to members of an orchestra, then executive function serves as the conductor. Many aspects of executive function have been studied, and these aspects typically show declines across the adult life span.

For example, one important role of executive function is inhibitory control. This refers to the ability to attend to one thing while ignoring another. Anyone who drives a car is familiar with deciding what requires attention and what can be ignored. Noticing children who are playing catch by the side of the road could require a sudden shift in attention, whereas a barn on the side of the road would not and could be safely ignored. An example of a laboratory task that assesses inhibitory control is the Stroop task, in which participants are asked to name the colors that words are printed in. However, the words themselves are color names, such as the word "red" printed in blue ink. The

automatic recognition of the word "red" interferes with subjects' ability to rapidly provide the correct response (in this case,
"blue"). If inhibitory control is affected by age, then we would
expect older adults to do worse on the Stroop task, and they do.[16]

Another role of executive function involves switching rapidly
between two different tasks, such as writing a memo and scan-
ning email as it arrives on a computer screen. Most people believe
that they are good at dealing with such multitasking, but in fact
each attentional switch incurs further processing costs. And as
you may have guessed by now, older adults experience more disruption in task switching than do those who are younger.[17]

Such cognitive declines give us legitimate cause for concern.
However, one should keep in mind several caveats to prevent
drawing overly pessimistic conclusions about the mental faculties of older adults. One of these is that people are highly variable in their susceptibility to the effects of cognitive aging. For
example, researchers who followed a set of older adults over a six-
year period found considerable individual differences: some participants showed significant declines, whereas others changed
hardly at all.[18] And though many people in their sixties and
early seventies believe they are experiencing significant cognitive decline, research suggests that meaningful changes don't
become common until after age seventy-five.[19]

Another important issue to keep in mind is that we know less
about what happens to our language abilities during middle age.
To some degree, this is a consequence of how research is typically
conducted. Experimenters need participants to study, and so language research is often carried out using so-called convenience
samples, such as schoolchildren or college students. Researchers
at the other end of the age spectrum have often drafted retired
college alumni and nursing home residents into their studies.

However, assuming an eighty-year life span, about half our lives is spent between the end of our formal education and retirement. Consequently, we know much less about language during middle adulthood (age range: 25–65). This "missing middle" problem makes it more difficult to tell a complete story about how language changes across the adult life span.

One final caveat: age-related cognitive decline can be offset in a variety of ways. These include cognitive and physical activity, social engagement, and proper nutrition.[20] Some training regimens for older adults, such as working-memory exercises, also appear to confer some benefits.[21]

So far, we have only considered outcomes linked to healthy cognitive aging. Other outcomes can have a far greater negative impact. A variety of brain diseases and neurocognitive disorders, collectively referred to as dementia, can have a devastating effect on a person's ability to think, reason, and remember. Although Alzheimer's disease is the most common form, there are many others as well, such as vascular dementia and Lewy body dementia. The cruelty of such disorders is that they strip away not only a person's cognitive abilities but also their personality and sense of self.

The decline into dementia is typically not a sudden one. Many individuals go through a transitional state during which they may be identified as having mild cognitive impairment (MCI). Doctors make this diagnosis when someone experiences mental difficulties that do not interfere with daily living. A variety of tools for assessing MCI have been developed. One commonly employed battery is the Mini-mental State Examination (MMSE), which clinicians use to assess whether someone is experiencing garden-variety forgetfulness and occasional lapses in judgment or something more serious.[22] MCI may or may not progress to dementia. In addition, we should note that many other conditions can mimic symptoms of dementia, including depression, stroke, urinary tract infections, brain tumors, head injury, and alcohol abuse.

Doctors today cannot definitively diagnose Alzheimer's disease while a person is alive. An autopsy of the brain is necessary to detect the telltale amyloid plaques and neurofibrillary tangles that are characteristic of the disorder. However, the presence of such plaques and tangles does not mean that someone exhibited signs of the disease when she was alive. In some cases, it appears that protective factors prevent the physiological changes in the brain from manifesting themselves as a loss of cognitive function. Researchers use the term *cognitive reserve* to refer to the sparing of cognitive abilities.

As an example, imagine you wanted to fly a rocket ship to the moon. You would probably make sure you had lots of extra fuel. That way, even if you went off course, you'd still have enough to get there. Cognitive reserve works in this way as well. Some people seem to have extra cognitive capacity that helps them function, even when their brains show neuronal degeneration.

A number of factors seem to correlate with increased cognitive reserve. These include higher educational and occupational attainment as well as participating in a wide range of different leisure activities.[23] And such protective factors also seem to be beneficial in the case of other causes of dementia, such as Parkinson's disease.[24]

Finally, we should stress that dementia is not an inevitable consequence of aging. A majority of people will experience normal aging—and normal cognitive decline—without the devastating cognitive effects of dementia. And the incidence of dementia may in fact be declining as educational levels rise and the rate of stroke is reduced.[25]

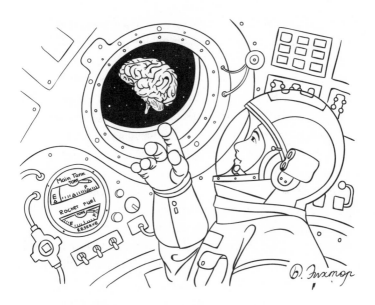

The Compensation of Language

When the ripe fruit falls
its sweetness distills and trickles away into the veins of the earth.

When fulfilled people die
the essential oil of their experience enters
the veins of living space, and adds a glisten
to the atom, to the body of immortal chaos.

For space is alive
and it stirs like a swan
whose feathers glisten
silky with the oil of distilled experience.
—D. H. Lawrence, "When the Ripe Fruit Falls"

What does it mean to age well? This is a difficult question to answer because it raises another question that must be answered first: what is the goal of aging? One potential answer could be to live as long as possible. But is outliving one's friends and family a worthy goal?

Maria Carney, a physician who specializes in gerontology and palliative care, estimates that 20 percent of Americans are elder orphans.[26] As the baby boom generation continues to age, this number is likely to grow. Carney and her colleagues define elder orphans as "aged, community-dwelling individuals who are socially and/or physically isolated, without an available known family member or designated surrogate or caregiver."[27] Sadly, these solo agers[28] are at an increased risk for untreated physical ailments, psychological problems, and in some cases elder abuse.[29] Although the needs of this group are beginning to be addressed, it seems clear that we should not define success solely by the number of candles on a cake.

Paul and Margret Baltes propose an alternative way to think about what it means to age successfully. Their approach measures success as the ability to adapt to the inevitable changes that come with aging by "forming a coalition between the human mind and society to outwit the limits of biological constraints in old age."[30]

The Baltes's approach posits that successful aging is the result of maximizing the gains and minimizing the losses of aging through a process of selective optimization with compensation (SOC). In other words, successful agers are those who select appropriate goals for themselves, find ways to optimize their own personal capabilities, and use external compensatory mechanisms to help achieve their goals. Defining successful aging as successful adaptation allows people to decide for themselves their own standard of success. In this way, SOC "enables people to master their goals despite, or perhaps even because of, losses and increasing vulnerabilities."[31]

Consider an example of how selective optimization with compensation worked for the artist who illustrated this book. Enkhtur Bayarsaikhan lives in Ulaanbaatar and grew up in the Mongolian countryside. He did not study English in school. Later he realized that his success as an artist was limited because he could not communicate with potential clients from other countries. But trying to learn English as an adult while working was a daunting task. And although he didn't know about SOC, he used its concepts to accomplish his goal.

First, he was careful to select an appropriate level of instruction. He found a school where other adults were also beginning English students and where he could arrange his classes around his work. Next, he optimized his English-language skills not only by going to class but also by seeking out extracurricular opportunities to practice. One way he did this was by taking advantage of the US Embassy's American Corner. There he was able to read English-language books and listen to presentations by native speakers. Finally, he compensated for his lack of fluency by always carrying a pad and pencil with him. When talking with English speakers, if the conversation reached an impasse, he could communicate by drawing pictures. These drawings later served as triggers for remembering his new vocabulary words.

Selective optimization with compensation can also serve as a roadmap for adults when they notice declines in certain abilities. For example, as processing speeds slow down, a person might start taking more time to solve a crossword puzzle. But since vocabulary size typically increases with age, the same person could choose more difficult puzzles to solve. In fact, it might be worth the trade-off. Finishing difficult puzzles slowly might be more satisfying than racing through easy ones. More practice

would be one way to optimize crossword puzzle ability, and the *New York Times* also offers a tutorial that could help improve skills in this area.[32] Finally, a cruciverbalist having difficulty coming up with answers to clues could compensate by keeping a crossword puzzle dictionary close at hand. Regardless of the task, therefore, selective optimization with compensation is one way to maintain a sense of accomplishment.

The appropriateness of the word "success" when it comes to aging has been called into question.[33] Using a word like success makes it seem like the variables that impact aging are all under a person's control, which is obviously not true. Moreover, claiming that there is a successful way to age could lead to blaming others for any perceived failure to do so. In addition, not all researchers who study aging would operationalize success the same way.[34] Inconsistencies in defining success might lead to ambiguity regarding what it means to succeed. Nevertheless, as we look at the impact of aging on language (and vice versa), we will point out examples of language helping us to select, optimize, and compensate for declines in cognitive and perceptual systems. Specifically, we now turn our attention to the changes in vision and hearing that can undermine the comprehension and production of language.

2 The Language of Sight and Sound

One of the ways that aging most noticeably affects both mind and body is our ability to see and to hear. In this chapter, we review the sensory and perceptual changes that directly affect the ability to comprehend spoken and written language.

Do You Hear What I See?

The terms *sensation* and *perception* are often used interchangeably. But they are not the same. Sensation refers to the act of getting an environmental stimulus (such as light or sound) to a place in the body where it can be converted into electrical (nerve) impulses. Perception, on the other hand, refers to the brain's interpretation of these impulses.

The process of converting an environmental stimulus into a nerve impulse is called transduction. Only certain, highly specialized cells in the body, called receptors, can do this. For example, the receptors in the eye are the rods and cones of the retina. The receptors for hearing are the hair cells of the cochlea.

Although we discuss only age-related changes in vision and hearing, transduction occurs for all our senses. In fact, if a researcher wanted to investigate extrasensory perception (ESP), then she would need to answer two questions: first, what is the environmental stimulus; and second, how is this stimulus converted into a nerve impulse?

Obviously, if someone shines a light in our ear, we don't hear light. But after transduction converts environmental stimuli into nerve impulses, all bets are off. For example, synesthesia is a condition in which the stimulation of one sense brings about additional perception in at least one of the other senses. Examples of this so-called blending, merging, or union of the senses would be seeing music or having the experience that chicken tastes triangular. The title of a recent study on olfactory-visual synesthesia exemplifies the concept: "Chocolate Smells Pink and Stripy."[1]

Researchers have identified at least sixty-one different kinds of synesthesia,[2] and it may be experienced by more than 4 percent of the population.[3] The most commonly studied variant is grapheme-color synesthesia, which occurs when a person associates specific colors with numbers or letters. The writer Vladimir Nabokov wrote about seeing distinct colors for letters of the alphabet. For him, the letter *t* was "pistachio," and the letter *u* was "brassy with an olive sheen."[4]

Although synesthesia is sensori-perceptual by definition, the psychologist Julia Simner points out that it may be primarily a linguistic phenomenon.[5] Approximately 88 percent of synesthetic experiences are triggered by speech sounds, words, letters, or numbers.[6] Likewise, synesthetes who use Sign language report linkages between colors and fingerspelled letters and signed numbers. It is interesting to note that the color associated with each manual sign seems to match its written counterpart.[7]

There are also developmental implications for synesthesia. Although it appears to run in families (Nabokov's mother and son were also synesthetes), consensus is building that the experience develops as a learning strategy. This hypothesis is supported by evidence that people who learn a second language later in childhood have higher rates of synesthesia. The language one learns may play a role as well. English is a language in which sounds and letters do not correspond to each other in a one-to-one fashion (think about how the word *yacht* would sound if all the letters were pronounced). The increased cognitive demand on learners of English appears to be reflected in higher rates of synesthesia.[8] Synesthesia can enhance memory for a wide range of tasks.[9] Grapheme-color synesthesia also appears to decline with age and is separate from age-related changes in the visual system.[10] Such a decline could reflect the primacy of synesthesia as a learning tool of childhood.

If synesthesia develops in children as a learning strategy, could adults learn it as well? The answer is an unqualified maybe. In their review of research aimed at teaching synesthesia to adults, Marcus Watson and his colleagues concluded: "Non-synesthetic participants in a number of training studies report experiences that sound quite similar to genuine synesthetic experiences. There are important differences between the effects of short-term training in adults and the long-term associations of synesthetes, but these are not enough to conclude that the two are qualitatively distinct."[11]

The idea that separate sensory systems can intertwine as perceptual systems has exciting implications for the sensory-related declines seen in adulthood. It should be clear that sensory problems are easier to correct than perceptual problems. For example, glasses adjust how light is focused on the retina. But a stroke in the visual cortex could leave a person blind, even though the eyes are not affected. Recent years have seen an explosion in the number of devices that bypass damaged sensory systems and create perceptual stimulation that the brain can interpret.

For example, the process of getting sound waves to the auditory cortex involves a Rube Goldberg–like chain of events. Sound waves travel down the ear canal and are converted into vibrations at the eardrum. These vibrations cause the three small bones of the middle ear to move in unison, sending pressure waves into the fluid of the cochlea. The disturbance of the fluid causes the hair cells to move, which sends neural impulses along the auditory nerve to the brain.

Damage to this system would have an immediate impact on hearing. For example, the ossification of the bones of the middle ear due to normal aging leads to declines in hearing. To correct for this problem, we can use hearing aids to amplify the sound waves as they begin the journey from the outer ear to the cochlea. But a device called a cochlear implant bypasses this pathway altogether and stimulates the auditory nerve directly. There is no age limit for receiving a cochlear implant. In fact, older adults who receive an implant after they have already learned language via hearing can rely on their previous experience to adapt to the implant. Cochlear implants try to mimic the action of the ear by converting sound waves into nerve impulses. But it is also possible to harness one sensory modality to improve perceptual awareness in another one.

For example, an artificial vision device (AVD) called a Brain-Port gathers visual stimuli through a small camera mounted in a pair of glasses. The device converts the visual information to an electrical signal and sends the signal to the tongue rather than to the optic nerve. (At present no AVDs can stimulate the optic nerve directly.) The tongue is chosen as the site for electrical stimulation because it has many tightly packed touch receptors (you know how sensitive the tongue is if you've ever literally bitten yours). Although this technology is new, results are encouraging, especially for object and word recognition for blind and low-vision adults.[12]

Devices designed to compensate for decrements in sensory input increase the efficiency of getting a stimulus to the receptors for transduction. But damage to brain cells from stroke or dementia, for instance, cannot be compensated for in this way. We explore the implications of this distinction for hearing and vision in the following sections.

A Look at Hearing

A man wondered if his wife had a hearing problem. One night he stood behind her while she sat reading.

"Honey, can you hear me?" There was no response, so he moved closer.

"Honey, can you hear me?" There was still no response, so he moved right behind her.

"Honey, can you hear me?"

"For the third time—*yes!*"

The inability to hear and understand spoken language is one of the most significant sensory issues that affects older adults. More formally, this inability is referred to as presbycusis (Greek for "old" and "to hear"). And although it creates a problem for hearing all types of sounds, we will limit our discussion to how presbycusis affects the comprehension of spoken language. Before discussing the causes of presbycusis, let's briefly consider the physics of the speech signal.

Children can hear sounds up to 20,000 cycles per second (which can be abbreviated as 20 kHz). Over time, we experience hearing loss at these high frequencies, and by age seventy-five, many people can hear sounds up to only about 13 kHz. Because hearing loss starts at higher frequencies, the sounds that make up speech are differentially affected. Vowels have most of their acoustic energy at lower frequencies, below 3 kHz, and so the perception of these sounds isn't greatly affected by hearing loss. Vowels are, however, the freeloaders; they're just along for the ride and don't do much of the work in making words sound different from one another. The heavy lifting is performed by the consonants, and some of them have a lot of their acoustic energy in higher registers (above 4 kHz). This is especially true for consonants that have a hissing quality, like /s/, /f/, /sh/, and /th/, as well as sounds like /k/ and /t/. To someone with significant hearing loss, phrases like "shake the sack," "face the facts," and "take the cat" might sound pretty much alike.[13]

A number of factors, unrelated to loud sounds in the environment, can cause or accelerate hearing loss. These include a genetic predisposition, conditions that stress the circulatory system, such as smoking and high blood pressure, and maladies such as diabetes and heart disease.[14] Having a high body mass may compromise blood flow to the auditory system and has also been identified as a risk factor for hearing loss. However, physical activity, even at moderate levels, reduces the risk.[15] Men are more affected than women, even when differences in occupational exposure to loud sounds are taken into account.[16]

Age-related hearing loss can also result from a variety of factors, only one of which is a person's cumulative exposure to loud sounds. Such exposure does damage and ultimately kills the hair cells in the cochlea. However, studies have demonstrated that even animals raised in completely quiet environments develop age-related hearing loss, so other factors must be at work as well. The most significant culprit may be the metabolic changes caused by aging. Specifically, humans experience an age-related decline in the efficiency of mitochondria, which function as the powerhouses for cells. This reduction makes it more difficult for the hair cells to generate the impulses that are sent to the brain.[17]

Hearing loss may also result from perceptual problems in the brain itself. The intelligibility of the speech of others can decrease over and above what one would expect based on the results of a hearing test. In such cases, traditional amplification via hearing aids is of limited use.[18] Training programs, such as learning to speechread, can help older adults optimize the hearing they do have.[19]

Furthermore, some linguistic environments are simply more challenging than others. Trying to follow one's conversational partner in a noisy environment offers a good example. Think of the din of competing voices in a busy restaurant, especially one with bare floors and walls, which cause lots of reverberation. To compensate, older adults try to make greater use of situational cues—relying, for example, on the predictability of words in particular contexts. However, compared to younger adults, they display poorer memory for the words they're trying to understand. Because they are trying to reallocate their attention to support the processing of speech, they have fewer cognitive resources available for memory.[20]

Paradoxically, though someone may have difficulty following a conversation, the problem might not be that their conversational partner's voice is too soft. In fact, many people suffering from age-related hearing loss report that noisy environments, such as in our restaurant example, are simply too loud. In such cases, the older adult may be experiencing an exaggerated perception of the loudness of sounds. This happens because the impaired hair cells mobilize neighboring cells to help out through a process known as recruitment. The net result is hyperacusis: a reduction in the range of the softest sounds that can be heard, and the loudest sounds that can be tolerated—truly the worst of both worlds.[21]

The joke at the beginning of this section illustrates an important truth about age-related hearing loss: the person with the problem may be the last one to acknowledge it. Many individuals who begin to struggle with hearing loss go through a period of denial; after all, it's easier to convince yourself that other people are mumbling than it is to confront a significant sensory problem.[22] Left untreated, the social isolation created by age-related hearing loss can adversely affect an older adult's quality of life.[23]

It may come as a surprise to learn that baby boomers, the first generation exposed to loud amplified music on a regular basis, may actually have better hearing than their parents' generation.[24] This could be due to a decline in smoking rates, lower rates of employment in industrial occupations, and a greater use of hearing protection. However, their own children may not be as fortunate, given the propensity of adolescents to listen to music via earphones at high volume.[25]

Tinnitus

Moving out from the cover of a tree, Treasury Department agent Brass Bancroft and his partner opened fire with their .38-caliber police pistols. A split second later, Lieutenant Bancroft fell back, suddenly gripped by pain, and grabbed at the side of his head. The injury that he had sustained was caused not by return fire but by the sound of his partner's gun, which had been fired six inches from his right ear.[26]

Although this incident was just a scene being filmed on a movie set, and caused by a pistol firing blank cartridges, the injury itself was all too real. Agent Bancroft was being played by the actor Ronald Reagan, the star of 1939's *Code of the Secret Service*, an otherwise forgettable Warner Brothers film about a counterfeiting ring and stolen Treasury engraving plates.[27] Reagan would appear in more than sixty movies during an acting career that spanned nearly thirty years. He would long remember this role, however, because the episode with the gunshot caused permanent damage to his hearing.

One of the most common outcomes of such acoustic trauma is tinnitus, which is frequently described as a ringing in the ears. By definition, such ringing is illusory: no such sound is present in the environment. Tinnitus caused by acoustic trauma can manifest itself in a host of ways and has been variously described as roaring, clicking, whistling, humming, chirping, hissing, sizzling, buzzing, or the constant ringing of a telephone.[28]

It is important to note that tinnitus isn't the same as presbycusis, the subject of the last section. Tinnitus caused by acoustic trauma is not age related, since such an episode can happen to anyone at any age. (Reagan was just twenty-eight when he starred in *Code of the Secret Service*.) However, as one's life unfolds, the odds of experiencing such trauma become greater. Simply put, the longer you live, the more likely you are to experience a variety of adverse events, such as being in a car accident, becoming the victim of identity theft, or experiencing acoustic trauma. And since most older adults suffer from presbycusis, many people mistakenly assume that tinnitus is just another facet of age-related hearing loss. It's also worth noting that ringing in the ears can be caused by a host of factors besides acoustic trauma, including a variety of disorders, diseases, viral infections, and even taking high doses of anti-inflammatory drugs, such as aspirin.[29]

Tinnitus from acoustic trauma and presbycusis share an underlying cause in that both result from damage to the hair cells in the cochlea. Although medical science has advanced a variety of theories to explain the perception of these phantom sounds, many researchers believe that auditory circuits in the brain become hyperactive to compensate for the loss of inputs from the damaged hair cells. An awareness of this fact, however, does nothing to mitigate the unbidden and unwelcome perception of the hissing, chirping, and roaring.

Unfortunately, the type of injury that Reagan experienced is far from being a rarity. At the milder end, many people may experience a ringing in one or both ears that lasts for only a few hours or days. However, about 5 to 10 percent of American adults experience chronic tinnitus, which can range from the merely annoying to the severe and debilitating.[30] Exposure to very loud sounds is, to some degree, an occupational hazard, with soldiers, musicians, and machine operators experiencing a greater degree of risk than accountants or librarians, for example.[31] Veterans of the US military who served in Iraq or Afghanistan commonly report issues related to hearing loss or tinnitus as the result of exposure to weapons fire or improvised explosive devices.[32] Pete Townshend, Neil Young, Eric Clapton, and Ozzy Osbourne are just a few of the many performing musicians who suffer from chronic tinnitus, which for them was likely caused by industrial-grade sound amplification.[33] In 2013, Liza Minnelli claimed her tinnitus was the result of her father shouting excitedly in her ear when she won the Academy Award for Best Actress in *Cabaret* in 1973—the month she turned twenty-seven.[34]

Tinnitus can also be caused by Ménière's disease, a relatively rare but debilitating condition marked by vertigo (feelings of dizziness and spinning). It can occur at any age but typically arises in one's forties or fifties. Some researchers have speculated that Vincent van Gogh suffered from this disorder, and that he cut off his ear in a desperate attempt to stop the auditory hallucinations that he was experiencing.[35] Another sufferer of Ménière's, the astronaut Alan Shepard, had his training cut short by the disease. He was much more fortunate than Van Gogh, however. Shepard underwent a surgical procedure for Ménière's and at forty-seven went on to command *Apollo 14*, becoming the oldest person to walk on the moon.[36]

Other actors besides Reagan have developed tinnitus by being subjected to the blanks and explosions employed on movie and television sets. Steve Martin, for example, experienced acoustic trauma from the sound of pistol shots during the filming of *¡Three Amigos!* in 1986, which led to persistent tinnitus. And both William Shatner and Leonard Nimoy experienced hearing loss and tinnitus as the result of pyrotechnic explosions during the first season of filming for the 1960s *Star Trek* television series.[37] Shatner went on to serve as a spokesperson for the American Tinnitus Association.

As with age-related hearing loss, living with the results of acoustic trauma can be difficult. The ability to hear speech that is being masked by phantom ringing or whistling can engender feelings of frustration and social isolation. When asked about his tinnitus, Steve Martin replied, "You just get used to it. Or you go insane."[38] A large-scale study of tinnitus sufferers has documented the impact it has on quality of life, such as increased awareness of bodily pain.[39] And although doctors have no cure for tinnitus, researchers are beginning to identify factors that may be protective. Women who ingest higher amounts of caffeine, for example, seem to have a lower incidence of tinnitus than women who consume less.[40]

The effects of tinnitus can, in some cases, be reduced by wearing hearing aids, since the amplification of environmental sounds can mask the ringing. The social stigma of using such devices was partly offset by Reagan himself, who began wearing one in his right ear in 1983, during his first term as president. In fact, he was the first chief executive to wear a hearing aid in public.[41] The device finally provided him some relief from the hearing loss that he had been living with for nearly forty-five years—ever since his star turn as Treasury agent Bancroft.

Voice Quality

When we hear someone that we can't see and don't know, such as during a voice-only phone call, we might have to guess his or her age and gender. When it comes to gender, we often base our guess on the pitch of the person's voice. Children and women typically have higher-pitched voices than men, in part because their vocal tracts are shorter. And the effects of testosterone lower the adult male voice.[42] We don't always guess correctly, however. Some readers might remember Dan, played by the actor Brian Reddy, the "high talker" from a *Seinfeld* episode. We're better at determining their approximate age, however. Why should this be? In this section, we explore the acoustic characteristics of the aging voice.

When people speak, air from the lungs is forced through the vocal folds, which are stretched across the top of the trachea, causing them to vibrate. These vibrations are then modified by other parts of the vocal tract, called articulators. Some of these are familiar: the tongue, teeth, gums, and lips all function as articulators. Less familiar articulators such as the palate, which is the roof of the mouth, and the nasal cavity can also get involved. In fact, certain sounds, such as /m/ and /n/, are produced by releasing the acoustic energy entirely through the nose instead of the mouth. (This is why your voice sounds different when you have a cold and your nasal cavity is partially blocked.)

A number of physiological changes in the older vocal tract lead to changes in voice quality. One result is that men and women begin to sound more alike: men's voices typically become higher pitched, and women's voices deepen. The aging process also leads to a decrease in control as the vocal muscles atrophy, which in turn causes the vocal tremor and hoarseness that many people associate with older voices.[43] Vocal muscle issues can also cause the glottis, which is the opening between the vocal folds, to close incorrectly. This so-called glottic incompetence creates turbulence and imparts a characteristic breathiness to the aging voice.[44] Rheumatoid arthritis can cause nodules to form on the vocal folds, and this also results in a hoarse-sounding voice.

Taken as a whole, these and other vocal changes are referred to as presbyphonia (old voice), or age-related dysphonia (difficulty in speaking).

The prevalence of presbyphonia is not easy to determine, since people seek medical intervention only when such problems become severe. In addition, voice quality is inherently subjective and difficult to quantify. However, a large-scale study using a random sample of Korean adults (average age: 72) provides an estimate. Researchers examined the vocal tracts of the participants with a laryngoscope and analyzed the resulting videos for the presence of abnormalities or nodules. Demographic, medical, and behavioral information was also collected. The researchers found that about 9 percent of their participants could be classified as dysphonic. Voice quality issues were associated with having a higher body mass index, asthma, COPD, and thyroid disease, among other factors. Participants who lived in cities were at greater risk than those who lived in rural areas.[45]

Significantly, voice quality issues did not increase with advancing age. And activities that many people associate with changes in vocal quality, such as smoking and consuming alcohol or coffee, did not emerge as culprits.[46] Cigarette smoking does seem to cause voice deepening and "creakiness," at least in men, but some of these effects are reversible; the voices of older men who stop smoking reverted to their normal pitch over time.[47] It is worth noting, however, that serious voice quality issues in older adults are uncommon and usually result from a separate underlying pathology, such as emphysema.[48] However, changes in voice quality are more consequential for some people than others. Singers often complain that their vocal ranges decrease with age.[49]

So what causes people to infer that a speaker is older? Think for a moment about how you might describe the stereotypical voice of an older person. Adjectives such as "hoarse," "weak," "squeaky," or "shaky" likely come to mind. When asked to describe an older voice, both younger and older adults readily generate such terms, suggesting that a stereotype really does exist. It's also worth noting that two-thirds of the terms were judged as negative (like those just listed), while only about a sixth, such as "gentle" and "considerate," were seen as positive. This is yet another reflection of ageist attitudes held by people of all ages, even older adults themselves.[50]

We should not discount the psychological effects of changing voice quality. In one study, researchers followed a group of older men over a five-year period to assess vocal changes. Even though these individuals weren't suffering from presbyphonia, their voices still underwent changes, such as becoming rougher and weaker. As a consequence, perhaps, these men were more likely to avoid social events like large parties.[51] Not surprisingly, this withdrawal from social participation is even more pronounced among those who seek treatment for voice disorders.[52] Commonly mentioned problems were the fatigue caused by talking for extended periods and concerns about being perceived negatively because of impaired voice quality.

These issues are significant because social isolation is associated with numerous negative health consequences for older adults.[53] Using the SOC metamodel described previously, rather than withdraw from social events entirely, people can choose to attend events where they don't need to raise or strain their voices to be heard. Examples might include meeting friends at coffee shops and restaurants without blaring music. In addition, they might choose to attend events for shorter periods of time or go to places where speaking would be at a minimum, such as the theater or a concert. They could also compensate for changes in vocal quality by texting rather than phoning.

Surgical procedures to address issues like the vocal fold bowing that leads to glottic incompetence include the injection of material, such as Teflon, into the vocal folds. An even more permanent solution can be obtained with implants that provide support for the vocal folds.[54] Noninvasive therapies for age-related voice disorders, such as vocal function exercises, can also be highly effective at optimizing a person's voice quality. One study found that just four voice therapy sessions, provided over a five-month period, led to improved quality of life scores for participants compared to those who chose not to undergo therapy.[55]

Speaking of Vision

The human eye is wondrous, complex—and inelegant. Basically, it's a kludge for converting light energy into vision. We won't discuss this entire process, but it's important to be aware of some of the points of failure that can lead to a loss of vision, especially in middle and older adulthood.

After light enters the eye through the pupil, it encounters the crystalline lens, a transparent structure that is thicker in the middle and thinner along the edges. Around the edges are ligaments attached to muscles, which can tighten or relax to change the shape of the lens. This change of shape results in sharp vision for nearby and faraway objects. When the muscles relax, the center of the lens becomes thicker, allowing us to see nearby objects clearly. In contrast, when the muscles tighten and the lens flattens, faraway objects come into focus. In both cases, the job of the lens is to direct the light to the central part of the retina, called the fovea. This tiny pit is packed with light-sensitive receptor cells that provide the sharpest vision.

For the lens to do its job properly, it must be transparent. And it is, mostly. However, a number of factors can cause the lens to become cloudy. Typically, this happens quite gradually over decades as proteins in the lens break down and clump together, causing a cataract in one eye or the other. However, some people are born with cataracts. In either case, the consequences can range from a blurring or dimming of vision to total blindness. Cataracts are, in fact, the most common cause of blindness throughout the world.[56]

So what causes cataracts to form? Some people are genetically predisposed to develop them. However, cataracts can be caused by a host of other factors, such as diabetes, high blood pressure, obesity, smoking, eye surgery, and the long-term use of steroids and statins. In addition, cataracts may be caused by those invisible wavelengths of light called UV (ultraviolet) rays—the same wavelengths that give you a bad sunburn.[57] All these factors, taken together, are reasons why the likelihood of developing cataracts rises with one's age. In the United States, more than half of all adults will develop cataracts by the age of seventy-five.

Fortunately, the debilitating effects of cataracts can be offset by a procedure that involves removing the crystalline lens and implanting an artificial replacement. In the past, the lens was surgically extracted from the eye, but the most common procedure today involves using ultrasonic sound waves to break up the lens, which can then be removed via suction through an incision.[58] A clear silicone replacement is then inserted to substitute for the natural lens. The procedure completely restores vision, and if a multifocal lens is implanted, it can also correct for other conditions, such as farsightedness and astigmatism.

While issues with the lens can be repaired in this way, plenty can still go wrong in other parts of the eye. For example, the light-sensitive lining at the back can separate from the layer below, much like wallpaper separating from a wall. Such retinal detachments can be surgically repaired, although depending on the severity, some vision may be lost.

Another age-related disorder has an unknown cause but is often signaled by the buildup of yellowish deposits called drusen in the area that surrounds the fovea. This macular degeneration doesn't lead to total blindness, but it does make many activities, such as reading, much more difficult. Although it's uncommon in people younger than sixty, with less than 1 percent of the population affected, its incidence increases to nearly 12 percent in people who are over the age of eighty.[59]

Glaucoma is another way that vision can become impaired. It is a disorder in which a buildup of fluid in the eye causes pressure and ultimately damages the optic nerve. Glaucoma is the leading cause of blindness in people over the age of sixty. People with diabetes are at risk of developing what is called diabetic retinopathy. It is caused by damage to the small blood vessels and nerve cells in the eye and subsequent reduced blood flow. It is the leading cause of blindness in middle age, although treatments, if employed before the retina has become highly damaged, can be extremely effective. These include cauterizing blood vessels with lasers, medication, and surgery.[60]

These visual disorders are important for us to consider because they can lead to serious issues with reading and writing. Older adults who lose the ability to read later in life may feel deprived of a significant source of information about the world, as well as the ability to read for pleasure. Because emails and texts have largely replaced telephone calls, losing the ability to write can also lead to a sense of social isolation. It's instructive, therefore, to see how several well-known authors did not let failing vision prevent them from practicing their craft.

Writers whose careers were affected by blindness include the English poet John Milton (1608–1674), who is thought to have suffered from either retinal detachments or glaucoma. Nonetheless, he compensated by dictating some of his greatest work, including *Paradise Lost*. The Irish writer James Joyce (1882–1941) struggled with failing vision caused by iritis, a painful inflammation of the iris, as well as a series of ill-fated eye surgeries. To compose *Finnegans Wake*, he wrote in crayon to make the letter stokes thick enough for him to read. The Argentine author Jorge Luis Borges (1899–1986) became totally blind by age fifty-five owing to an inherited disorder and largely shifted from writing short stories to poetry so that he could keep an entire work in his mind at once.

Modern medical interventions, such as cataract surgery, have greatly reduced the incidence of blindness. And tactile reading systems designed for blind or low-vision individuals have also been developed. The best known of these was developed by the French educator Louis Braille (1809–1852). He lost his vision early in life and perfected his system in the 1820s and '30s. Patterns of raised dots in a 2 x 3 grid stand in for the letters, numbers, and punctuation used in visual writing systems. By the mid-twentieth century, more than half of blind and low-vision American schoolchildren could read Braille. Since then, its popularity has declined as these children have been mainstreamed into public schools. In 2009, fewer than 10 percent of legally blind Americans could read Braille.[61]

A reliance on Braille has also been offset by newer technologies, such as the Kurzweil reading machine developed in the 1970s. This device uses optical character recognition and text-to-speech software to read printed material out loud. Later developments, such as the JAWS screen reader for Microsoft Windows, have had an enormous and positive impact because they allow low-vision and blind people to work in any office environment.[62] And audiobooks recorded onto cassettes, and later CDs and digital formats such as MP3 files, provide individuals with impaired vision access to an enormous amount of written material. Clearly, these technologies are helpful to older adults who develop vision problems as well.

Presbyopia

Most people will never develop glaucoma or macular degeneration, and although cataracts are common in older adulthood, they can be remedied through surgery. Another process, however, affects the vision of nearly everyone who reaches middle age: losing the ability to clearly see objects that are close at hand. This condition is referred to as presbyopia (from "old" and "eye").

To understand why this happens, we need to consider the physiology of the eye once again. In the last section, we described how muscles tugging on the crystalline lens allow the lens to change its shape. The process is called accommodation. Like any system that relies on mechanical action, however, the parts can wear out, and accommodation becomes less effective over time. Although the exact causes of presbyopia are still a matter of debate, several processes are at work. For example, over time the lens becomes stiffer and less able to alter its shape. In addition, because the lens continues to grow throughout one's life, this thickening may play a role as well.[63] Cellular and chemical changes also occur in the lens over time.[64] The net result is that the light entering the eye is no longer focused when it reaches the fovea, and the consequence is blurry vision for nearby objects.

Unfortunately, an important part of our visual world is the region a couple feet from our eyes. This is where we hold things in our hands to examine or read them. The development of presbyopia causes us to hold things farther away so that some degree of accommodation can occur. In the case of text, the letters become smaller and harder to read. When things are too small to see, our natural tendency to bring them closer only serves to make them blurry. It's a lose-lose situation. The development of presbyopia is gradual, and the age of onset varies, but many people begin to notice a problem in their mid-forties, and virtually everyone is affected by age fifty. Put another way, many people will spend half their lives coping with this problem.[65]

Just as a defect in the Hubble space telescope was fixed with corrective lenses, so middle-aged and older adults can resort to eyeglasses to offset insufficient accommodation. But glasses designed for close-up vision don't correct for other kinds of visual problems. As a result, an individual may need multiple kinds of correction. One solution to this difficulty is to equip glasses with lenses of different optical powers. Since people tend to look down when examining close-up objects, bifocals correct for presbyopia in just the bottom part of the lens. Benjamin Franklin has traditionally been recognized as the inventor of these "double spectacles."[66] The later development of trifocals by John Isaac Hawkins in the nineteenth century allows for correction in viewing middle distances as well. The twentieth century saw the development of progressive and multifocal lenses, which provide a gradient of correction across the lens, as well as the deployment of similar techniques in wearable contact lenses.[67] Surgical interventions have also been devised.[68]

But glasses, contact lenses, and surgery only correct for problems in getting light to the retina. Changes in vision can also occur after the light has been converted into nerve impulses. For example, although we normally think of visual acuity in terms of how well we can read an eye chart, other dimensions are also important. One of these is contrast sensitivity, or the ability to distinguish the bright and dim elements of a visual scene, which declines with age.[69] It's possible, for example, to have 20/20 vision and still have difficulty reading when there isn't sufficient contrast between the letters and background, as in low-light situations. Given that the source of this problem lies in the brain, not the eyes, we need a different type of correction.

A group of psychologists led by Denton DeLoss explored whether perceptual training would benefit older adults. The researchers had college students and older adults (average age: 71) engage in training designed to improve performance thresholds under conditions of low contrast sensitivity. Their task was to judge whether patterns turned in a clockwise or counterclockwise direction on a computer screen. The researchers found that, after just ninety minutes per day of perceptual learning over five days, the performance of the older adults was as good as it had been for the younger adults before training.[70]

Given that sort of success, might it be possible to retrain one's brain to read smaller type more comfortably? Uri Polat and his collaborators asked middle-aged adults to practice the demanding visual task of detecting patterns on a computer screen for thirty minutes a day, at least twice a week, over a three-month period. By the end of training, the visual acuity of all the participants increased to a point where they could read newsprint without optical correction, and they read more quickly as well. Perceptual learning, therefore, may improve the brain's ability to discriminate images that are blurred.[71] Note that the participants in the study were mostly in their early fifties, and it is an open question whether such training would benefit adults in their sixties and beyond. In addition, it's unclear how generalizable the results may be, because the study employed only a small number of control (comparison) subjects.[72]

Although the effectiveness of so-called brain training to combat the effects of presbyopia is unresolved, it is something that everyone can try. A variety of smartphone apps are now available that are similar to the perceptual learning regimens used by researchers; try searching for "no glasses" in the online app stores.[73] It's encouraging to think that the brain may be able to adapt to at least one of the visual challenges of older adulthood.

Making Sense of Feelings

> The great enemy of communication, we find, is the illusion of it.
> —William H. Whyte (1950)

Although we usually think of comprehending spoken language as something we do with our ears, our eyes play a major supporting role as well. In face-to-face interactions, conversational participants rely on a host of nonverbal cues. People must pay attention to their partners' facial expressions and gestures to understand their intended meaning. And as we will see, prosodic cues (such as pitch, loudness, and timing) go beyond the words being spoken to convey communicative intent as well. We also use tone of voice to interpret emotional state. Is someone angry or resigned? Certain or uncertain? Being literal or sarcastic? Understanding what a person means requires the integration of the words being spoken, *how* they are spoken, and visual cues to the speaker's state of mind. Given the complexities of such multimodal sensory integration, we might expect to see age-related declines in emotion recognition. This appears to be the case.

Declines in older adults' ability to recognize affect in facial expressions has been well documented. For example, one study assessed participants' ability to identify basic emotions, such as happiness, fear, and surprise. The researchers also varied the intensity of the expressions (slightly surprised, surprised, or very surprised). The accuracy of the oldest subjects in the study (average age: 88) was lower than a somewhat younger older group (average age: 73). They in turn performed less well than a younger group (average age: 29). Participants in the oldest group required intense displays of emotional expression before they were able to identify them accurately.[74]

Facial cues can also give someone away when he is lying: a person may, for example, suddenly break off eye contact when he is being deceitful. Older adults do not seem to use this information as easily as younger adults and are therefore worse at identifying deceit.[75]

People also use gestures to clarify or reinforce the meaning of their spoken words. For example, a person might accompany an utterance like "I paid by check" (instead of with cash) by pantomiming the act of writing in the air with an imaginary pen. In an experiment that used such iconic gestures, younger participants (age range: 22–30) benefited more from such multimodal expressions of a person's meaning than a group of older adults (age range: 60–76).[76]

Interpreting other forms of body movement can become problematic as well. Joann Montepare and her colleagues asked younger (average age: 19) and older (average age: 76) participants to watch videos of actors displaying positive, negative, and neutral emotional states. For example, a person might clap her hands after reading some good news in a letter she has received. The videos seen by the subjects were silent, and the actors' faces were obscured, which made their bodily movements the only salient clue about the emotion being displayed. Both the younger and the older adults performed at above-chance levels in determining which emotion was being shown, but the older participants made more errors. In addition, they were worse at identifying negative emotions and tended to misidentify displays that were affectively charged as being emotionally neutral.[77]

Researchers have also found age-related declines in processing emotions through verbal cues. César Lima and his colleagues asked participants to rate the emotionality of vocal sounds associated with positive and negative emotions, such as sighs, sobs, and laughter. Older adults (average age: 61) were less accurate than younger adults (average age: 22), even after the effects of hearing loss and differences in intellectual abilities were taken into account.[78]

Older adults also tend to perform more poorly when the speaker's tone does not match the words that someone is saying (for example, when the tone is positive but the meaning is negative). However, evidence suggests that compensating strategies, like a simple restatement of the words, suffices to mitigate this effect.[79] Although a mismatch of prosody and spoken intent may seem unlikely to occur outside the lab, it is actually an important cue for understanding sarcasm, which is something that older adults often struggle with as well.[80] We will return to this topic in chapter 5.

In summary, studies have consistently found that older adults have a harder time recognizing some emotional cues. This leads to a deficit in recognizing affective states in other peoples' facial expressions, their voices, and their bodily movements and posture. It also holds true for recognizing a variety of different basic emotions.[81]

Part of the problem may be that older adults show a positivity bias. Simply put, they are better at processing positive than negative information.[82] This positivity effect has been primarily discussed in terms of attention and memory, such as a preference for looking at happy versus sad or angry faces.[83] This bias also influences how emotional cues are interpreted. For example, older adults performed more poorly in recognizing facial displays of sadness.[84] The ability to accurately recognize the emotions of others plays a role in other abilities, such as empathy and emotional intelligence.[85] So although a positivity bias may be beneficial for older adults' emotional well-being, it may exact a cost in terms of effective communication.

These cognitive deficits are amplified in nonhealthy aging. In one study, participants suspected of having Alzheimer's disease experienced difficulty in recognizing and identifying the non-verbal aspects of emotional displays, such as facial expressions and emotional prosody, in comparison to older adults who were aging healthily.[86]

As we have seen, age-related changes to hearing, vision, voice, and emotion recognition can all have a deleterious effect on language production and comprehension. However, many of these changes are gradual and vary a great deal from person to person. In addition, it is possible to use selection, optimization, and compensation to offset the effects of these declines.[87] In the next chapter, we turn our attention to spoken language and examine how it changes as we grow older.

3 The Story of Speech

Word Finding

> The signs of it were unmistakable; he would appear to be in mild tor-
> ment, something like the brink of a sneeze, and if he found the word
> his relief was considerable.
>
> —psychologists Roger Brown and David McNeill (1966)

Have you ever had trouble thinking of someone's name? Perhaps
you can even see the face of the person in your mind's eye, and
you would immediately recognize the name if a friend suggested
it to you. Although this happens frequently with names, it's the
same for any word. It's not that you can't remember the *concept*
but that you can't find the language label for it.

Word-finding problems are an almost stereotypical aspect of
the cognitive issues that plague middle-aged and older adults.
These failures occur without warning for even the most familiar
words and names a person knows. The most troublesome words
are proper nouns and the names of objects.[1] This retrieval inability
can last anywhere from a split second to minutes or even hours.
And as the epigraph above suggests, they can be exasperating.

In fact, older adults frequently mention word-finding problems when asked about the annoyances of aging.[2]

In such cases, a person is certain she knows the word she is searching for. It may seem as if the AWOL term is just on the tip of her tongue, but for some reason she can't produce it, at least at that moment. In fact, psychologists refer to such experiences as tip-of-the-tongue (TOT) states. But are they really the harbingers of befuddlement that they appear to be?

Studying TOT presents certain challenges to psychologists who want to understand how and why such states occur. Much like astronomers who study ephemeral phenomena like supernovas, researchers know that TOT states will eventually happen, but not exactly when. This uncertainty has led to two distinctly different ways of investigating TOTs: via naturalistic methods and by experimentally inducing word-finding failures in labora-tory settings.

Researchers studying word finding and TOT have tried to quantify two aspects in particular: how often these states occur, and the likelihood that they are resolved—that is, the sought-after word is spontaneously recalled by the person without exter-nal assistance (such as looking the word up or having a friend offer the solution). Diary studies, in which people write down every time they experience a TOT state, allow researchers to assess both frequency and resolution rates. The results suggest that college students experience about one to two TOT states a week, while for people in their sixties and early seventies, the rate is slightly higher. Research participants in their eighties, how-ever, experience TOT states at a rate almost twice as high as col-lege students.[3] Diary studies have shown that TOT episodes are likely to be resolved: the typical success rate in such studies is more than 90 percent.[4]

We need to be cautious, however, when interpreting such naturalistic data. It may be the case that older adults, who are more concerned about their memory lapses, will be more likely to record such instances. They may be more conscientious about writing them down, perhaps because their lives are less hectic than those of younger participants. It may also be the case that participants are simply more likely to record resolved TOT states than episodes that are not resolved.[5]

The alternative method for studying word finding is to experimentally induce a TOT state. A method for doing this was developed by Roger Brown and David McNeill. They found that simply giving participants dictionary definitions of uncom-mon English words would often trigger a word-finding failure. An example from their study was "A navigational instrument used in measuring angular distances, especially the altitude of the sun, moon, and stars at sea."[6] (If this example has caused a TOT state for you, sorry! The word is "sextant.")

In this study, the participants were often able to provide the desired word without difficulty. On other occasions, the subjects had no idea what word the definition was describing. However, if they found themselves in a TOT state, Brown and McNeill asked them additional questions. The researchers discovered that, while in such a state, people can report partial information about the sought-after word, even as the word itself eludes their grasp. For example, the participants performed far above chance when asked to guess how many syllables the word had, or what its initial letter might be. And not surprisingly, when people made errors, they often produced words that had a similar meaning. When given the definition for "sextant," the participants sometimes responded with "astrolabe" or "compass." However, they also sometimes offered up words that only sounded like the intended term. The definition for "sextant" also led to responses of "sextet" and "sexton." If we assume that sailors wielding their sextants are neither members of six-person musical groups nor gravediggers, then these errors suggest something important about how our knowledge of words is arranged in memory. Studies with older adults, however, suggest that partial information (such as the initial letter of the word) is less available for them.[7]

As with many issues in cognitive aging, we can view the increase in TOT states as a glass half empty or half full. On the one hand, these retrieval failures can be taken as evidence of weakening connections between the meanings of concepts and the words that denote them in long-term memory.[8] It's also possible that the increase in word-finding problems with age reflects something very different. Donna Dahlgren has argued that the key issue is not one of age but one of knowledge. If older adults typically have more information in long-term memory, then as a consequence they will experience more TOT states.[9] It's also possible that TOT states are useful: they can serve as a signal to the older adult that the sought-for word is known, even if not currently accessible. Such metacognitive information is beneficial because it signals that spending more time trying to resolve the word-finding failure may ultimately lead to success.[10] Viewed this way, TOT states might represent not retrieval failures but valuable sources of information.[11] If you are an older adult and still worried about the number of TOT states that you experience, research suggests you might have fewer such episodes if you maintain your aerobic fitness.[12]

Word Naming

These days I have to put in a request to my brain as one does at the library. And then a little worker takes my slip and disappears into the stacks. May take him a while, but he always comes back with the goods.

—Coral Upchurch (age 95), a character in Gail Godwin's *Grief Cottage* (2017)

When it comes to plucking words out of memory, researchers have also employed a separate, but similar, task: word naming. Also known as confrontation naming, picture naming, or cued recall, it is typically assessed by asking research participants to identify line drawings of familiar objects as quickly as they can. Word-naming ability has been explored with a variety of groups, such as children or people with language or memory impairments caused by brain injury. Researchers investigating word naming often use the Boston Naming Test (BNT), which is a standard-ized set of line drawings that increase in difficulty. Easier items require people to name familiar objects like a toothbrush, whereas a harder item to identify is a drawing of a protractor.[13]

You might suspect, given what we have already reported about processing speed, that older adults would perform more slowly on a naming task than younger adults. The results of experiments designed to measure such a difference, however, have been inconsistent. Some have found no difference between younger and older adults, whereas others have found that older adults are slower. This inconsistency may be due to the fact that some studies didn't control for extraneous variables that might affect word-naming ability, such as the taking of prescription medications or the health status of the participants.[14] A study that synthesized and analyzed the results of previous word-naming studies concluded that while performance may decline with age, it does so only after age seventy.[15] Likewise, a separate study that included a large number of participants with a wide age range (30–94) also documented a performance decline with age, but the effect was fairly small: only about 2 percent per decade.[16]

An analysis of the types of errors made on the Boston Naming Test is also instructive. Rhoda Au and her colleagues gave the BNT to people ranging in age from thirty to seventy. These participants were tested on three occasions over a seven-year period. Consistent with previous studies, older adults tended to make more mistakes than younger adults. But they also made certain types of errors more often than their younger counter-parts. For example, older adults produced more circumlocutions, in which multiple word responses were produced instead of the desired term (such as "it adds numbers" for an abacus, or "it draws circles" for a compass). Although circumlocutions were counted as errors, they might ultimately have helped the subject to retrieve the name of the object. By describing its shape or function, participants gave themselves additional cues that guied them to the sought-after word. In addition, older adults also produced more quasi-word responses. These aren't real words but sound like the intended term ("spinwheel" for pinwheel and "ocupus" for octopus, for instance).[17] The underlying issue therefore seems to be an increasing difficulty in selecting the appropriate word from long-term memory.[18]

Other factors besides aging could also influence word naming. A research group led by Christopher Randolph looked for patterns in a large sample of participants who were given the BNT. Predictably, they found that older participants did worse. But people who had more years of education performed better, a result that has also been found in other studies.[19] It is interesting to note that men outperformed women. However, this result may be an artifact of the items that are employed on the battery. Men were faster and more accurate at naming test items like "tripod," "compass," and "latch," while women outperformed men on items like "mushroom," "trellis," and "palette." Since the BNT employs several drawings of tools and related objects, a gender difference may be due to differential familiarity with the test items.[20] There may be generational effects with the BNT items as well: a different study found that older adults outperformed younger participants on items like "yoke," "trellis," and "abacus."[21]

It seems, therefore, that word-naming ability does decline with age. And since there appears to be an age bias in the questions themselves, the decline may be larger than has already been reported. However, having a higher education may compensate for some of this age-related decline. Gender bias related to the test items means that the jury is still out on differences between men and women.

Finally, as we saw with word naming, health issues that may seem unrelated to cognition have been shown to influence performance on this task. Martin Albert and his colleagues determined a relation between performance on the BNT and high blood pressure. The researchers speculate that changes in the tiny blood vessels of the frontal lobes negatively affect executive function and contribute to word retrieval difficulties.[22] Such studies demonstrate that high blood pressure isn't just bad for your heart; it's also bad for your head.

Speech Disfluency

> Sometimes I'll start a sentence, and I don't even know where it's going. I just hope I find it along the way.
> —Steve Carell as Michael Scott in *The Office*

When we have trouble naming an object or finding the right word, we might buy time by using a filler word—like "uh" or "um." Although doing so is quite natural, these filler words nevertheless disrupt the normal flow of speech. Other examples of these types of speech interruptions include starting and then restarting a sentence or correcting oneself midsentence. Mothers sometimes do this when they can't hit upon the name of the child they want to scold ("Rick, I mean Jay, I mean Patrick ... BECCA—stop it!"). In addition, whole word repetitions ("I'm not, *I'm not*, going to say this twice") and interjections ("He's, *like*, really cute") are all considered speech disfluencies. Such self-interruptions do not, in and of themselves, indicate a speech disorder. In fact, there are both qualitative and quantitative differences between the kinds of disfluencies we discuss in this section and those of a speech disorder such as stuttering, which we discuss in the following section.[23]

In normal speech, disfluencies occur fairly frequently: several studies have estimated that they occur about six times for every hundred words that are spoken. They also tend to increase when tasks are difficult, such as when one is giving directions. The topic under discussion matters too. One study has shown that university lecturers in the natural sciences, in which the subject matter is more structured and formal, employ fewer filled pauses than lecturers in the humanities.[24]

In the laboratory, the psychologist Heather Bortfeld and her colleagues found that the disfluency rate, which they defined as repeats, restarts, and fillers, was higher for older adults (an average of 6.7 per hundred words) than for middle-aged (5.7) or younger adults (5.6). Compared to the other two groups, the older adults (average age: 67) were especially prone to utter disfluent fillers within a phrase ("and a brown, *uh*, belt") as opposed to between phrases ("and a brown belt and, *uh*, a white shirt").[25]

When it comes to public speaking, such filler words have a bad reputation. Because they can cause speakers to sound unprepared or lacking in confidence, filler words have been referred to as "credibility killers."[26] About two-thirds of a sample of college students reported that they try to avoid using them, with varying degrees of success.[27]

Let's consider two filler words that have received considerable attention from psychologists and linguists. At first blush,

"uh" and "um" may seem interchangeable, but research suggests that their usage isn't equivalent. Herb Clark and Jean Fox
Tree analyzed the way these fillers were used by British English
speakers, and found that "uh" tends to signal a relatively short
delay in speech. "Um," on the other hand, was more commonly
employed when the following pause was longer.[28] So these fillers actually serve the useful function of giving the listener some
idea of how long the speaker's pause will be.

Other factors also seem to influence how people use filler
words. The use of "uh" and "um," for example, varies by gender. Eric Acton examined the use of these fillers by analyzing
thousands of telephone conversations and transcripts of people
on speed dates. He found a large difference, with women using
"um" more, and men employing "uh."[29]

Do these disfluencies become more common with age? Unfortunately, we can't give a simple answer to this question. As we
have seen, processing speed declines as people get older, so if
one's thoughts can't keep up with one's words, the result might
be an increased reliance on filled pauses. But it turns out that the
type of filler word plays a role. Mark Liberman found the same
"um" versus "uh" gender difference as Eric Acton, but he also
found an age difference: the use of "uh" is higher in people in
their sixties compared to those in their twenties and thirties. The
pattern for "um" is reversed: its use decreases with age.[30] It seems
that more research is called for.

A number of studies have compared the speech disfluencies
of younger and older adults when given specific tasks, such as
describing pictures. Some studies found no differences.[31] One,
however, found that, relative to younger participants, older adults
became more disfluent when describing pictures with negative
content.[32]

In general, older adults more frequently use ambiguous ref-
erents and so-called extenders ("that sort of thing," "stuff like
that"). They also use sentences that are shorter and less complex.[33] It's encouraging to note that the speech disfluency
rate for centenarians is not much different than it is for older
adults in their seventies, eighties, and nineties.[34] Moreover,
the rate of filled pauses for people with Alzheimer's disease is
no different than for a comparison group without cognitive
impairment.[35]

Although not technically a type of disfluency, formulaic language also functions to fill pauses in conversations. These expressions include prefabricated phrases that can be easily retrieved
from memory, as opposed to laboriously constructing a novel
way of expressing something.[36] Formulaic expressions include
idioms ("once in a blue moon," "wake up on the wrong side of
the bed"); proverbs ("actions speak louder than words," "look
before you leap"); and conventionalized expressions ("you don't
say," "have a nice day").[37]

Although everyone uses formulaic language to some degree,
older adults with cognitive impairment or dementia rely heavily
on such phrases.[38] However, even though they use these phrases
more often, people with Alzheimer's disease still use formulaic
language appropriately.[39]

Taken as a whole, differences in speech disfluencies between
men and women, younger and older adults, and those with and
without cognitive impairment are relatively minor. It is interesting to note, however, that negative content seems to invoke
more disfluent speech among older adults. This finding is consistent with the fact that older adults may have a more difficult
time identifying negative emotions, and harkens back to the
positivity bias discussed in the section on emotion recognition.

Stuttering

> If you can live through a childhood of stuttering, you can live
> through anything. And if you go into adulthood still stuttering, you
> can handle anything.... You have been tempered by the fire.
> —David Seidler, speech to the National Stuttering Association (2011)

In late 2010, filmgoers were treated to a major motion picture about a somewhat unusual subject: the speech disorder of a future ruler of the United Kingdom. Specifically, *The King's Speech* depicted the struggles of "Bertie" (the future George VI, portrayed by Colin Firth) to overcome a severe stuttering problem via the ministrations of Lionel Logue, an Australian speech therapist portrayed by Geoffrey Rush. David Seidler's screenplay has been criticized for deviating significantly from historical events.[40] However, the film serves as an important reminder to its audience that stuttering is not just a problem faced by some children: it is a disorder that adults may struggle with throughout their lives.

Virtually everyone has heard examples of stuttering (or stammering; the words mean the same thing). The most common elements of this speech disfluency are repetitions of words or syllables, prolongations of the same sound or syllable, and periods of silence that break up the flow of speech. Even before *The King's Speech*, stuttering had been depicted fairly frequently onscreen. Such depictions, however, were often offensive, since the speech impediment was frequently employed for supposed comic effect (as in the case of Porky Pig's catchphrase "Th-Th-The, Th-Th-The, Th-Th ... that's all, folks!"), or as shorthand to imply that a character was mentally challenged.[41] An example of this stereotype can be seen in the 1988 film *A Fish Called Wanda*:

Michael Palin plays a character with a pronounced stammer who is repeatedly mocked for his impediment by costar Kevin Kline. The local chapter of the National Stuttering Project protested the film's release outside the Culver City offices of its producer, MGM.[42]

Stuttering typically begins in childhood, with an incidence rate of about 5 percent, but the majority of children overcome it, either on their own or through the assistance of a speech language therapist. In about a quarter of all cases, however, the problem is chronic and persistent and remains an issue for about 1 percent of adults.[43] One percent may not sound like a large number, but it equates to more than 2.5 million US adults—more than the population of Houston, Texas.

Many people think of stuttering as a manifestation of anxiety, and that is certainly part of the story. People who stutter tend to score higher on tests of anxiety as a trait, and they do report higher levels of social anxiety than those who don't stutter.[44] However, stuttering is not caused solely by anxiety. Research suggests there might be a genetic component: as with other heritable conditions, males are more likely to be affected than females. In addition, the rate is higher among identical twins in comparison to fraternal twins, who share on average only half of their genes.[45] Environmental factors may also play a role, but to date researchers have identified no single cause. Research on underlying neurological factors, while promising, has not yet yielded insights that have translated into specific treatments.[46]

In some ways, stuttering resembles other muscular movement disorders that lead to a partial loss of voluntary control. For example, stuttering has been compared to the "yips," which are involuntary spasms that disrupt the small stroking motions golfers employ when they are putting.[47] Similar problems have been observed among competitive darts players (a condition dubbed "dartitis"). Viewed from this perspective, stuttering could be characterized as a specific example of a larger family of movement disorders called action dystonias.[48]

People who stutter often report having an awareness that they are about to stammer.[49] This is referred to as anticipation, and it is one of the ways that chronic stuttering differs from other types of disfluency. Of course, everyone makes mistakes while speaking, but people who don't stutter typically do not experience such awareness beforehand. It's also not the case that episodes of stuttering can be predicted. Measures of the rate of stuttering for specific individuals show wide variability from day to day, and from task to task (such as spontaneous speech versus reading from a text). This variability does not correlate with the perceived severity of a person's stammer.[50]

A number of studies have assessed the impact of stuttering on quality of life. For example, a study of South African adults who stutter (age range: 20–59) found they generally did not believe that stuttering had affected their occupational choice or personal relationships. However, they also reported that it had negatively affected their performance in school and their relationships with classmates. With regard to the present, several participants asserted that stuttering affected their performance on the job, as well as their promotion chances.[51] A study conducted in Israel found that older and married adults who stutter reported being less affected by their impediment than those who were younger and unmarried.[52]

A number of adults who stutter have achieved notable success in life: the list includes the Roman emperor Claudius, Isaac Newton, Lewis Carroll, Ty Cobb, and Alan Turing. More impressive, perhaps, the list can be extended to include individuals who achieved prominence in fields that require acting or public speaking: Thomas Jefferson, Theodore Roosevelt, Anthony Quinn, Marilyn Monroe, and James Earl Jones (as well as the aforementioned George VI).

It's also possible to point to individuals whose severe stammer was debilitating. An example would be Annie Glenn, the wife of John (who in 1962 was the first American to orbit the Earth). She struggled with mundane activities like giving an address to a taxi driver or interacting with store clerks.[53] (Annie's struggles were briefly depicted by the actress Mary Jo Deschanel in the 1983 film *The Right Stuff*.) However, even Glenn's story has a happy ending: in 1978, at the age of fifty-three, she underwent several weeks of intensive therapy for her disfluency, which focused on factors like controlling breathing and speech rate.[54] Although she didn't consider herself to be cured, the therapy did allow her to start making speeches on behalf of her husband, who served for twenty-five years as a US senator from Ohio. In Glenn's case, a strong desire to overcome her stammer, combined with appropriate therapy, allowed her to participate more fully in her role as the spouse of a political figure.

But therapy doesn't help everyone. Many adults who stutter have mixed feelings about the role of speech therapy. Some respondents in a survey said that they had negative experiences with therapy, but they also reported that it had been helpful. Over and above such ambivalence, some also felt that to change the way they talk would be to reject the person they had become.[55]

Another survey of older adults who stutter found that although the severity of their stuttering had not declined with age, they perceived their stuttering as "less handicapping" than when they were younger.[56] This is not to say, however, that stuttering has no impact on aging. Older adults who stutter may still experience fear of negative evaluation and may limit their social interactions to avoid situations that require them to speak. The choice to self-isolate could cause them to avoid seeking outside assistance, even in important areas such as health and finance.[57]

Aphasia

> **Doctor** What brings you to the hospital?
>
> **Patient** Boy I'm sweating. I'm awful nervous, you know, once in a while I get caught up, I can't mention the tarripoi, a month ago, quite a little, I've done a lot well, I impose a lot, while, on the other hand, you know what I mean, I have to run around, look it over, treb-bin and all that sort of stuff.
>
> —Howard Gardner, *The Shattered Mind* (1975)

The human brain is seemingly well protected from damage. The skull forms a bony bulwark that shields the brain from external threats, and the meninges and cerebrospinal fluid function like shock absorbers, providing additional protection. The blood-brain barrier serves as an internal shield, preventing pathogens from entering the central nervous system. The brain is, however, vulnerable to another internal threat that many a homeowner can relate to: problems with the plumbing. Just as a clogged or burst pipe can wreak havoc within a building, so a blocked or ruptured artery or blood vessel in the brain can compromise basic cognitive functions. These include a person's ability to speak and comprehend language.

Although a stroke can occur at any point in one's life, it becomes more common as a person ages. The majority of strokes occur after age sixty-five. Risk factors include smoking, irregular heartbeat, and high blood pressure. Advances in medicine and prevention have significantly reduced the incidence of stroke, but it remains the third most common cause of death in the United States and is the leading cause of long-term disability. Survivors of stroke may experience paralysis, weakness, numbness, pain, and problems with vision. They may tire easily or experience sudden bursts of emotion. Many develop depression.

Cognitive issues resulting from a stroke include impairments in thinking, memory, learning, and attention. In addition, about a third of stroke victims experience some form of language disruption. The effects on a person's linguistic abilities can vary considerably and provide important clues about how language is represented in the brain. These language deficits are referred to as aphasia, and there are many different types.

Traditionally, researchers and clinicians have distinguished between expressive and receptive aphasia. People who suffer from expressive aphasia experience considerable difficulty in speaking. Their speech is typically slow, halting, and effortful. Anomia, or difficulty in finding words, is also common. Despite all of this, however, what they say does make sense, and with a little patience on the part of their partners, it is possible for them to participate meaningfully in conversation.

In contrast, those with receptive aphasia have difficulty in understanding speech. And as the epigraph at the beginning of this section suggests, a person with receptive aphasia may produce fluent but impaired speech, running the gamut from the merely odd to a confused jumble that has been likened to "word salad." Their mistakes include paraphasias (substitutions of related words, such as "window" for "door") and neologisms (made-up words with no actual meaning, like "doopid" or "peka-kis" when asked to identify a picture of a tricycle).[58] Strangely, individuals with receptive aphasia don't seem to be aware that

what they're saying is wrong or doesn't make sense. The same is not true for people with expressive aphasia: they are very much aware of their linguistic limitations and, as result, often withdraw from communicating with others.

Expressive aphasia has traditionally been associated with injury to a brain region called Broca's area. It is named after Paul Broca, a nineteenth-century French physician who made the connection between expressive language disorder and its anatomical location in the brain. Receptive aphasia, on the other hand, has traditionally been associated with damage to a different region, one called Wernicke's area (after the German physician Carl Wernicke). Broca's area is found toward the front of the brain, whereas Wernicke's is located toward the back. The two brain regions are connected by a tract of nerve fibers that also play a role in language. Individuals with stroke damage to this tract display yet a third form of impairment, called conduction aphasia. In this disorder, speaking and understanding speech are relatively unaffected, but the ability to repeat words or sentences may be greatly impaired.

Because aphasia can manifest itself in different ways, it can be difficult to diagnose. This is especially true when a person arrives at a hospital unable to communicate effectively. Patients who have had a stroke and are suffering from aphasia can be misdiagnosed as having a psychotic episode, schizophrenia, epilepsy, dementia, or a host of other conditions.[59] Misdiagnosis is particularly worrisome in the first few hours after a stroke occurs. If the stroke is the result of a blood clot, and the patient receives a drug called tPA (tissue plasminogen activator) soon afterward, there is a chance the stroke can be "reversed" and the person will regain much of his normal function.[60]

We know that expressive aphasia is a cognitive and not a motor problem because people who communicate via Sign language display similar deficits. They experience great difficulty in producing the physical motions that are required in Sign languages. However, these individuals are relatively unimpaired in their comprehension of the signs of others. In another parallel, a Sign language user with receptive aphasia will display poor comprehension of the signs of others and will produce signs that are meaningless: a "gesture salad."[61]

But what about writing and reading? Since these abilities can also be characterized as expressive and receptive, you might suspect that these skills are preserved or disrupted differentially— and you would be correct. Individuals with expressive aphasia can write meaningful sentences, but they find the act of writing to be effortful. Those with receptive aphasia will write fluidly but produce largely meaningless verbiage. People who suffer from expressive aphasia can read fairly well (paralleling their relatively intact comprehension of spoken language), whereas those with receptive aphasia comprehend the written word poorly.[62]

Strange as it may seem, brain injury that leads to a loss of the ability to read—referred to as pure alexia—does not necessarily entail the loss of an ability to write. A person with alexia can write something and not be able to read what she has just written! Some individuals with alexia seem to process numbers better than letters, but the same may also be true of cognitively intact individuals.[63] People who suffer from alexia can learn to read once again but must do so in a letter-by-letter fashion, which can be tedious and frustrating when words are long.[64]

Although the impairments caused by such language deficits can be severe and long lasting, most people with aphasia experience some degree of improvement, called spontaneous recovery, during the first weeks and months following onset. Not surprisingly, recovery is influenced by a variety of factors, such as the location and extent of the brain injury, type of aphasia, and environmental considerations such as family support.[65] People with aphasia also benefit from speech and language therapy (SLT). A comprehensive review of the research on this topic has found that SLT does improve the functional communication of people with aphasia and is most effective when it is intensive and continues over an extended period.[66]

Other treatment options are in the works. These include transcranial direct-current stimulation (tDCS), which is a noninvasive electrical stimulation aimed at changing brain function.[67] Tablet-based home treatment programs have been effective. They are generally liked by patients, can be used independently, and can be customized for each person. In addition, virtual reality and virtual therapist protocols are also being developed.[68]

Dyslexia

Like alexia, which we discussed in the previous section, dyslexia also relates to difficulty in reading. The terms "reading disability" and "dyslexia" are often used synonymously, although the former term refers to a host of factors, whereas dyslexia specifically refers to difficulties in word recognition and spelling. Researchers use the term "developmental dyslexia" to differentiate it from language deficits like alexia that occur later in life as a consequence of brain injury or stroke. These definitional issues are complicated because dyslexia frequently co-occurs with other language development disorders. For example, in language impairment, children experience difficulty with vocabulary and grammar. In speech sound disorder, children have problems in producing speech sounds. Dyslexia also co-occurs with dyscalculia, which refers to difficulties with numbers, mathematics, and calculation.[69]

Estimates of the incidence of dyslexia are affected by the arbitrary nature of selecting assessment cutoff scores, but a commonly cited figure is 7 percent.[70] Dyslexia is not the same as having a low IQ, since the term is reserved for individuals who struggle with word decoding despite having normal or above-average intellectual ability.

Researchers have long debated the heritability of dyslexia, and as is typical with such research, it is difficult to tease apart the relative contributions of nature and nurture. However, a growing consensus suggests that genetic factors play an important role.[71] The higher incidence seen in boys may also be due to other factors, such as attention-deficit/hyperactivity disorder (ADHD).

Are the effects of dyslexia greater for the learners of languages like English, in which the mapping of sound to spelling is less consistent than in other languages? In English, for example, /f/ can be rendered as *f* (as in "flower"), *ff* (as in "suffer"), *ph* (as in "philosophy"), or *gh* (as in "enough"). However, a study comparing children with dyslexia who were learning both English and German (which is more regular than English) found more similarities than differences. This finding suggests that the issue for people with dyslexia is a general phonological decoding deficit and not a language-specific correspondence problem between spelling and sound.[72]

Before the development of diagnostic assessments that could identify this disorder, children with dyslexia were often labeled as being "slow" or "underperformers," which only added to the frustration that they experienced as they struggled to keep up with their peers in reading. It's also the case that many people with dyslexia attempt to conceal their difficulties out of shame or fear.[73] The stigma of dyslexia was on full display in September 2000, when an article by Gail Sheehy in *Vanity Fair* suggested that then-candidate for president George W. Bush had dyslexia.[74] As evidence, she pointed to Bush's younger brother Neil, who had been diagnosed as having dyslexia, as well as Bush's tendency to utter non sequiturs and malapropisms. (As we have seen, however, dyslexia refers to written and not spoken language.) In an interview on ABC's *Good Morning America* after the article's publication, Bush denied Sheehy's assertion, although he added that he had never been assessed for the condition.[75]

Many adults who struggle with dyslexia are not diagnosed as children and go through life assuming that they are simply poor readers and spellers. And according to a study of people with dyslexia in Norway, it is poor spelling, even more than reading difficulties, that leads adults to the conclusion that they might have dyslexia.[76] In addition, adults with dyslexia report having more memory issues than those without dyslexia.[77]

Because dyslexia is often thought of as a disorder of childhood, it is also important to screen adults when making a diagnosis of dementia. Both conditions are defined by difficulty with language, attention, and memory. Failure to recognize that a person has underlying dyslexia can lead to misdiagnosis and the selection of inappropriate treatment options.[78]

It would be a mistake to conclude that people with dyslexia are unable to compete in a world that places a premium on linguistic ability. A list of adults with dyslexia who have achieved fame or fortune in their respective fields would include hundreds of individuals. It is difficult, however, to retrospectively identify historical figures as having had dyslexia (but that hasn't stopped people from trying). Leonardo da Vinci, Napoleon, Beethoven, and Einstein are all frequently found on lists of famous people with dyslexia. They may well have had problems with word recognition and spelling, but a lack of diagnostic criteria during their lifetimes precludes a definitive diagnosis. We are on firmer ground if we consider individuals from the mid-twentieth century onward. A partial inventory would include entrepreneurs and financiers (Richard Branson, Charles Schwab), actors and comedians (Danny Glover, Anthony Hopkins, Jay Leno), filmmakers (Steven Spielberg, Quentin Tarantino), athletes (Caitlyn Jenner, Magic Johnson, Nolan Ryan), and authors (John Irving, John Grisham). The fashion designer Tommy Hilfiger and the journalist Anderson Cooper would be included as well. And the actor Henry Winkler, who did not receive a diagnosis until he was thirty-one, has gone on to coauthor a popular series of children's books about Hank Zipzer, a boy with dyslexia.

Many adults with dyslexia develop compensatory strategies to deal with their reading difficulties. Winkler, for example, could barely read as a child and therefore used memorization and improvisational skills to get through auditions and college coursework. And a study of French university students with dyslexia found that they have greater vocabulary depth, in terms of word meaning and semantic knowledge, than their peers.[79]

It has been claimed that adults with dyslexia may also benefit from specially designed typefaces. For example, users of electronic book readers like Amazon's Kindle can view text in a variety of sizes and fonts, including one called OpenDyslexic. This typeface, which is also available as an extension in Google's Chrome web browser, has thicker or heavier lines at the bottoms of letters and numbers. These features purportedly make the characters easier to distinguish from one another. In theory, this may be helpful, but a study designed to assess the efficacy of OpenDyslexic found no improvement in either reading speed or accuracy when compared to traditional fonts like Arial or Times New Roman.[80] Another specially designed font, Dyslexie, was found to increase reading speed, but this result seems to be due to the wide spacing employed by the typeface. When the researchers adjusted the spacing of a comparison font (Arial) to match the spacing used in Dyslexie, they observed no differences in reading speed.[81]

Although the difficulties experienced by people with dyslexia are all too real, a countervailing narrative has also been advanced. Because their brains work somewhat differently, people with dyslexia may possess superior reasoning skills in particular domains. The authors of *The Dyslexic Advantage*, for example, argue that many people with dyslexia possess excellent spatial ability and are heavily represented in fields like computer graphics and architecture.[82] However, one should take such claims with a grain of salt, since many people with a wide range of learning disabilities may simply use the term "dyslexic," and the perception of surfeits in certain professions may in fact represent motivated reasoning and confirmation bias.

As we have seen, our language abilities and our identity are closely intertwined. In the chapter's final section, we delve into an unusual condition that highlights how even subtle shifts in the way we speak can have a dramatic impact on how we (and others) see ourselves.

Foreign Accent Syndrome

> I think we are wise, we English speakers, to savor accents. They teach us things about our own tongue.
>
> —David, in Anne Rice's *Merrick* (2000)

On September 6, 1941, the German-occupied city of Oslo was attacked by the British Royal Air Force. The frightened citizens caught in the open frantically sought refuge from the falling bombs. One of the casualties of the air raid was a twenty-eight-year-old woman named Astrid, who was hit by shrapnel as she ran toward a shelter. She was seriously wounded on the left side of her head. Hospital staff feared she would not survive. After a few days, however, she regained consciousness and was found to have paralysis on the right side of her body. She was also unable to speak. Over time her paralysis receded, and she gradually recovered her ability to talk. Her speech, however, had changed, and people who heard her detected a pronounced German-like accent. This was a serious problem in Norway, where the military occupation had created intense antipathy toward anything

German, and her speech caused shopkeepers to refuse to assist her. Clearly she had no desire to speak as she did. Even more mysteriously, she had never lived outside Norway, nor had she interacted with foreigners.[83]

Two years after her injury, Astrid's strange case came to the attention of Georg Herman Monrad-Krohn. He was a professor of neurology at the University of Oslo and had a particular interest in language disorders. He was also struck by Astrid's distinctly foreign accent and initially thought that she must be German or French.

Astrid's case is not unique: an occurrence of what is now called foreign accent syndrome (FAS) was described as early as 1907 by Pierre Marie in France, where a Parisian had acquired an "Alsatian" accent.[84] Over the next century, physicians and language researchers reported dozens of similar cases. As the case studies piled up in the medical journals, scholars struggled to understand what was going on. (FAS has also happened to at least one well-known person today: in 2011 the British singer George Michael, who grew up in London, came out of a three-week coma and initially spoke with a West Country accent.)[85]

A shared element in many FAS cases involves injury to specific areas of the left hemisphere of the brain. In most individuals, language functions are localized in this hemisphere, which controls the right side of the body (this is why most individuals write with their right hand). Brain injury is rarely selective, and in two-thirds of the FAS cases that have been studied, such individuals have some other language deficit, such as aphasia or apraxia (a motor planning problem).[86] This was the case for Astrid as well. However, in a small number of cases, the syndrome seems to have been caused by a psychological disorder rather than physical damage to the brain. In some of these cases, the foreign accent seems to have faded away as the underlying condition, such as conversion disorder or schizophrenia, was treated successfully. In other cases, however, the foreign accent persisted.[87]

What is it that makes individuals suffering from FAS sound like foreign speakers of their native language? A common element is that the prosody of their language production has changed in some way. Prosody refers to the rhythm, pitch, and intonation of a language as it is spoken. In a language like English, flat intonation is used for statements of fact ("I owe you twenty dollars"), whereas questions are accompanied by rising intonation ("I owe you twenty *dollars*?"). Languages differ in their prosodic contours, and so any disruption of normal rhythm and flow might be perceived as nonnative or foreign sounding.

For Astrid, the brain injury caused by the shrapnel wound led to prosodic changes in how she spoke her native language. For example, she tended to raise the pitch on the last word of short sentences. (In English, this phenomenon goes by various names, one of which is "upspeak." It is associated with the speech of younger women in Britain and the United States.)[88] In addition, whereas Norwegian has fixed pitch on syllables that receive stress, languages like German have a less-consistent relation between pitch and stress. In German, because of this variable pitch, the word that receives the stress depends on the intonation pattern of the sentence. Another characteristic of Astrid's talk after her injury is important as well: her speech was not always entirely grammatical.

When all these features are combined, it becomes easier to understand how other Norwegians might have perceived Astrid's speech as foreign sounding. The relatively subtle prosodic and grammatical errors that she made would be consistent with someone who had learned Norwegian as a second language.[89] Recall that Monrad-Krohn initially thought that Astrid might be a native speaker of German or French. This probably reflects the fact that the nonnative speakers of Norwegian whom he and others encountered hailed from nearby, populous European countries—like Germany and France.

The subjective nature of how we perceive others' accents is exemplified by the case of Linda Walker, a sixty-year-old British woman from Newcastle who suffered a stroke in 2006. Her sister-in-law asserted that, after regaining consciousness in the hospital, Linda sounded Italian. Her brother, on the other hand, claimed that her speech resembled someone from Slovakia. Others thought they detected a French Canadian or even a Jamaican lilt to her speech. In cases like this, even small changes in the way vowels are pronounced seem to drive major differences in how speech is perceived.[90]

Such variability has been demonstrated in the laboratory as well. Experiments in which participants heard recordings of FAS speakers, as well as a control group of native speakers, also showed a great deal of inconsistency with regard to accent attribution. For example, a Scottish FAS speaker was correctly perceived by some participants to be Scottish, but by others to be Irish, Welsh, English, or even Spanish, German, Portuguese, and Polish. In contrast, the control Scottish speaker was always identified as a native speaker of some variety of English (Scottish, English, Irish, or American).[91] Clearly, many of the study participants heard something that didn't sound quite right, but they didn't agree about what that "something" actually was. In a similar study, participants were able to reliably distinguish between native and foreign speakers but perceived FAS speakers as existing in some sort of linguistic netherworld: clearly not native, but not totally foreign either.[92]

Perhaps not surprisingly, therefore, people afflicted with FAS often feel that their sense of self has been undermined. Linda Walker, for example, said, "I've lost my identity, because I never talked like this before. I'm a very different person and it's strange and I don't like it."[93] An American woman with FAS, who sounded British to her Midwestern neighbors, went so far as to travel to England "in search of someone who sounded like me."[94] People in England, however, thought that she sounded South African! As these examples make clear, our self-concept is intimately tied up with how we speak and how we sound to others.

4 Word Domination

Stressed Out

> It's "Assess the window," not "Asses the window." You put the wrong emPHAsis on the wrong sylLAble.
>
> —Mike Myers as John Witney in *View from the Top* (2003)

Spoken language entails a great deal more than just the words that someone says. *How* words are spoken is also important. Words are composed of syllables, and people selectively emphasize certain syllables for a variety of reasons. In some cases, it's simply conventional to accentuate a particular syllable within a given word. In other cases, speakers use what linguists refer to as stress to help disambiguate their message or to make clear their intentions. Let's consider each of these forms of stress in turn.

In many of the world's languages, speakers will utter one syllable of a word more loudly or at a different pitch relative to the other syllables of that word. Some languages, like Czech and Hungarian, usually stress the first syllable of a word. In Armenian, stress typically falls on the last syllable. In Polish, it's the second to last. And some languages, like French and Japanese, play no favorites: in general, all syllables are treated the same.

How about English? Well, it's complicated. English has what is called variable stress: one syllable will be given emphasis, but not in any predictable way. And speakers of different dialects may stress different syllables; for example, the Brits typically stress the first syllable of words borrowed from French (*adult*, *garage*, and *salon*), whereas US speakers stress the last syllable. Speakers of variable-stress languages must learn which syllable receives the stress in each word.

Speakers of languages like English and German also use what is called lexical stress to differentiate between words like the noun "*con*tent" (the subject matter of a book) and the adjective "con*tent*" (the state of feeling at peace). Speakers also use lexical stress in phrases to disambiguate meaning. A *light*house keeper is someone who maintains a navigational beacon, whereas a light *house*keeper is someone willing to tidy up your house, but who probably won't wash your windows. In a similar way, "I saw a black *bird*" means "I saw a bird that was black in color," whereas I saw a *black*bird" means "I saw a thrush belonging to the species *Turdus merula*."

Another type of stress is called prosodic stress. This is what allows speakers to differentiate between making statements, which are spoken with a flat intonation ("I'm supposed to wash the windows"), and asking questions, which employ rising intonation ("I'm supposed to wash the *windows*?"). Prosodic stress also allows clause boundaries to be marked, as in "The employee said the boss is angry" and "The employee, said the boss, is angry." In written form, the clauses can be disambiguated by commas, but in spoken form, the crucial cue is timing, or the pauses and relative durations of the words in question. In sentences like the examples just given, small timing differences allow listeners to understand who is angry (the boss in the first case, and the employee in the second). In all these ways, stress plays an important role in making clear the meaning of potentially ambiguous words and sentences.

In general, the ability to use prosodic cues like stress and timing is well preserved in older adults. The psychologist Margaret Kjelgaard and her colleagues found that college students and adults in their sixties and seventies similarly use prosodic information to identify clause boundaries in ambiguous sentences.[1] However, there are several different prosodic cues, such as loudness, pitch, and timing. Are these cues equally important, and do older adults use them in the same way as younger people?

Ken Hoyte and his collaborators studied the relative contribution of these prosodic factors by using a computer to manipulate prosodic cues in ambiguous sentences. They used sentences like "The employee said the boss is angry" and systematically reduced or removed the loudness, pitch, and timing cues that listeners would normally rely on to figure out who is, in fact, angry. The college students and older participants (average age: mid-seventies) listened to these doctored sentences and were asked to identify, as quickly as possible, the subject of each one (the employee or the boss in our example). The researchers found that both groups were highly accurate in their identifications, although it took the older adults a little longer to make their judgments. Furthermore, both groups relied on the same cues: both younger and older adults principally used subtle timing differences to make their decisions.[2]

This is not to say that older adults don't experience difficulties in spoken-language comprehension. One line of research has shown that older speakers of English have more difficulty in understanding accented English spoken by some nonnative speakers.[3] Although age-related hearing loss is one possible culprit, many languages have lexical stress patterns that are unlike those of English. As a result, second-language learners of English might not sufficiently differentiate their pronunciation of words like *con*tent and con*tent*. In an experiment designed to explore this issue, younger (age range: 18–35) and older (age range: 65–90) native English speakers listened to recordings of such words being spoken by other native English speakers and also by native Spanish speakers with varying degrees of accent. The participants' task was to identify which word was intended. Both the younger and older adults were less accurate when the words were produced with a heavy Spanish accent, although the older adults experienced more difficulty than the younger participants. This was true even for older adults with normal hearing.[4]

An important caveat to this finding is that it doesn't take into account the effects of prolonged exposure to a given speaker. Everyone finds it easier to understand other speakers as they hear more of their speech, and this process of adaptation occurs for both younger and older adults.[5] However, older adults with hearing loss may depend more on being able to both see and hear the speaker.[6]

Spelling Ability

It is a damn poor mind indeed which can't think of at least two ways to spell any word.
—attributed to Andrew Jackson (1833)

A synonym is a word you use when you can't spell the other one.
—Baltasar Gracián (1601–1658)

The English language is infamous for its spelling eccentricities. Consequently, as children learn to write, they must commit to memory a large number of spelling rules, as well as their many exceptions. Children's spelling is commonly tested in spelling bees, which are popular because they make a boring task more interesting by turning it into a competition. The result of such contests and other forms of testing is that most of us stumble into adulthood with tolerably good spelling abilities. Modern conveniences, such as the spellchecking and autocorrect functions in software, have made this task easier. And Google's "Did you mean" prompt is smart enough that users need only supply an approximation of the intended word in a search query. For many lazy typists, a search engine serves as an ersatz dictionary.

Every day we read large numbers of correctly spelled words in books, periodicals, and online material. Because we see the correct spelling of words over and over again throughout our lives, it is reasonable to assume that our spelling ability should improve over time. As a memory researcher might put it, the representation of the correct forms in long-term memory is being strengthened through repeated exposure. And this seems to be true in general: we do find it easier to recognize someone if we have seen them repeatedly as opposed to just once or twice. But is this the case with words? Does familiarity truly breed accuracy?

Think for a moment about what the US penny looks like. Americans routinely handle these coins several times a day in their financial transactions, and everyone would agree that the one cent piece is extremely familiar. It should be a simple task, therefore, to describe the elements of the coin—especially its front side, since the design hasn't changed in over a century. You can probably recall that Abe Lincoln appears in profile. But is he facing to the left or the right? What words, if any, appear

over his head? Does anything appear to the left and right of the president? Does the date appear somewhere on the front? Don't feel bad if you are having difficulty remembering these details; you have plenty of company. In a classic study from the late 1970s, the psychologists Ray Nickerson and Marilyn Adams asked undergraduates at Brown University to draw the penny's front and back faces from memory, and the results were "remarkably poor."[7]

Later studies have demonstrated that people also misremember the appearance of other common objects, even those for which the layout of the elements is important, such as keypads on telephones and the placement of characters on keyboards.[8] These studies converge on the same surprising result: even frequent exposure to something does not mean that someone will be able to recall it later with a high degree of accuracy.

This fragility of memory has real-world implications for being able to spell words correctly. We encounter misspelled words more frequently than we may realize. Corporations frequently use so-called divergent or sensational spellings, such as "Froot Loops," "Krispy Kreme," and "Chick-fil-A," to call attention to their brands and products. Moviegoers watched Will Smith perform in a film titled *The Pursuit of Happyness*. And over the years, bands like the Beatles, the Monkees, and Def Leppard have enjoyed varying degrees of popularity. If our ability to remember the appearance of coins or the layout of keyboards can be compromised, does exposure to such misspellings have any effect on our spelling ability? As you might have guessed by now, the answer is yes. The cognitive psychologist Larry Jacoby demonstrated that exposing people to misspelled words in the laboratory made them slower to recognize the correctly spelled forms of the words and impaired their spelling ability.[9]

We might assume that such effects are transitory, but Jacoby reports that his coauthor, Ann Hollingshead, may have sustained long-term damage from her repeated exposure to the misspelled versions used in their experiments. Before joining Jacoby's lab, Hollingshead had worked as an executive secretary, with a high degree of confidence in her spelling accuracy. However, after serving as the lab technician in a series of such studies, she found that she was making more errors in spelling words, and her confidence in her spelling ability also declined.[10] And just as certain occupations are more *physically* dangerous than others, it may well be the case that some professions are more *cognitively* dangerous. Teachers who grade their students' spelling quizzes, or professors who must decipher their students' handwritten essay examinations, may be at high risk for losing their spelling confidence and accuracy. As Jacoby and Hollingshead put it in

the title of their paper, "Reading student essays may be hazardous to your spelling."[11]

Assuming someone is not a member of these high-risk pools,
what is the typical trajectory of spelling ability over one's lifetime? It turns out that this skill seems to be well preserved
throughout adulthood. The ability of people in their sixties and
early seventies to detect misspellings, for example, is generally
on par with college-aged students.[12] Another study documented
more spelling inaccuracies for subjects in their eighties compared to participants in their sixties.[13] However, this disparity
may reflect other differences between the groups of subjects. The
participants in their sixties performed better on a measure of
general cognitive ability (the Mini-mental State Examination)
than those in their eighties, and they also had more years of education. So we can't conclude that the decline in spelling among
the oldest participants can be ascribed only to their age. And
if you fined this sentens anoying, then your spelling skills are
probably in fine shape.

Vocabulary Size

> "Will I have to use a dictionary to read your book?" asked Mrs.
> Dodypol.
> "It depends," says I, "how much you used the dictionary before
> you read it."
> —Alexander Theroux, *Darconville's Cat* (1981)

How many words do you know? The question is easy to ask, but
hard to answer. What does it mean to "know" a word, anyway?
Some words are used very frequently and are part of everyone's
active vocabulary, such as "table" or "happy." However, there

are many others that make up a person's *receptive* vocabulary: someone may not use words like "adjudicate" or "quiescent" in conversation, but she knows what those words mean when she encounters them in print. And then there are words that are even less commonly encountered, whose meanings may be only partly understood. These so-called frontier words might include terms like "anathema" and "obsequious."[14] Most people would be hard-pressed to provide precise definitions of these two words, although they are probably aware that they mean something negative. And if you do know what "obsequious" means, should you automatically get credit for also knowing its derived forms, like "obsequiously" and "obsequiousness"? And how could you measure the size of someone's vocabulary without asking him about each of the hundreds of thousands of words that make up a language like English? Clearly, you would need to use some sort of sampling technique.

A common method for estimating vocabulary size involves selecting a number of words from a dictionary at random. Researchers then give these word lists to people to see how many they know. The percentage of known words is then multiplied by the total number of words in the dictionary. And voilà—there's your answer! However, as we have already pointed out, the issue of derived forms complicates such estimates, and even the size of the dictionary turns out to be a factor. Not surprisingly, therefore, such estimates vary widely, although an oft-cited number is about 17,000 base words for the "average educated native" speaker of English.[15]

So do older adults know more words than younger adults? This seems likely, since older adults have had more years of exposure to print than their younger counterparts. As usual, however, we have to be wary when comparing younger apples to older oranges.

You might think, for example, that younger adults of the early twenty-first century read less than their elders. But you would be wrong: they report reading just as much, if not more, albeit in different ways, such as via online sources.[16] It's also the case that different measures of vocabulary yield different results for younger and older participants.[17]

With these caveats in mind, researchers have consistently found larger vocabularies for older adults compared to younger adults. Eugene Zechmeister and his colleagues, using a variation of the dictionary approach just described, estimated that college students have an average vocabulary size of about 16,000 words. Individuals in a group of older adults (average age: 76) living in a retirement village near Chicago were estimated to have a vocabulary size of over 21,000 words.[18] In another study, a sample of older adult speakers of Hebrew (average age: 75) outperformed younger and middle-aged counterparts on a vocabulary task. In this study, the participants were also asked to report how confident they were that they knew each word. The older adults were justifiably more confident in their ratings. This greater metacognitive awareness seems to arise from "a feeling of mastery of their vocabulary knowledge [gained] over a lifetime of word usage."[19] In short, older adults know more words, know what they mean, and know that they know them.

Joshua Hartshorne and Laura Germine conducted a large online study with participants ranging in age from ten to sixty-nine. They administered parts of the Wechsler Adult Intelligence Scale (WAIS-III) and found that vocabulary knowledge peaks in the mid-sixties, which is decades after performance peaks for cognitive processes like short-term and working memory.[20]

It is tempting to conclude that the word-finding problems we discussed earlier may be the unfortunate consequence of knowing lots of words. After all, it would be easier to find a particular book in a small library of a few dozen volumes than to locate a book in a large library with thousands of tomes—particularly if the books aren't well organized. And as we mentioned earlier, older adults are less able to inhibit information that is irrelevant to the task at hand. So maybe all those words sloshing around in one's head create more interference than would be the case for a smaller vocabulary.

The psychologist Meredith Shafto and her colleagues put this idea to the test by asking adults from ages eighteen to eighty-eight to identify real words when given word and nonword pairs, which is one way to assess vocabulary. The participants were also given a task designed to measure word-finding ability through the induction of tip-of-the-tongue (TOT) states. As expected, the older subjects had larger vocabularies than the younger ones. In addition, the older adults also experienced more TOT states. But a closer inspection of the results yields a more complex picture. As the vocabularies of the younger adults increased, so did the number of TOT states. However, for the older adults, as their vocabulary size increased, the number of TOT states decreased. It seems, therefore, that the larger vocabularies of older adults can serve as a compensatory mechanism for word-finding difficulties.[21]

Researchers have also used vocabulary size to see if it might predict people developing cognitive impairment. Older adults in Japan were assessed for signs of mild cognitive impairment (MCI). They were also asked to write and to talk about a happy event. Based on their clinical scores, the participants were classified as either cognitively unimpaired or as having MCI. Although the written versions of the happy events did not differ between the two groups, the spoken versions did. Specifically,

participants classified as experiencing MCI used a more extensive vocabulary. The authors suggested that individuals with
MCI employ larger vocabularies to compensate for their cognitive deterioration. Describing an event to another person must
be done in real time. Those experiencing MCI tried to mask their
impairment with their garrulousness. In the writing task, with as
much time as they wanted to craft a response, the task was less
taxing, and no such compensation was necessary.[22]

Vocabulary size, therefore, is one area where older adults consistently outperform their younger counterparts. This is encouraging, since a larger vocabulary can help offset the changes in
cognitive processing that lead to slower word-naming and word-
finding abilities.

Verbal Fluency

Here's a test for you: how many words starting with the letter
f can you say out loud in one minute? If you give this a try,
you might begin with a rapid-fire stream-of-consciousness reci-
tation of words like "father," "February," "fantastic," "fox," and
"four" and then find yourself mentally ransacking specific categories, such as occupations ("florist, "firefighter," "foreman")
or mental states ("fear," "frustration," "fury"). Like a wildcatter
searching for oil, you might quickly abandon any wellhead that
is becoming less productive and move on to fields that appear
more promising. If you are a younger or middle-aged adult, you
can probably rattle off forty or so words in sixty seconds.[23]

What might seem like an exercise in trivia turns out to be an
important technique for studying peoples' ability to retrieve linguistic information. Although ostensibly a memory task, letter
fluency is thought to involve higher-order cognitive processes
like inhibition ("the word 'phone' doesn't begin with an *f*, so

I shouldn't say it") and self-monitoring ("February starts with an *f*, but I've already said it").[24] Tasks of this kind often use the letters *f*, *a*, and *s* because most English speakers are easily able to think of words beginning with those letters. For that reason, the letter fluency task is sometimes called the FAS test (not to be confused with foreign accent syndrome, which we described earlier). A variant of this task is the category task, in which people are prompted to name all the animals, fruits, or vegetables that they can think of in one minute. Because the animal category is frequently employed, this task is usually referred to as the animal-naming test.

Taken together, tests of letter fluency and category fluency are tests of verbal fluency. Researchers often use them as screening devices to identify individuals who may have suffered some form of brain injury, such as stroke. Verbal fluency tasks can also identify individuals with some other form of cognitive impairment, such as Parkinson's or Alzheimer's disease. These tests have often been conceptualized as measures of executive function, which involves planning and search strategies.[25] In contrast, other researchers have concluded that verbal fluency performance is more closely tied to processing speed.[26] The most recent research on this topic, however, suggests that verbal fluency is best conceptualized as a measure of language processing.[27]

What factors are related to verbal fluency in adults without cognitive impairment? Once again, level of education is one of the strongest predictors of high performance.[28] People with more education tend to have larger vocabularies and consequently possess a larger pool of candidates to draw on as they attempt to recall words beginning with a particular letter.

Does one's age affect verbal fluency? That question is harder to answer, because factors like age and education are often correlated. Since younger adults tend to have more years of formal education, it is difficult to untangle the relative contributions of these two factors. Consequently, the results of this research are mixed. Some studies of verbal fluency have found an effect for education, but not for age,[29] whereas others have found an effect for age, but not for education.[30] And in at least one study, older adults outperformed younger adults.[31] The psychologist Danielle Barry and her colleagues combined the results of 134 previous studies to assess the relation between fluency, age, and education more precisely. The researchers found effects for both education (the more years of schooling, the better the performance on the task) and age (younger people perform better than older).[32]

Performance on verbal fluency tasks also depends on the type of task. Although the impact of age on verbal fluency is mixed when researchers employ the FAS test, a more consistent trend appears when the participants are asked to name as many animals as they can think of. In studies that use this measure of fluency, older adults typically perform more poorly than younger adults. Although the letter and category tests may seem quite similar, some researchers have suggested that different brain regions are responsible for performance on the two tasks.[33]

But what does a decline in verbal fluency really mean? The puzzling pattern of results across studies, as well as the fact that performance varies by type of test, suggests that the full story may be even more complex. For example, expertise plays a role in verbal fluency performance. Competitive Scrabble players, who frequently attempt to find words beginning with particular letters, do very well on the letter test. They outperform age-matched control participants who do not play Scrabble. However, when given the animal-naming task, which is unrelated to playing Scrabble, the experts were no better than their peers.[34]

Taking things one step farther, Michael Ramscar and his colleagues have argued that what appear to be declines in the verbal fluency of older adults might be better thought of as the consequence of higher levels of knowledge.[35] Simply put, the more you know, the harder it is to find what you're looking for. This would explain why older adults consistently perform less well on category tasks: they have large vocabularies of extraneous words to sort through. This may be less of an issue for letter tasks like the FAS, since older adults have access to more word candidates or particular expertise that comes from playing games like Scrabble. It is controversial to claim that cognitive decline due to age is a myth, as Ramscar and his colleagues have. However, their research underscores that what may appear to be cognitive decline could result from other factors, some of which may be beneficial depending on the context. For verbal fluency, a lot of knowledge may be a dangerous thing, but overall, isn't that a good problem to have?

Grammatical Complexity

> Grammar is to a writer what anatomy is to a sculptor or the scales to a musician. You may loathe it, it may bore you, but nothing will replace it, and once mastered it will support you like a rock.
> —Beatrice Joy Chute (1913–1987)

During their first years of life, children progress from expressing themselves with simple one-words utterances ("Juice!") to two-word constructions ("More juice!") to more complex sentences ("I would like some more orange juice, please"—if you happen to have a very polite child). Sentences become longer as people get older, and they also become more grammatically complex.

In languages like English, a principal way in which complexity increases is by the number of clauses that are embedded in a sentence.

Linguists differentiate between left-branching and right-branching clauses. In a left-branching clause, the hearer has to remember the first part of the sentence to make sense of the last part. An example might be "The juice that was bought yesterday and left on the counter until this morning is now in the refrigerator." In this case, the subject of the sentence ("juice") must be kept in working memory until the end of the sentence is reached—assuming you'd like to know where the juice can be found, anyway.

In contrast, right-branching sentences are easier to process. This is because the subject and verb are both in the first clause. Compare the earlier sentence with its right-branching equivalent: "The juice that is now in the refrigerator was bought yesterday and left on the counter until this morning."

Given that working-memory constraints can be problematic for older adults, we might expect to see a decline in grammatical complexity with age. Susan Kemper and Aaron Sumner explored this possibility by asking both college-aged and older adults (average age: 76) to talk for about five minutes about an interesting life experience or an influential person in their lives. These monologues were transcribed and scored to measure sentence length and grammatical complexity. They found that the older adults' sentences were about 30 percent shorter than those spoken by the younger adults. In addition, the older adults' grammatical complexity was about a half point lower on an eight-point scale. The researchers also assessed the participants' working memory and found that, for both groups, the better the memory, the more complex the grammar.[36]

In another study from Kemper's lab, younger and older adults were given sentence stems to memorize. The stems varied in grammatical complexity: some were of the more complex left-branching variety ("What Billy found") whereas others were the easier right-branching type ("Robert ordered that"). The task of the participants was to provide a full sentence using the stem. When younger adults were given right-branching stems to complete, their sentences were longer and more varied than when provided left-branching stems. Older adults, however, showed no difference in sentence length or grammatical complexity in completing the two stem types; they seemed to be operating at the limits of their working memory in both cases. In addition, compared to the younger participants, the older subjects were slower and made more errors when given the more taxing left-branching stems. Once again, these results suggest a working-memory limitation for the older participants.[37]

Later research by Kemper and her colleagues attempted to determine when an age-related decline in grammatical complexity might become apparent. They asked a group of healthy older adults to provide samples of their spoken language on an annual basis for up to fifteen years. When the grammatical complexity of the participants' language use was plotted, the researchers found relative stability up to about age seventy-five, and then a fairly large drop, with further declines continuing over time.[38]

Marilyn Nippold and her collaborators also assessed the complexity of speech produced by participants in their twenties, forties, and sixties, but with a twist. To get a baseline of their speech patterns, participants were recorded as they engaged in a relatively unstructured conversation with an experimenter. Then, after listening to descriptions of situations that involved interpersonal conflict, they described the conflict and gave ideas about how it could be resolved. The researchers found no difference in grammatical complexity among the three groups. However, all groups showed more complexity in their grammar for the natural conversations. Conversely, grammatical complexity declined for all groups when asked to discuss conflict.[39]

Fermín Moscoso del Prado Martín explored how grammatical complexity interacts with vocabulary, sex, and aging. He analyzed a corpus of telephone conversations and found age-related differences over time in grammatical complexity for men and women. Moscoso del Prado Martín found that the diversity of the grammatical forms used by men increases more steeply than it does for women—but only up to about age forty-five, when it falls off again. The diversity of syntactic forms for women showed a steadier increase and a more gradual decline over time. (Note that the oldest speaker in his sample was only sixty-seven.)[40]

Grammatical complexity therefore appears to differ based on a variety of factors, such as age, gender, and topic of conversation, to name but three. Beneath such variability, however, may be two underlying constants: grammatical complexity appears to be constrained by the limits of working memory and by executive function.[41]

However, Moscoso del Prado Martín sounded a note of caution, which applies more broadly than to just his study. He pointed out that the changes he observed, while real, did not correspond to any observed difficulties in the communicative abilities of the participants.[42]

If declines in working memory and executive function are the primary reason for the changes in grammatical complexity, then we would expect to see more rapid declines in grammatical complexity among individuals diagnosed with Alzheimer's disease (AD).[43] And we do.[44] However, although sentence fragments become more common as AD progresses, the fragments themselves remain fairly grammatical.[45] Researchers have also observed the same preservation of grammaticality in the written sentences of individuals suspected of having AD.[46]

In sum, grammatical complexity may have a "ceiling" based on the limits of working memory and executive function.[47] Tasks that strain these two cognitive processes appear to result in shorter, less grammatically complex sentences. That said, older adults have had a lifetime to become more skilled communicators and have acquired a great deal of world knowledge and a large vocabulary. Therefore subtle declines in grammatical complexity may not be particularly noticeable outside the laboratory and probably do not interfere with everyday communication.

Off-Topic Verbosity

My liege, and madam, to expostulate
What majesty should be, what duty is,
Why day is day, night night, and time is time,
Were nothing but to waste night, day and time.
Therefore, since brevity is the soul of wit,
And tediousness the limbs and outward flourishes,
I will be brief: your noble son is mad:
Mad call I it; for, to define true madness,
What is't but to be nothing else but mad?
But let that go.
—Polonius, Shakespeare's *Hamlet*, act 2, scene 2

The humorous story may be spun out to great length, and may wander around as much as it pleases, and arrive nowhere in particular.
—Mark Twain, *How to Tell a Story* (1897)

After Polonius's long-winded delivery, is it any wonder that Gertrude responds by exclaiming, "More matter, with less art"? And haven't we all been trapped in similar situations, listening to a discursive monologue and wishing the speaker would finally get to the point? Of course, people can be verbose and rambling at any age, but older adults seem particularly liable to drift off topic and to engage in lengthy digressions. This is referred to as off-topic speech or off-topic verbosity (OTV).

An essential criterion for designating speech as off topic is that it wanders away from the original subject. The psychologist Dolores Pushkar and her colleagues, who were among the first to study the phenomenon, describe it as "a prolonged series of loosely associated recollections, increasingly remote from, relatively unconstrained by, and irrelevant to the present [context]."[48] They conducted life history interviews with Canadian army veterans of World War II (average age: 65). They found that nearly 20 percent could be classified as "extreme talkers" who produced substantial amounts of off-topic speech. Later research confirmed that OTV is not a matter of sheer garrulousness: the talkativeness and OTV of the veterans were shown to be independent factors, with age predicting OTV but not talkativeness.[49]

Older adults are not the only ones who wander away from the main point of what they are talking about, of course; younger adults may be just as guilty as their grandparents. A study by Guila Glosser and Toni Deser, however, found that older adults performed more poorly on measures of global connectedness in comparison to middle-aged participants. This was true even though performance for the two groups was comparable for grammatical complexity and lexical mistakes.[50] As we have seen, one must take care when comparing younger and older adults. A longitudinal study tracking the same older participants found that verbosity was a relatively stable attribute of their speech over time. However, only fifteen months separated the two assessments, so we don't know what might happen over longer periods.[51]

Psychologists have several competing theories about the cause of OTV. One is that as adults get older, they are simply less able to keep task-irrelevant information from intruding into their thoughts and speech.[52] However, studies have also shown that such off-topic verbosity is task dependent. Lori James and her colleagues asked participants to describe pictures instead of answering open-ended autobiographical questions. The older adults did not produce any more OTV than their younger counterparts.[53] If the underlying issue were simply a matter of reduced inhibition, then the researchers should have found comparable levels of OTV for the two tasks.

Does off-topic verbosity have any real-world implications? It could be the case, for example, that younger adults tend to discount such rambling and perceive older adults as less credible. In simulated courtroom contexts, Elizabeth Brimacombe and her colleagues compared the eyewitness testimony of younger adults (average age: 20) and two groups of older adults: younger seniors (average age: 68) and older seniors (average age: 79). In one study, participants watched a video of money being stolen from a wallet. When asked to describe what happened, a third of the older seniors produced off-topic speech. This included personal experiences that were not relevant to describing the theft. None of the younger seniors or younger adults did this. However, these tangential comments occurred only when the older seniors were describing contexts that were familiar to them (one version of the video had been recorded at their own senior center). This finding suggests that the meandering testimony resulted from reduced inhibition, since the familiar contexts could trigger irrelevant memories of prior experiences in the locations that appeared in the video. Fortunately, however, the off-topic speech was not held against them. A different group of undergraduates, who watched videos of all three groups giving testimony, rated the three groups of participants as equally credible.[54] (We should note, however, that other studies have found older eyewitnesses to be less believable.[55])

Of course, judgments about what is on or off topic are subjective by definition. In the James study mentioned earlier, younger and older adults seemed to have different standards for what constitutes OTV: "Older adults adopt communicative goals that emphasize the significance of life experiences rather than conciseness in their personal narratives."[56] When life experiences are valued, it becomes more acceptable to inject personally relevant observations into a conversation about a different topic.[57] The communicative goals and preferences of younger and older adults may differ as well. Dunja Trunk and Lise Abrams found that younger adults had distinct preferences for how different communicative goals should be expressed. Older adults were more tolerant of diverse expressive styles.[58]

In addition, there may be different degrees of OTV. At one end of the spectrum, "disruptive topic shifts," accompanied by speech that also includes aborted phrases, repetitions, and empty phrases, have been observed in older adults with dementia.[59] At the other end of the spectrum, autobiographical stories that have an internal coherence but are only tangentially related to the topic at hand may be nothing more than an older adult's desire to tell a good yarn.

Although being on the receiving end of OTV can be a frustrating experience, the production of off-topic speech has other implications as well. When younger adults hear such meandering dialogue, it can evoke negative stereotypes about the elderly.[60] We return to the topic of negative stereotypes in the next chapter.

Just one more thing: off-topic productions don't necessarily mean the speaker doesn't have a larger goal in mind. The fictional homicide detective Columbo, played on TV by Peter Falk, told seemingly irrelevant stories that actually ensnared the guilty. In short, pertinence is in the eye (or ear) of the beholder.[61]

Telling Stories

> After nourishment, shelter and companionship, stories are the thing we need most in the world.
> —Philip Pullman

Humans have told stories to each other for thousands of years. Before the advent of widespread literacy, the oral transmission of stories was a primary form of entertainment and instruction. Some of these stories have been preserved as folktales or epic poems and can be quite lengthy, running to thousands of lines. Storytelling thus exemplifies a complex cognitive task, placing great demands on short-term, working, and long-term memory. To offset this cognitive load, storytellers have used mnemonic aids to assist them. These include the repetition of certain phrases, such as the many instances of "swift-footed Achilles" in the *Iliad*, as well as metrical lines with rhyming couplets, used by English poets and dramatists like Shakespeare. When Hamlet exclaims, "The play's the thing, wherein I'll catch the conscience of the king," the word "thing" serves as a retrieval cue for "king." Of course, most of us can't write like Shakespeare, but we all tell stories of one type or another. What happens to the storytelling ability of people as they grow older?

As might be expected, age-related declines in working memory seem to exact a toll on several aspects of older adults' storytelling abilities. Susan Kemper and her colleagues asked participants (age range: 60–90) to "tell us a story—a made up story like you might tell a child.... You could decide to retell a familiar story or make one up from scratch."[62] The researchers then analyzed these personal and fantasy narratives in terms of their narrative structure, grammatical complexity, content, and cohesion (in other words, how well the parts of a narrative are linked to one another). Participants in their eighties produced narratives that were more structurally complex than those provided by participants in their sixties. (More structurally complex stories had more causally connected elements, or they included a coda or a moral.) However, the older group's sentences were less grammatically complex and less cohesive. The researchers suggested that this pattern reflects declines in working memory. However, the increase in structural complexity may be due to deliberate choices made by the older adults to provide information about a story's setting and the narrator's personal opinions about the tale they were telling.[63]

Experiments comparing college students to older adults also suggest differences in storytelling. In one study, when asked to retell a story, older adults produced narratives that were more integrative or interpretive than those told by the undergraduates.[64] Nonetheless, both younger and older participants recalled stories with similar degrees of accuracy.[65] Younger and older adults also agreed on what constitutes a good story, probably because they possess a similar, albeit implicit, understanding of story quality.[66]

Does a lifetime of experience telling stories lead to *better* storytelling? Some evidence points in that direction. Kemper and her colleagues found that judges characterized the stories of older adults (age range: 60–92) to be more clear and interesting than those produced by younger adults (age range: 18–28).[67] A similar study by Michael Pratt and Susan Robins found that the personal narratives of older participants were perceived to be of higher quality than the productions of younger subjects.[68]

Why are older adults better storytellers? Nancy Mergler and her collaborators asked college students to recall sections of prose that had been recorded by three groups of people: peers (aged 20 and 21), middle-aged adults (40 and 49), and older adults (67 and 82). The students remembered more of the incidental details in the segments recorded by the older adults, and when the passages were stories, the students evaluated the older speakers more favorably than the other narrators. However, this was not the case when the passage was simply a descriptive one. The researchers speculate that the physical characteristics of the voices of older people "lead to more effective oral transmission."[69] In addition, the difference in favorability ratings suggests that people have expectations about receiving particular kinds of information from older people. Older adults tend to speak more slowly and may alter their pitch and rhythm in ways that add interest to what they are saying.[70] Finally, such effects may reflect a conscious attempt by older adults to make stories as entertaining as possible, as opposed to being objectively accurate.[71] Or perhaps the experiment evoked memories in the participants of being read to by their parents and grandparents when they were younger!

Although a storyteller is just one person, people often tell stories together. For example, a couple at a dinner party might relate an amusing anecdote to the other guests, with each partner taking turns, or perhaps interrupting each other to fill in

important details or provide an alternate version of events. A study that compared how younger and older couples cope with the demands of collaborative storytelling found few differences between the age groups. With regard to the amount of information recalled, older male participants recalled less than the younger adults, whereas older women did not. The reasons for this difference are unclear. In addition, the study found no difference in the ability of older and younger adults to tell stories collaboratively. They tell them just as well with people they know as they do with new acquaintances.[72]

Differences in collaborative storytelling become more apparent, however, in the ways in which couples tell their stories. For example, in a study where couples were asked to discuss a vacation, older couples talked more about people and places, while younger couples talked more about their itinerary. In addition, older couples tended to tell different parts of the story individually—taking over from each other as the topic shifted. Younger couples interacted more with each other and told all parts of the story together.[73] In a similar vein, older couples also appear to do well in tasks of collaborative problem solving.[74]

Since older couples seem to work well together telling stories and solving problems, working with a partner might be another way to help compensate for any age-related declines in cognitive ability.[75] It seems, therefore, that two heads really are better than one.

5 Using Language

Pragmatic Competence

What does it mean to be a pragmatically competent language user? Among many other factors, pragmatic competence includes being polite, socially appropriate, and responsive to the needs and wants of others.[1] A good example of pragmatic competence would be making small talk. Using language as a way to congenially pass the time requires a sophisticated understanding of context, social conventions, and shared knowledge. Another skill one needs to be pragmatically competent is knowing how to vary the level of deference depending on the size of a request. Minor impositions, such as asking for a sheet of paper, may only require the use of the word "please," whereas more consequential requests, like a ride to the airport, might require a greater display of need and gratitude.

One important aspect of the pragmatic skill required to carry on a conversation is the ability to remember what is (and is not) in the shared common ground. It appears, however, that older adults may not always take into account what their listeners know and do not know. In one study of this phenomenon, younger (age: 24) and older (age: 68) Dutch adults were asked to

narrate comic stories to another person who was either familiar or unfamiliar with the story. When the story was new to the
other person, the younger adults were more accommodating and
included more words and gestures in their storytelling. The older
adults did not accommodate to the needs of the listener as much.[2]

A frequent complaint of older adults is that they experience
difficulty in following and understanding conversations. If cognitive decline, such as changes in memory and executive function, occurs in tandem with perceptual decline—poorer vision
and hearing—then it becomes less clear which factor is responsible. Disentangling cognitive and perceptual deficits can be a
challenge, but some research suggests that older adults' difficulty
with conversation is more perceptual than it is cognitive.[3] For
example, in a group setting, older adults may not effectively use
auditory cues that indicate who is speaking. However, they still
know how to carry on a conversation.

Studies of spontaneous language use by older adults suggest
that there may also be important gender differences. Impromptu
descriptions of a picture by younger, middle-aged, and older
Spanish-speaking participants revealed age-related decreases
that were small for female subjects, but more pronounced for
males.[4] The paucity of spontaneous speech produced by the
men could be construed as a lack of interest or even rudeness.
Consequently, even the amount of language that one produces
is significant. The study did not explore whether the difference
between men and women was due to cognitive, social, or cultural factors, but it does suggest that pragmatic changes in older
adulthood may play themselves out differently for men than for
women.

Pragmatic competence is not limited to verbal expression.
For example, in face-to-face interactions, people are typically

sensitive to the eye gaze of their conversational partners: they will follow the other person's glance at an object or a third party as a means of creating joint attention. In an experiment involving younger (average age: 20) and older (average age: 73) adults, researchers asked participants to view faces appearing on a computer screen and to decide when the person appeared to be looking slightly to their left or right or straight ahead. The older adults were slower in making such judgments, as well as in following the direction of the gazes, suggesting that older adults may be at a disadvantage in using this important social cue.[5]

Pragmatic deficits in adulthood have been implicated in various neurodegenerative diseases. People suffering from Parkinson's disease show an impaired ability to size up the level of politeness required to make appropriate requests.[6] People with multiple sclerosis (MS) may not provide the appropriate amount of information to a conversational partner.[7] Similar deficits are seen in people with amyotrophic lateral sclerosis (ALS).[8]

Everyone needs to interact with health-care professionals to report symptoms and to receive medications and instructions for using them. However, it's especially important for practitioners to be aware of the aspects of pragmatics that may be problematic for their more senior patients. For example, given the difficulties that older adults can have in following conversations, it might be better if just one person provides a patient with information about a procedure than to have several caregivers engage in a multiparty conversation.[9] In addition, practitioners must take care to avoid making an incorrect assumption about why someone does not maintain appropriate eye gaze (for example, they are lying) or fails to follow correct turn-taking protocol (they are pushy).

Nonliteral Language

> Life is like riding a bicycle. To keep your balance, you must keep
> moving.
> —Albert Einstein, in a letter to his son Eduard (1930)

A great deal of the language we use isn't meant to be interpreted
literally. For example, when someone asserts that it's a million
degrees outside or that a waiter took forever to appear, she is
using exaggeration to emphasize hotter-than-usual temperatures
or slower-than-normal service. One has to infer the intended
meaning of such utterances by taking into account context,
world knowledge, and information about one's conversational
partner. So one could interpret a statement about impossibly
high temperatures as a complaint about the weather by an overly
dramatic friend.

Exaggeration is just one example of figurative or nonliteral
language commonly employed in both speech and writing. Language researchers have studied how nonliteral language competence develops in children and the ways in which people use
these language forms to achieve specific discourse goals, such as
to be humorous or to provoke thought,[10] as in Einstein's simile
quoted earlier. Researchers have also studied how the aging process affects the comprehension of nonliteral language. In this
section, we briefly review some of the research on aging and four
types of nonliteral language: metaphor, idiom, verbal irony, and
proverbs.

Metaphors involve a comparison between two dissimilar things
that have an underlying connection, such as lectures and sleep-
ing pills (things that can induce sleep). Some metaphors are rich,
and invite many such connections. Consider Jaques's assertion

in *As You Like It* that "all the world's a stage." His monologue runs to over two hundred words as Shakespeare explicates the varied ways in which our lives are like acts in a play. Because metaphors require the simultaneous consideration of apparently dissimilar concepts, they can be quite complex. This suggests that they tax cognitive processes like working memory and the inhibition of irrelevant information. Does it follow, then, that older adults experience difficulties in interpreting metaphors?

Research to answer this question is equivocal. In one study, in comparison to younger adults (average age: 25), older adults (average age: 70) made more errors when asked to identify metaphors as being literally false (responding "no" to statements like "The singer killed the song"). This study concluded that older adults found it more difficult to inhibit the metaphorical interpretation of such sentences.[11] However, in another study, younger (19) and older (74) participants read sentences like "The lawyer for the defense is a shark." These sentences were followed by metaphorically relevant statements (such as "Sharks are tenacious") or by metaphorically irrelevant ones ("Sharks are good swimmers"). The subjects were asked to decide whether these statements made sense. Both the older and the younger participants were faster when the second statement was relevant to the metaphor ("tenacious"), and slower when the second statement was metaphorically irrelevant ("good swimmers").[12] This result suggests that older adults can inhibit the irrelevant meanings of metaphors, at least in some situations.

In comparison to metaphors, idioms are relatively frozen expressions with just one fixed meaning (such as "letting the cat out of the bag" for "revealing a secret"). Given their additional years of linguistic experience, older adults might be expected to outperform younger adults with regard to their familiarity with

such expressions and knowledge of their meanings. Once again, the results are mixed. In a study in which subjects were asked about such phrases, participants in their sixties outperformed those in their twenties.[13] However, another study found that, compared to younger adults, older subjects performed more poorly at tasks that required them to inhibit the literal meaning of idioms.[14]

Verbal irony and sarcasm in particular present the interpretive challenge of figuring out why someone would assert the opposite of what they literally intend (such as saying "Fabulous weather!" during a downpour or "You're a genius!" to a forgetful friend). In face-to-face communication, sarcastic utterances are often accompanied by affective cues like exaggerated facial expressions or a particular tone of voice. And as we have already seen, older adults are less able to recognize affective cues in others' expressions. In a study of sarcasm detection, younger,

middle-aged, and older adults watched videos that depicted conversations in which characters made either sincere or sarcastic
statements. Although the three groups performed similarly in
figuring out the meaning of the sincere utterances, the older
adults had more difficulty in correctly identifying sarcastic asser-
tions. The authors of the study suggest that older adults are less
able to use affective cues and situational context to decipher the
nonliteral intent of the speaker.[15] It comes as no surprise, then,
that older adults with mild cognitive impairment have even
more difficulties inferring the mental states of others and perform even less well in identifying verbal irony in such tasks.[16]

The comprehension of proverbs provides another window
into the language abilities of older adults. In some respects, we
might expect performance to parallel that of idioms, since they
are also phrases that have a specific meaning within a culture
(as in "Look before you leap" as a way of urging caution). Older
adults should have greater familiarity with such phrases, and
one study shows that the ability to explain less-familiar proverbs increases throughout adolescence and young adulthood.
This ability remains stable through midlife until a small decline
in the sixties and then a more pronounced decline in the seventies.[17] However, Hanna Ulatowska and her collaborators found
that research participants in their eighties and nineties performed
quite well when summarizing or interpreting proverbs.[18] On
the other hand, another study has shown a decline in proverb
interpretation for a group of participants in their sixties and
seventies when compared to a younger group in their twenties
and thirties and a middle-aged group in their forties and fifties.
These researchers also found decreases in working memory and
inhibitory control in the older group, which may explain why
such a decline occurs.[19] The evidence, therefore, is mixed, but

it suggests that proverb familiarity and comprehension may be preserved for at least some older adults.

As we have seen, older adults do benefit from their greater experience with language, outperforming younger research participants in their knowledge of idioms and maintaining an ability to explain less-familiar proverbs until late in life. However, a decline in some of the cognitive foundations that language comprehension is built on, such as working memory and the inhibition of irrelevant information, ultimately affects the comprehension and interpretation of nonliteral language. In addition, a decrement in the monitoring of affective and contextual cues makes it more difficult for older adults to interpret verbal irony and sarcasm. Yet even younger adults can find these forms of language to be challenging (as fans of the children's book series about Amelia Bedelia, who always interprets figurative language literally, may attest).

Finally, keep in mind that the experiments summarized here were designed to highlight differences that may not matter as much in the real world. An idiom like "quitting cold turkey" may cause an older person to momentarily think about Thanksgiving leftovers, but that doesn't mean she can't also understand that a friend has declared his intention to stop smoking.

Can Spring Chickens Teach Old Dogs New Tricks?

> It is no exaggeration to say that languages change because speakers want to change them.... They do not want to express themselves the same way they did yesterday, and in particular not the same way as somebody else did yesterday. To this extent, language is comparable to fashion.
> —Christian Lehmann (2004)

Almost by definition, the story of language is the story of language change. Speakers of modern English who attempt to read Old English poetry written a thousand years ago must approach the task as if they were learning a foreign language. Students who are assigned *The Canterbury Tales*, written in Middle English about four centuries later, still require extensive glosses to fully appreciate Chaucer's stories. Not until we reach the seventeenth century (the King James Bible and Shakespeare's plays) do most English speakers today feel comfortable reading literature in their native language without annotation. So if language change is a given, then how do these changes play themselves out on shorter timescales, such as within the lifetime of one individual? And what are the implications of language change on aging?

Researchers have employed a variety of techniques to study these questions. Corpus linguists, for example, have analyzed large numbers of texts to identify trends in literature over time.[20] Psychologists have surveyed the written output of individuals across several decades to identify changes in grammatical usage, vocabulary, or particular word categories.[21] Sociolinguists have studied language change within specific speech communities by comparing audio recordings at varying intervals to identify shifts in pronunciation. More recently, researchers have sifted through social media postings on sites like Facebook to identify age-related differences in language use.[22] Not surprisingly, perhaps, these studies have found a great deal of variation, although linguistic stability at the level of the individual seems to be the most common outcome, even as the culture or society undergoes significant shifts.[23]

The claim of linguistic stability for individuals seems paradoxical if we consider the extensive changes that can occur in a particular language over time. This can be explained, however, if we consider the ways in which language is acquired. Although most people assume that children learn language from their parents, a body of research now suggests that one's peers play a major role as well.[24] Many parents who relocate to a different part of the country are surprised when their children pick up the accent or dialect of the new region. And these linguistic shifts can occur quite early in life: one study documented changes occurring in children as young as twenty months.[25] Adolescents in particular are motivated to fit in with their classmates and neighbors and will change their speech—consciously or unconsciously—to conform to their peers. These changes are perhaps most noticeable in how words are pronounced, but there can be many other, more subtle differences.

The issues involved in language change may be clearer if we zero in on just one linguistic component, such as word choice. The vocabulary that people acquire during childhood, and specifically the terms they use to refer to things, tend to remain stable over time. Many of these words and labels, however, drift out of fashion through a process of technological, cultural, or generational change. The end result is that, simply through their word choices, middle-aged and older adults come to be perceived as old-fashioned by members of younger generations. Many children and adolescents have been mortified by their parents when they hear them referring to objects with names that have fallen out of contemporary usage or have otherwise been displaced. Examples would include calling a backpack a knapsack or a rucksack or referring to a sofa as a davenport or a chesterfield. Five-and-dime stores have been replaced by dollar stores, parlors have evolved into family rooms, and iceboxes have transformed into refrigerators. In a similar way, many once-common idioms, similes, and metaphors gradually drop out of contemporary

"Please get your rucksack off the davenport!"

usage, and using them marks a speaker as a member of an older generation.

From this perspective, we can make sense of the seemingly incompatible ideas of language change across time and language stability within individuals. The speech of a particular person may change extensively while she is younger and striving to be accepted by her peers. In other words, language change is a young person's game, with adolescents and young adults promoting sometimes sweeping changes in linguistic fashion. And since middle-aged and older adults spend much of their time talking with their peers, the culture reinforces a certain linguistic orthodoxy across the adult life span.

But don't people want to be perceived as being as youthful as possible? The demand for procedures like facelifts suggests that we should see middle-aged and older adults taking on the linguistic trappings of the young. Older speakers, however, can run into difficulties by attempting to incorporate more contemporary terms into their speech. People in their fifties or sixties who use contemporary styles of speech or youthful slang may well be ridiculed for their awkward attempts to appear younger than they are. They may also be resented for trying to appropriate the culture of those who are several decades younger.

In a classic study of the issues involved in intergenerational communication, Angie Williams and Howard Giles asked college students to recall conversations with older adults. (For the purposes of the study, they were asked about people aged 65 to 75 who were not family members.) For conversations perceived as dissatisfying, many of the study participants asserted that the difficulties were caused by their older interlocutors. Specifically, they characterized their older partners as being insufficiently accommodating, such as when they were perceived to be closed-minded or out of touch.[26] Being "out of touch" may result from a variety of factors, and one of these could be the use of unfamiliar or "old-fashioned" terminology.

Taken as a whole, the research on language change across the life span suggests that individuals try to find some middle ground between stability (consistency in language use over time) and flexibility (acquiring new terms and new ways of using the language as the culture changes).[27] Just as with clothing styles, so there are clear dangers for adults in being too linguistically fashion-forward. As with many other things in life, however, most people are able to find a balance between the old and the new that works for them.

Elderspeak

When people talk to each other, they consciously and unconsciously make changes in how they talk. Someone giving directions to a young child, for example, might speak more slowly and distinctly than he usually does. The homesick college student may speak to her parents during a video chat with more of a twang in her voice than when she interacts with her classmates. And when younger people talk to older adults, they also make changes in their speech. Because of its similarity to so-called baby talk, the practice was referred to by that term when Linnda Caporael first documented its use in nursing homes in 1981.[28] It has since been dubbed "elderspeak."[29]

Both baby talk and elderspeak are examples of a phenomenon called accommodation, whereby speakers attempt to alter their speech to be more easily understood by their conversational partners.[30] People make this kind of adjustment routinely when conversing, for example, with nonnative speakers. If a speaker assumes that her partner's vocabulary is not as extensive as her own, she may be more careful in her choice of words than she would be otherwise. Viewed in this way, the accommodation can be helpful, reflecting consideration on the part of the speaker. And in the case of elderspeak, a person may be trying to convey empathic concern or warmth toward the older partner. However, this way of speaking also reflects negative stereotypes of older adults, who are often thought to have diminished cognitive capacity. Not surprisingly, therefore, such speech is often perceived as patronizing.[31]

Baby talk and elderspeak have much in common. Speakers attempt to simplify their vocabulary and grammar and use collective nouns, such as substituting "we" for "you," as in "Are we ready for our pills?" Shorter sentences, repetitions, and paraphrases are also common.[32] The use of tag questions, such as "You want to go to dinner now, don't you?" deprive the recipient of making independent choices. Perhaps the most characteristic aspect of such speech, however, is a distinct change in prosody. Elderspeakers talk more loudly, more slowly, and at a higher pitch. They may also use a singsong intonation, with the vocal pitch swooping up and down.[33]

The use of such speech directed to older adults is not monolithic, however. Younger speakers seem to take into account factors such as whether the person being addressed seems to be independent and in good health, and whether the interaction is taking place in the community or in a hospital setting.[34] This accommodation is consistent with the idea that speakers adjust their speech when they think it is necessary. The problem may be that younger people assume older adults are frail and hard of hearing and use elderspeak unless they have clear evidence that it is unnecessary.

One negative aspect of elderspeak is the effect that it has on institutionalized individuals. A major issue faced by caregivers working with older adults with dementia is that their patients may become resistive to care. For example, residents in a long-term care facility may show aggression, have verbal outbursts, or withdraw and become less engaged with their surroundings. A team led by Kristine Williams has found that the use of elderspeak is related to such problematic behaviors.[35] It seems likely, therefore, that such patronizing language fosters an attitude of dependence and diminished capacity.

Even for older adults who are aging healthily in their communities, the use of elderspeak is rampant. Particularly offensive for many are terms of endearment, such as "honey" or "sweetie." An eighty-three-year old woman, for example, when asked about her experiences with such language, complained about the use of the word "dear." "People think they're being nice, but when I hear it, it raises my hackles." A seventy-eight-year-old man objected to people decades younger than he, such as store clerks, referring to him by his first name, calling it "faux familiarity." Another common complaint is simply being ignored by others, such as doctors who might address questions to the patients' adult children, or by restaurant servers, who make small talk with younger patrons at the same table, but not with the older diners.[36]

Elderspeak also has pernicious long-term effects. Becca Levy argues that such language promotes negative stereotypes of aging, which are internalized by people when they are younger, and then become part of their self-concept when they grow older. And these self-perceptions can have health consequences. Levy's work has shown that older adults with positive self-perceptions about aging live, on average, 7.5 years longer than people with more negative self-perceptions.[37]

On the other hand, it's worth noting that the use of elderspeak does have some positive attributes. In one study, older adults who heard medication instructions presented in elderspeak remembered more of the information than when it was presented using normal speech. The study also found that perceptions of elderspeak were not uniformly negative but were, in fact, mixed, and for both young and old. It seems that perceptions of caring and kindness—that is, the intentions behind elderspeak—can coexist with its being perceived as patronizing and disrespectful.[38] And some aspects of elderspeak are more helpful than others. Susan Kemper and Tamara Harden gave younger and older participants a task in which they followed verbal directions to trace a route on a map. The researchers found that directions that provided elaborations and used syntactically less complex sentences were beneficial for the older subjects. Other aspects of elderspeak, such as short sentences, a slower speaking rate, and a higher vocal pitch, did not help and created communication problems.[39]

Although there's no such term as "youngsterspeak," young adults have also reported being put off by the way in which older people talk to them. When asked to describe conversations with older adults they found dissatisfying, younger adults recalled these conversations as being ones in which the older person complained, showed negative emotion, and stereotyped the younger generation as irresponsible and naive. In addition, younger people disliked when the older person disclosed inappropriate personal information or was pushy.[40] In general, then, it seems that younger adults do not like when older adults "underaccommodate" to the conversational task at hand by not taking the younger partners' conversational needs into consideration. And older adults do not like when younger people "overaccommodate" and end up talking to them as if they were children.

We have at least some reason to be hopeful that this infantilizing behavior can be corrected. Nursing assistants benefit from training to reduce their use of elderspeak, and positive effects were observed after just three one-hour training sessions.[41] So even though people may acquire negative stereotypes about older adults through socialization, the resulting negative behaviors can be overcome fairly easily.

Living with More Than One Language

A different language is a different view of life.
—Federico Fellini

Throughout the world, a majority of people acquire more than one language during their lifetime. In the United States, 20 percent of individuals older than five speak a language other than English at home.[42] Most commonly, this happens because such individuals were exposed to two (or more) languages early in life. In other cases, they chose to become proficient in a second language in adolescence or adulthood and then invested the time and effort necessary to achieve fluency.

Proficiency in a second language, however, is not a fixed, unchanging ability. Many children who are exposed to a heritage language not spoken outside the home will mostly lose their ability to easily speak or understand it as they grow older. This is the fate of many second-generation Americans, who may stop using a heritage language entirely once they leave their parents' homes. In addition, many people required to learn a second language as part of their formal education rapidly lose their ability to speak or understand it once they leave school, although vestiges of this knowledge may persist for decades.[43]

It's helpful, therefore, to imagine multiple-language proficiency as existing on a continuum, with monolinguals at one end and people completely proficient in two (or more) languages at the other. But even these so-called balanced bilinguals tend to use their languages in different contexts and for different purposes. In large parts of Africa and Asia, multilingual individuals may speak one language at home, a second at school or at work, and even a third in the marketplace. However, singing a lullaby to a young child, negotiating with an uncooperative supplier, and purchasing ingredients for the evening meal are quite different in terms of their social and cognitive complexity.

In addition, even people who are completely proficient in two languages may feel less fluent if they haven't used one of their languages for a while. The first author of this book remembers the account of a postdoctoral researcher in his academic department. She was from Germany and had completed her graduate studies in the United States. After spending several years in America, she returned to her hometown for a visit and found herself hesitant and tongue-tied when using her native language. It was terrible, she lamented; she got the impression that her friends and family concluded she had gone to America and "become stupid." So even proficiency in one's native language can be blunted by the exclusive use of a second language over an extended period.

There may also be cognitive limits with regard to how many languages a person can have active at any point. In his survey of the world's most accomplished polyglots, Michael Erard found several who, although able to speak many languages, admitted that they would need time to "reactivate" one that they had not employed recently.[44]

The consequences of bilingualism have been a focus in developmental psychology, and researchers have found that children exposed to more than one language accrue certain advantages in comparison to their monolingual peers. As just one example, bilingual children performed better on measures of inhibitory control. Stephanie Carlson and Andrew Meltzoff conducted an experiment with bilingual kindergarteners and found they were better at playing "Simon Says" (which requires *not* doing something on certain trials) than their monolingual peers.[45] However, researchers have also noted certain linguistic deficits. For example, compared to monolinguals of the same age, bilingual children's vocabulary development is slower.[46] This is not particularly surprising, since these kids have to acquire twice as many words for concepts.

An individual might acquire more than one language, but she might also lose one as well, perhaps because she has left the community in which one of her languages is spoken. Such language attrition may be a common consequence of multilingualism, but language loss can also be driven by other factors. In 1881 the French psychologist Théodule-Armand Ribot proposed that when cognitive functions are disrupted, more recently learned knowledge or skills are affected to a greater degree than those acquired earlier. Ribot's law, or the regression hypothesis, is consistent with recovery from retrograde amnesia, in which earlier memories are unaffected but recall for more recent events is impaired. Can we make a similar generalization about the languages spoken by bilinguals?

Ribot's regression hypothesis predicts that the language acquired later in life is at greater risk if a person experiences some sort of cognitive impairment, such as aphasia, mild cognitive impairment (MCI), or Alzheimer's disease (AD). Consistent with this hypothesis, bilinguals with AD perform better on language tasks in their dominant language. But the same holds true for bilingual individuals who are not cognitively impaired.[47] Furthermore, a study that followed a group of Catalan-Spanish MCI and AD bilinguals over time found equivalent deterioration in both languages.[48] Therefore the evidence appears not to support Ribot's hypothesis that the last language learned is the first language lost.[49]

What does it feel like to be bilingual? At one level, it is no different from possessing any other specific skill, such as being able to play the flute or contract bridge, or having knowledge of a particular subject, such as organic chemistry or entomology. These abilities and knowledge exist in a latent state until they are called on by the individual. And just as with chemistry students or flautists, so people have a wide range of proficiency and fluency in language use.

At another level, some bilinguals report that it feels as if they switch personalities when they switch languages. In his classic book on bilingualism, *Life with Two Languages*, François Grosjean included several such accounts. For example, a French-English bilingual asserted, "I know that I am more aggressive, more caustic, when I speak French." A Greek-English speaker reported that when she speaks Greek, she talks "more rapidly, with a tone of anxiety and in a kind of rude way." And a Russian-English bilingual opined that when he speaks Russian, he feels "like a much more gentle, 'softer' person," whereas when speaking English he feels more "harsh [and] "businesslike."[50] As these examples illustrate, language, culture, and personality can interact in complex and not entirely predictable ways and underline how language can affect one's sense of self at any age.

The Benefits of Bilingualism?

Researchers who study bilingualism have long assumed that possessing two or more languages confers certain cognitive benefits in comparison to monolingual speakers. This bilingual advantage might manifest itself in a variety of ways, such as through better working memory or superior executive functioning. However, owing to the complexity of the issues involved, it is difficult to draw any unambiguous conclusions about a bilingual advantage.

First, we need to differentiate between potential bilingual advantages that might be possessed by children and the effects of bilingualism for younger and older adults. It's possible, for example, that children exposed to two or more languages accrue cognitive benefits that may diminish later in life. In addition, direct comparisons of bilingual and monolingual children are problematic, since the two groups may differ systematically on other relevant dimensions, such as their parents' socioeconomic status or level of education.[51] Comparisons between adult bilinguals are also fraught, since many bilinguals are immigrants and therefore differ in significant ways from monolinguals who have spent their lives in one linguistic community. Even the cognitive measures that researchers use can be an issue, since they don't always agree about which tasks tap into which cognitive processes.[52] Finally, the paths to bilingualism vary, and individuals who are equally fluent in two languages probably represent the exception rather than the rule.

With these caveats in mind, let's consider some of the reasons why bilingualism might confer cognitive benefits. Bilinguals possess the ability to shift rapidly back and forth between two languages, sometimes even within a single sentence. Such code switching, as it's called, might lead to greater overall cognitive flexibility and control. However, carefully controlled studies using a number of different measures of executive processing have not revealed any general advantage for bilinguals over monolinguals.[53]

Another potential advantage for bilinguals could come in the area of attentional control. Researchers can study this ability via the Stroop task, which we described in the first chapter (participants are asked to name the color of a word that is also a color name; for example, a response of "red" when confronted by the word "green" printed in red ink). This task requires active inhibition of a dominant response (reading the word). Since bilinguals may inhibit one language while using the other, they should perform better on such tasks than monolinguals. Once again, however, a study with good controls failed to find a bilingual advantage for either younger or older adults.[54]

We should note that the way in which scientists conduct and then publish their research could have led to the initial preponderance of evidence in favor of superior executive control for bilinguals. In general, experiments that uncover a significant difference between two groups are deemed more publishable than those that fail to detect a difference. And an analysis of conference presentations on this topic reported more nonsignificant and mixed results in comparison to supportive results in the published literature. The supposed bilingual advantage may therefore be the result of publication bias,[55] although other researchers have called this conclusion into question.[56]

Bilingual advantages may manifest themselves in specific contexts with specific populations. A study by Brooke Macnamara and Andrew Conway, for example, documented greater cognitive control and working memory for hearing students of American Sign Language as they progressed through a two-year program of study. The scientists hypothesized that these improved abilities result from simultaneous interpretation, which requires juggling the demands of frequent switches between languages, as well as simultaneous comprehension and language production.[57]

It may also be the case that growing up with two languages is fundamentally different from later exposure to a second language. Bilinguals who learned English and Spanish or English and Mandarin early in life have been shown to learn and retain novel words and their meanings better than monolinguals.[58]

But how about learning a second language later in life? Do we have any evidence that acquiring another language in younger or older adulthood might prove beneficial? This notion makes a great deal of intuitive sense. It ties into the larger cultural belief that the brain is like a muscle that requires exercise to stay in shape. The admonition to "use it or lose it" has spurred tremendous growth in the "brain-training" industry. If engaging in cognitive and memory tasks on a phone app can theorietically stave off cognitive decline or dementia, then surely learning another language should provide even more cognitive benefits.

As compelling as this line of reasoning might seem, the evidence suggests otherwise. A detailed analysis of the research literature on the effectiveness of brain-training regimens produced three major conclusions. First, and least surprising, is that performance on the tasks used in brain training leads to better performance on those tasks. In other words, your mother was right: practice does makes perfect, and practicing word searching makes you better at—word searching. However, the researchers also looked at transfer to similar tasks and found much less evidence for brain-training effectiveness. Finally, they found virtually no evidence that such training improves cognitive performance in general.[59]

Furthermore, most accounts of research on bilingual brain benefits in the popular media leave out an important detail. Scientists who explore the benefits of bilingualism have primarily studied individuals who have been bilingual since early in life and who regularly use both of their languages.[60] Learning a second language in one's fifties or sixties may not confer the same cognitive benefits that exist for those who have always been bilingual. But that doesn't mean you shouldn't do it. There are many, many reasons to learn a second language later in life, and contrary to popular belief, older adults can be highly successful at it.[61] Learning a second language, even late in life, can expand one's cultural horizons, increase career opportunities,[62] and perhaps even make people more empathic.[63] But the notion of learning another language as a means of staving off cognitive decline is not supported by research at this time.

6   The Write Stuff

Healing through Language

Throughout their lives, people experience traumatic events that can have long-term negative consequences for them. The quintessential example is post-traumatic stress disorder (PTSD), in which people experience unwanted and distressing feelings and thoughts related to an earlier traumatic event. These feelings and thoughts can persist for years and can be debilitating in some cases. Another, less well-known consequence of trauma is complicated grief disorder (CGD). This most typically occurs as the result of bereavement. Although the death of a loved one will have a significant negative impact for most people, people who suffer from CGD experience high levels of distress long after their loss.

A fundamental assumption of psychotherapy is that talking about distressing experiences can lead to improvements in well-being. However, psychotherapy can be both expensive and time-consuming. Could simply *writing* about traumatic episodes be beneficial as well? The University of Texas psychologist James Pennebaker and his colleagues sought to answer this question. Some of the undergraduate participants in their study were asked to write about the most upsetting or traumatic event they had ever experienced and to express their deepest feelings and thoughts about the trauma. Participants in a control group were asked to simply write about an assigned topic, such as their plans for the rest of the day. Both groups wrote for just twenty minutes on four consecutive days. Perhaps not surprisingly, participants who had written about traumatic events, such as the loneliness they experienced at college or conflicts with romantic partners, reported higher levels of subjective distress immediately after these writing sessions. Remarkably, they reported being happier than the control group at a three-month follow-up. In addition, Pennebaker's team found that students who had written about their trauma had fewer illnesses and visits to the university's student health center in the weeks after the writing sessions. The researchers even observed physiological changes: blood tests revealed improvements in two measures of cellular immune function.[1]

In fact, additional research has linked a host of positive outcomes to writing or talking about traumatic experiences. Several other studies have also found reductions in doctor visits after writing about trauma. In addition, scientists have documented improvements in several physiological health markers besides cellular immune function. And several other behavioral changes, such as improvement in student grade point averages, finding a new position after a job loss, and reduction in work absenteeism, have been reported.[2] Writing about emotionally traumatic experiences can even lead to improvements in people who suffer from rheumatoid arthritis and asthma.[3]

Of course, one could argue that undergraduate homesickness or adolescent relationship problems are only pale shadows of the kind of trauma that can lead to PTSD and CGD. However, Pennebaker also conducted interviews with Holocaust survivors living in the Dallas area in the 1980s. He found that the majority of these survivors had not talked about their horrific experiences with anyone else, either because they wanted to forget or because they thought no one else would understand. Pennebaker and his colleagues conducted one- to two-hour, highly emotional interviews with more than sixty survivors. The sessions were videotaped, and each interviewee's heart rate and skin conductance were also measured. (Skin conductance is a measure of how much someone is perspiring. It is a commonly used measure of physiological arousal, which is often associated with strong affective states.) Based on these physical measures and the degree of traumatic content of the interviews, the researchers classified each survivor as being a low, midlevel, or high discloser. High disclosers remained physiologically relaxed as they described their suffering, whereas low disclosers displayed signs of tension during their interviews. When they contacted the participants about fourteen months after the interviews, the researchers found that both high and midlevel disclosers were healthier than they had been before participating in the interviews. The low disclosers, however, were more likely to have seen their doctors about an illness in the year after the interviews.[4]

Other research by Pennebaker and his colleagues suggests that specific types of words may be responsible for the beneficial effects of writing about traumatic experiences. Their work suggests that improved mental and physical health is seen when participants employ positive emotion words (such as "happy," "joyful," and "elegant") relative to negative emotion words (like "angry," "wrong," and "sad"). Using words from other linguistic categories had positive but less universal effects. Words associated with insight (like "see," "understand," and "realize") and terms associated with causation (like "infer," "thus," and "because") were correlated with better physical, but not psychological, health.[5]

An important qualification to this line of research is necessary. Talking or writing about trauma proves most beneficial when people use language to create a narrative structure about their experiences. In other words, one must think about the traumatic event as a meaningful story, not just a pattern of unconnected experiences and sensations. When college students were asked to write about traumatic events in their lives as coherent narratives, they subsequently reported fewer bouts of illness than a group who described their trauma in the form of a fragmented list.[6] Others have also echoed the importance of constructing a coherent self-narrative.[7]

It would be a mistake, however, to regard writing about traumatic events as some sort of magic cure-all. Pennebaker himself points out that writing about trauma seems to confer no benefit if it occurs right after the event itself. And writing a lot about negative events, perhaps via extensive journaling, may actually be harmful: it could turn into rumination, which might worsen anxiety or depressive symptoms.[8]

Reminiscing

Again, you can't connect the dots looking forward; you can only connect them looking backward. So you have to trust that the dots will somehow connect in your future. You have to trust in something—your gut, destiny, life, karma, whatever.

—Steve Jobs (2005)

The founder of Apple famously spoke these words during a commencement address at Stanford.[9] He was speaking to young people on the verge of a new life. But at the opposite end of life's journey, it's important to think about something Jobs didn't say: in looking backward, the dots won't connect themselves.

As we saw in the previous section, talking or writing about traumatic events has been shown to have positive health benefits. But there's a catch—two actually: it's best if some time has passed since the event, and the events need to be conveyed in the form of a coherent, meaningful narrative.

Erik Erikson speculated that one of the natural consequences of coming to terms with the approaching end of life is the desire to look back and make sense of it all.[10] Erikson divided our life span into eight stages of development that begin at birth and continue through the end of life. He theorized that during each of these stages an individual is faced with a crisis. The theme of the crisis is tied to the most salient aspect of identity formation at that time. As we age, the successful resolution of one stage prepares us to cope with the upcoming crisis of the next. For Erikson, identity development is a lifelong process in which "*different capacities use different opportunities* to become full-grown components of the ever-new configuration that is the growing personality."[11]

The first six crises, from infancy through one's thirties, center on struggles related to trust, autonomy, initiative, competence, identity, and the experience of intimacy. Regardless of how these crises are resolved, adults in their forties, fifties, and early sixties next turn to figuring out how to give back to others and nurture future generations. Erikson conceptualized this struggle as one between *generativity* and *stagnation*. Although often expressed through child rearing and the guidance given by parents and grandparents, the goals of this stage can also be viewed more broadly. At this point, men and women start to think about their legacy and to reevaluate the direction their life is taking. Some people may recommit to previously established goals and find new strength and energy in seeing these goals through. Others may make a change and take their lives in a new direction.

For most people, it would be a dramatic overstatement to call this evaluation a midlife crisis. But certainly such a reexamination is likely to be taking place in middle age. A failure to use generativity as a way to model positive values sets an example of greed and selfishness for the next generation.[12] And language is key to the realization of generativity. Mentoring, guiding, parenting, and teaching are just some of the ways people use language to give back to others.

After an individual has figured out how to be generative, he begins to think more about his own mortality. This new stage generally begins when a person retires, around age sixty-five. An individual who sees his life as whole and complete can make the most of the time he has left and face death with a sense of calm. A person who can only look back and feel that he hasn't accomplished anything worthwhile becomes depressed and despairs of his eventual death. Based on Erikson's ideas about this crisis between *integrity* and *despair*, Robert Butler created life review therapy[13] to help adults reflect in a way that brings about reconciliation, peace, and a sense of life satisfaction[14] and empowerment.[15]

Life review therapy is not the only technique for discovering the integrity of one's life. For example, Guided Autobiography (GAB) is a structured life review process that occurs in a group setting.[16] In GAB, people write down memories of events that relate to specific themes. They then share these memories with others in a small group. Through this kind of reminiscence, we can develop "a deeper understanding of who we are, where we have been, and where we are going in the future."[17]

But not all searches of lost time are effective remembrances of things past. To separate adaptive kinds of reminiscence from maladaptive ones, Paul Wong and Lisa Watt created a taxonomy of reminiscence.[18] Theirs is not the only way to specify types of reminiscence,[19] but for our purposes, their categories illustrate some important ways in which the language used to describe the past has an impact on the present.

Of the six types of reminiscence that they discuss, the category called integrative reminiscence is the one most closely aligned with the goals of Erikson, life review therapy, and GAB. Integrative reminiscence involves coming to terms with failures and disappointments to understand the overarching trajectory of one's life. "To the extent that one is able to resolve these negative sentiments from the past, life review should contribute to successful aging."[20] Integrative reminiscence also allows people to understand how they have lived their life according to their own system of values. It is empowering to see how one's life has coherence, meaning, and purpose, even though things did not always work out as planned.

A second type of helpful reminiscence is instrumental reminiscence, which allows people to draw on past experiences to overcome present circumstances. Remembering a particularly difficult time and then thinking about what it took to overcome that difficulty can build resilience. Therefore, practicing instrumental reminiscence as a coping strategy is a skill worth developing much earlier than one's sixties.

Unlike instrumental reminiscence, which has a practical goal, transmissive reminiscence occurs when an older person tells a younger person about her life and the lessons she learned from it. This kind of reminiscence is meant to instruct and guide. In Erikson's terms, transmissive reminiscence is generative. Mentors often use this kind of reminiscence to help their mentees. A great deal of satisfaction can come from knowing that one's past experiences will help others in the future.

Narrative reminiscence also occurs when someone tells stories about past events. But here there is no attempt to integrate the events, solve a problem, or instruct. Even so, this kind of reminiscing is not *un*healthy. Children love to hear the stories of their parents and grandparents almost as much as they enjoy telling them. These kinds of stories can be entertaining or can allow people to bond over a shared history. Nevertheless, while not harmful, the mere narration of past events does not bring about a sense of closure or resolution.

When reminiscing takes the form of glorifying the past as a way of denigrating the present, however, it devolves into escapist reminiscing. There may be times when escaping into the past provides a sense of relief from the burdens of the present. But too much escape may keep a person from coping effectively (think Norma Desmond in Billy Wilder's *Sunset Boulevard*).

Even worse, rumination on negative past events without any attempt to make sense of them could be seen as the definition of despair. This kind of obsessive reminiscence merely recycles the memories that keep a person feeling guilty and powerless. They are ultimately "destructive, if left unresolved."[21]

Effective life review techniques teach individuals how to put past experiences into language that facilitates meaningful integration. They help people come to terms with unresolved issues and reconnect with the past. But life review is not necessarily the end of the story.

In the 1990s, Erikson's wife Joan added one more stage to the theory after Erik had died. Called simply the Ninth Stage, this is a time when each of the crises of the previous eight stages is reexperienced all at once. People in their eighties and nineties may no longer trust their own abilities: they may feel a loss of the autonomy, sense of purpose, and competence it took a lifetime to develop. Experiencing such reversals could lead to a further loss of identity and a sense of isolation, uselessness, and despair. The crisis of the Ninth Stage, therefore, is existential in nature. Fittingly, successfully resolving this stage involves moving beyond the physical and into the realm of transcendence.[22]

Late Bloomers

> Our united opinion is entirely against the book. It is very long, and rather old-fashioned.... Does it have to be about a whale?
> —from a publisher's rejection of Herman Melville's *Moby-Dick*

> Keep scribbling! Something will happen.
> —attributed to Frank McCourt (1930–2009)

The literary world is replete with authors who achieved fame early in life by writing critically acclaimed debut novels. Bret Easton Ellis, for example, was just twenty-one when *Less Than Zero* was published in 1985, and F. Scott Fitzgerald was twenty-three when *This Side of Paradise* was released in 1920. Other novelists who made their mark at a young age include Truman Capote (*Other Voices, Other Rooms*: age 23), Zadie Smith (*White Teeth*: 24), and Norman Mailer (*The Naked and the Dead*: 25). The author as prodigy is not a modern phenomenon, either: a century before Fitzgerald, Mary Shelley was just twenty when *Frankenstein* appeared in 1818; and a century before that, the twenty-four-year-old Alexander Pope made a splash with *The Rape of the Lock*, which appeared in its first version in 1712.

Based on examples like these, one could argue that literary ability is simply something that a person is born with. Such a narrative is reinforced by wunderkinds like Stephen Crane, who was writing stories at fourteen and self-published *Maggie: A Girl of the Streets* at twenty-two. Perhaps even more impressive, just two years later, he wrote *The Red Badge of Courage*, in which he convincingly described a Civil War battle, despite never having served in the military. And despite being deaf and blind from infancy, Helen Keller wrote her autobiography, *The Story of My*

Life, when she was twenty-two. She would go on to write eleven more books over her lifetime.

The accomplishments of young authors like these are impressive, but is such precocity typical? In 2010 the Humber School of Creative and Performing Arts in Toronto undertook a survey to determine the average age of authors when they published their first book. The survey excluded academicians and included only prose writers who had published their first work with a traditional publisher (as opposed to self- or online publishing). The surveys were distributed to 1,500 authors, and 475 responded. When the numbers were crunched, they showed that the average age of first-time published authors was forty-two.[23] In other words, first-time authors who secured a book contract had probably been writing, either full- or part-time, for twenty years or more before they were published. This suggests that successful writers do not need to be kissed by the Muse at birth. It's also in line with current research on the development of expertise, which suggests that success is not a matter of innate talent but rather the result of years of deliberate practice.[24]

In fact, we can cite many examples of writerly success at the other end of the age spectrum. The phrase "late bloomer" is often applied to such antiprodigies and reflects a cultural expectation that notable accomplishment is more common early in one's career than later. According to the *Oxford English Dictionary*, the term was originally applied to plants, like the black-eyed Susan, that produce flowers relatively late in the summer or early fall. As early as 1921, the English psychologist Charles Spearman used the phrase metaphorically to refer to the intellectual abilities of children. And late blooming has always been the secret hope of plenty of parents with regard to seemingly directionless offspring.

Many authors, however, take to writing later in life, after pursuing a variety of other careers. And some only come into their own after producing a series of less successful works. Bram Stoker began writing as a theater critic and authored short stories and nonfiction while working as a civil servant in Dublin. In his forties, he published several unsuccessful novels, with titles like *The Snake's Pass* (1890) and *The Shoulders of Shasta* (1895). *Dracula*, the gothic horror novel that made him famous, did not appear until 1897, the year he turned fifty. Anna Sewell wrote her first and only novel, *Black Beauty*, during her fifties, and it was published in 1877, just a few months before she died at the age of fifty-eight.

Other impressive examples of late-blooming authors include the British civil servant Richard Adams, who told his children a story about a group of talking rabbits during a car trip. His kids encouraged him to commit it to paper, and the result, *Watership Down*, was published in 1972, when Adams was fifty-two. The Irish American writer Frank McCourt had a career as a teacher before his wife encouraged him to write down the stories that he told about his impoverished childhood in Limerick. This led to *Angela's Ashes*, published when McCourt was sixty-six. The memoir won a Pulitzer Prize for its author in 1997.

Many of the best-selling authors in history persevered despite receiving multiple rejections. *Watership Down*, which would become one of the fastest-selling books in history, was rejected by four publishers and three writer's agencies before it was finally accepted. J. K. Rowling's agent received twelve rejections from publishers unwilling to take a chance on a book about a boy wizard named Harry Potter. Both Stephen King and John Grisham had their debut novels rejected by dozens of publishers and literary agents. Zane Grey, the frustrated dentist who took up writing, was reportedly told at one point, "You have no business being a writer and should give up." Another writer of Westerns, Louis L'Amour, received two hundred rejections before finding a publisher. Both Grey and L'Amour went on to write dozens of novels about the Old West, and both enjoyed sales of hundreds of millions of copies. Agatha Christie endured five years of rejections before she experienced her first success and eventually became the best-selling novelist of all time. But for sheer determination, it's hard to top Jack London. His estate in San Francisco has preserved many of the six hundred rejections that came his way before he published his first story.[25]

Finally, some authors have been late blooming and also extremely prolific. A good example would be the British author Ted Allbeury (1917–2005). His life reads like a novel, or perhaps several of them. He was an intelligence officer and parachuted into Nazi Germany during World War II (he is thought to have been the only British secret agent to do so). During the Cold War, he ran agents across the border between East and West Germany and was once captured and tortured by the KGB. After coming in from the cold, he ran his own advertising agency and later became the managing director of a pirate radio station.[26] So when he turned to writing, in his early fifties, he had plenty of material to draw on. Although he is not as well known as some of his contemporaries, like John le Carré or Jack Higgins, for many years Allbeury was one of Britain's most popular espionage writers. His first novel, *A Choice of Enemies*, was published in 1972, and over the next twenty-one years, he penned forty-one novels, many under his own name, and others under two pseudonyms. At his most prolific, during the early 1980s, he published as many as four novels a year and continued to write until his early eighties. His final work appeared in 2000.

It seems fair to say that Allbeury, had he begun writing in his early twenties, could not possibly have been so prolific within his chosen genre. Because he started writing relatively late in life, he was able to bring his wealth of experiences to his fictional creations. Being prolific is certainly an important part of achieving literary success. But it also helps if the author has something to say.

Writer's Block

> Writing is easy. All you do is stare at a blank sheet of paper until drops of blood form on your forehead.
> —attributed to Gene Fowler (1890–1960)

As Fowler pointed out, many authors struggle mightily to put their thoughts into words. The inability to write easily or consistently is usually referred to as "writer's block," a term coined by the Austrian psychiatrist Edmund Bergler in 1947. Bergler's Freudian interpretation that the problem was rooted in "oral masochism and a superego need for punishment" has not fared well in the marketplace of ideas.[27] The phrase itself, however, had become firmly entrenched in the popular imagination by the 1970s. And any number of self-help books are available that purport to "conquer," "cure," or "break through" writer's block.

The term may be well known, but it is also notably imprecise, as writers can get hung up at many different points in the writing process. In some cases, a blockage of words or ideas really does seem to occur. However, an inability to write can have many other causes, such as procrastination, perfectionism, fear of criticism, and garden-variety melancholy. In other cases, a writer may have too many ideas and find himself unable to choose among

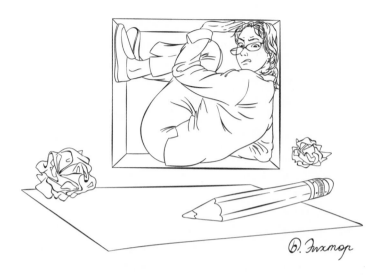

them. As a result, some researchers who study this condition employ the term "writing anxiety" instead. No one is immune, it seems: in a study of successful academic authors, the word most commonly employed to describe the writing process was "frustration."[28] And authors who claim to suffer from this malady can still be impressively prolific: even Fowler, quoted earlier, managed to produce dozens of novels, biographies, and Hollywood screenplays during his career.

Novelists who meet with initial success may be especially prone to becoming blocked. This is an example of a more general phenomenon, sometimes referred to as the "sophomore slump," which can also affect initially promising college students (hence the name), as well as athletes and musicians. After a promising debut, many authors fear that their second creation will not measure up to the first, and this anxiety may lead to a loss of confidence and a delay in creating a follow-up work. In fact, such anxiety is warranted, since probability theory predicts that unusual performances (in this case, a much-lauded premiere) tend to be followed by less stellar showings.

In some cases, the blockage can become permanent. The list of authors who have suffered this fate is both long and varied. Samuel Taylor Coleridge produced his well-known serious poems at the beginning of his career, and although he continued to write as a journalist and literary critic, was never able to recapture the genius of his early years.[29] More recent examples include Ralph Ellison and Harper Lee, who never published another novel after their first successful works (*Invisible Man* and *To Kill a Mockingbird*, respectively, although both authors left behind manuscripts that were published posthumously). During the final two decades of his life, Truman Capote was unable to produce another novel to follow *In Cold Blood*.[30] And perhaps the most extreme example is Joseph Mitchell, the celebrated contributor to the *New Yorker*. He published *Joe Gould's Secret* in 1965, when he was fifty-six. For the remaining thirty years of his life, he went to his office every day but never again produced anything of significance.[31]

It may be helpful to consider the solutions to blocks that professional authors have devised. After writing more than a dozen books, the British novelist Graham Greene became blocked in his fifties. He found that keeping a dream journal helped, since it was writing that was not meant to be read by anyone but him.[32] After a fallow period, Greene went on to write another dozen books, including some of his best-known work. His last novel was published in his early eighties.

The American neurologist Alice Weaver Flaherty has suggested that we can better understand writer's block by thinking of it as a brain state, and she contrasts it with a less well-known syndrome called hypergraphia, or the overwhelming urge to write. Flaherty suggests that both conditions can be triggered by underlying clinical syndromes, such as mania and epilepsy. With regard to writer's block, she suggests that the ultimate culprit may be decreased activity in the frontal lobes of the brain, which may be offset by medications that are used to treat depression and anxiety.[33] But as everyone knows, cause and effect are difficult to disentangle. It may be that writer's block is *caused* by anxiety and depression, but it is also likely that the state of being blocked can *lead* to feelings of anxiety and depression.

We should note that not all writers believe in writer's block. Authors such as Allan Gurganus and Mark Helprin have pointed out that such blockages do not occur in other professions. They disparage this idea by suggesting that it may simply be an excuse for sheer laziness. After all, plumbers and electricians don't suddenly lose the ability to repair pipes and run wires.[34]

Gathering data on writer's block turns out to be rather difficult. Many writers are reluctant to discuss their creative practices with researchers.[35] And some fear that the simple admission of having writer's block could turn a temporary slowdown into a more serious problem—a kind of self-fulfilling prophecy.[36] As a result, studies of writer's block have often involved college students: they represent a convenience sample for researchers, but they must also frequently write against assignment deadlines.

Mike Rose, an American education researcher who was one of the first to study writer's block in college students, suggests that students are often overly constrained by the inflexible rules they have been taught about how they "ought" to write. He also points to premature editing, problems in planning and writing strategies, and problematic attitudes and assumptions about the writing process itself. Although these conclusions were drawn from a small number of participants and were based on interview data, they provided an important starting point for later investigations.[37]

College students have also served as participants in studies designed to alleviate writing anxiety. In one study, a treatment group received a combination of cognitive-behavioral therapy aimed at reducing stress and instruction about how to write better. They were compared to a second group who received only the writing instruction. Both treatment groups reported that their anxiety about writing decreased, but only the group that received both therapy and instruction showed an improvement in writing quality.[38] The results of this study suggest that anxiety plays a major role in writer's block.

Does the incidence of writer's block increase or decrease over the adult life span? It's difficult to say, since, as we have seen, the term can be used to refer to many different types of writing difficulties. A selection bias may also be involved: individuals who are frequently blocked may, over time, gravitate to professions that do not require extensive amounts of writing. Finally, older writers may confront changes in motivation and energy levels. An author may retire from writing because she is blocked, but the reason may also be that she simply lacks the stamina for the sustained cognitive effort that writing requires. When Philip Roth was asked if he ever missed writing, he replied, "I was by this time [about age 77] no longer in possession of the mental vitality or the verbal energy or the physical fitness needed to mount and sustain a large creative attack of any duration on a complex structure as demanding as a novel.... Not everyone can be fruitful forever."[39]

The Destroyer of Minds

Consider the following passage from a late-twentieth-century novel:

> Benet had taken a taxi from his house to Anna's house near Sloane Square. From here he had taken a taxi to Owen's house. Now he was taking another taxi to Rosalind's little flat off Victoria Street. He rarely drove his car in London. As he sat in the taxi he felt a pang of painful miserable guilt.

Although this excerpt is just fifty-eight words and five sentences long, it is full of repetition. The phrase "taken a taxi" appears twice in the first two sentences, along with "taking another taxi" in the third, and "in the taxi" in the fifth. The word "house" is used three times in the first two sentences. An English teacher would undoubtedly be itching to take a red pen to such writing to remove the repetitions, or at least to suggest alternate word choices.

It might come as a surprise, therefore, to learn that the author of this passage is Iris Murdoch, the acclaimed British novelist and philosopher (1919–1999). She published twenty-six novels over a forty-year career that began in the mid-1950s, and the passage quoted here is from her final fictional work, *Jackson's Dilemma*.[40] Earlier in her career, Murdoch's work had won awards, including the coveted Man Booker Prize for Fiction, and she was made a Dame Commander of the British Empire in 1987. Murdoch was, in fact, considered one of the most significant British writers of the postwar period.

When *Jackson's Dilemma* was published, however, critical opinion was decidedly mixed. The *New York Times*, for example, praised the work for being "psychologically rich" but also noted that it was "strewn with imprecisions and blatant redundancies," with "pet words [scattered] like so many nails in the reader's road." In short, the reviewer declared, "the writing is a mess."[41]

What the reviewers did not know was that Murdoch was already struggling with cognitive impairment and would be diagnosed with Alzheimer's disease (AD) in 1997. She died two years later at the age of seventy-nine.[42] Her battle with the disease is well known because of her husband's memoir and the 2001 movie *Iris*, in which she was played by Kate Winslet and Judi Dench.[43]

As mentioned previously, a diagnosis of AD cannot be made definitively during one's lifetime, and in Murdoch's case, it was confirmed only after her death. Peter Garrard, the neuroscientist who made the initial diagnosis and conducted her autopsy, went on to coauthor a paper that examined her literary output. The researchers compared samples of the prose in *Jackson's Dilemma* with samples from her first novel (*Under the Net*, 1954), as well as the midcareer work that won the Man Booker Prize (*The Sea, the Sea*, 1978). Although the syntax used in the three books did not vary greatly, her final novel uses a smaller vocabulary, and the words she employs are more common.[44]

Building on Garrard's work, a group of researchers at the University of Toronto conducted a computerized analysis of the complete texts of all of Murdoch's novels and examined a wider variety of linguistic markers. They also found an abrupt decline in the breadth of vocabulary that Murdoch employed in *Jackson's Dilemma* when compared to her other novels. In addition, they found increases in phrasal and word repetitions (as seen with "taxi" and "house" in the passage quoted earlier), as well as an increased use of lexical fillers, such as "um" and "ah." Significantly, some of these changes in her writing had begun to occur when she was in her fifties, more than twenty years before she died.[45]

Of course, it's unwise to make generalizations from a single case, and the Toronto researchers also analyzed the works of Agatha Christie (1890–1976), the enormously successful British crime novelist, as well as P. D. James (1920–2014), another British crime writer. The researchers chose Christie because she was suspected of having developed dementia during her final years, although no postmortem confirmation was undertaken. James was included as a control, since she showed no signs of cognitive impairment during her lifetime. Just as with Murdoch, the researchers found that Christie's vocabulary size suddenly declined in her later novels, and she also greatly increased her use of word repetitions and fillers. P. D. James, on the other hand, displayed none of these trends: none of the lexical or syntactic fluctuations during her career were statistically significant.[46]

The availability of machine-readable texts and the development of sophisticated linguistic analysis tools have led to something of a cottage industry in this field. Ian Lancashire, part of the Toronto group of researchers, has analyzed the works of Murdoch as well as two other writers who are known to have suffered from dementia: Ross Macdonald (1915–1983), a crime fiction novelist; and Enid Blyton (1897–1968), the incredibly prolific English writer who penned hundreds of children's books. Lancashire compared these authors to L. Frank Baum, James Hilton, and R. A. Freeman, none of whom showed cognitive impairment during their lives. The nonimpaired authors were similar in that their vocabulary sizes either remained the same or increased during their careers, and their rates of employing phrasal repetitions remained unchanged. Macdonald and Blyton, however, showed the now familiar pattern of increased repetitions over time and, in the case of Macdonald, a shrinking vocabulary size.[47]

Sadly, many writers become painfully aware that something is very wrong with their mental faculties. Murdoch, for example, talked of feeling like she was falling and being in "a very, very bad, quiet place" during an interview in the year after *Jackson's Dilemma* was published.[48] And Terry Pratchett (1948–2015), the popular English fantasy writer, made his diagnosis—a type of early onset AD—public in 2007, when he was fifty-nine. He spent the remaining years of his life advocating for more funding for medical research and was able to complete several more novels "through the haze of Alzheimer's."[49] However, he was unable to complete his autobiography.

Several prominent politicians, including Ronald Reagan and Margaret Thatcher, were diagnosed with dementia, a fact that raises questions about whether their cognitive impairments began while they were in office. Most politicians are not novelists, but they do engage in linguistic performances at events like press conferences. Unlike speeches, which can be ghostwritten, encounters with the press are unscripted and provide a means for assessing the language abilities of political leaders. Visar Berisha and his colleagues analyzed transcripts of press conferences for Presidents Reagan and George H. W. Bush, who aged healthily. As might be expected by now, the researchers found a reduction in Reagan's vocabulary size over time, as well as an increase in his use of lexical fillers (well, uh) and less-specific nouns (we, they, something, anything). The researchers found no similar trends in Bush's press conference remarks.[50]

Even historical figures who have been dead for centuries are having their written words scrutinized for signs of cognitive impairment. King James VI/I (1566–1625) also got the treatment. During his long reign, James united the Scottish and English crowns and sponsored the translation of the Bible that bears his name. He also left behind fifty-seven letters that cover a twenty-year period of his life. His letters show a pattern of decreasing grammatical complexity over time, but also an increase in vocabulary size. As we have seen, such changes are not unusual, but since he had circulatory problems, the authors of the study speculate that the king suffered from vascular dementia.[51]

Most writers never develop dementia. But its debilitating effects are echoed in Martin Amis's quote that "writers die twice: once when the body dies, and once when the talent dies."[52]

Lessons from the Nuns

In the early 1930s, two young women in Mankato, Minnesota, were asked to write short narratives about their lives. They were novices in the School Sisters of Notre Dame, a Roman Catholic order, and their mother superior had decreed that all novices write a brief autobiographical sketch before taking their vows.

The approaches taken by the two novices were very different. Consider the first sentence in the narrative written by "Sister Helen" (a pseudonym):

> I was born in Eau Claire, Wis., on May 24, 1913, and was baptized in St. James Church.[53]

And now "Sister Emma":

> It was about a half hour before midnight between February twenty-eighth and twenty-ninth of the leap year nineteen-hundred-twelve when I began to live and to die as the third child of my mother, whose maiden name is Hilda Hoffman, and my father, Otto Schmitt.[54]

These sketches, along with many others, were filed away in the convent's archives in Mankato. They would remain there undisturbed for decades, but when rediscovered, they would have an enormous impact on the field of cognitive aging.

In 1986, David Snowdon, an epidemiologist, then at the University of Minnesota, contacted the religious order in search of volunteers for an aging study. Because of their communal life in convents, eating the same food and working in the same profession, these teaching nuns constituted an ideal group for the study of aging. The nuns who agreed to take part completed a battery of cognitive tests each year. And crucially, they also consented to having their brains autopsied after they died. Because of this, it was possible to definitively assess whether any of the sisters had developed Alzheimer's disease (AD). The project expanded to include six other Notre Dame convents, and ultimately 678 members of the order joined the study.

Then one day, quite by accident, Snowdon discovered the room that contained the archives of the Mankato convent. Within the archives, in a couple of olive green metal file cabinets, he found the records of the nuns who had taken their vows at Mankato. He unearthed a wealth of information, including the narrative sketches of Sisters Helen and Emma, as well as dozens of others. Suddenly, instead of being limited to studying the sisters from the beginning of his research, he now had a time machine; he could journey decades into their pasts. Specifically, he could look for clues in the ways the novice nuns had written about themselves more than a half-century earlier, and correlate the writing styles with the mental status of the nuns in the present.[55]

To analyze the autobiographies, Snowdon teamed with James Mortimer and Susan Kemper. They initially focused on two linguistic measures: idea density and grammatical complexity. Idea density was operationalized as the number of ideas expressed per ten words. In the earlier examples, Sister Helen's sentence was scored as having an idea density of 3.9, whereas Sister Emma's received a score of 3.3. Sister Helen's grammatical complexity was coded in the lowest category, while Sister Emma's received the highest possible score.

When Snowdon's group published their first paper examining language and aging, fourteen of the nuns had passed away, and AD was confirmed in the brains of seven. Of the seven, the researchers found that all of them had written autobiographies with low idea density. None of the nuns whose essays contained high idea density had AD. And low grammatical complexity was also associated with AD, although not as strongly.[56] By 2000, seventy-four of the nuns who had written essays had passed away, and once again, idea density in the essays was a strong predictor of a diagnosis of AD postmortem.[57] A later study found an association between these linguistic factors and other declines in cognitive function, including mild cognitive impairment in old age.[58]

The essays also yielded another surprising finding: the expression of positive emotions was associated with longer life. Deborah Danner, a psychologist involved in the Nun Study, led a group that analyzed 180 of the nuns' essays, identifying words associated with positive emotions (happy, love, hope), as well as those that denoted negative emotions (sad, afraid, anxious). The researchers found a seven-year difference in life expectancy between the nuns who used the largest number of positive emotion words and those who used the fewest.[59]

This pioneering work showing an association between linguistic factors and dementia has inspired others to undertake similar projects. A team at Utah State University has studied personal journals and letters that are part of the Cache County Memory Study. Intriguingly, the mere fact of keeping a journal was associated with a 53 percent risk reduction in all forms of dementia. However, the only linguistic variable associated with journal content and dementia was the percentage of long words (six letters or more). The use of long words was associated with a reduction in the risk of being diagnosed with AD.[60]

And what of the two nuns whose autobiographies were mentioned earlier? When they were assessed by Snowdon's team in 1992 with a standard cognitive test, Sister Helen earned the lowest possible score: zero out of thirty points. She died a year later at age eighty, and a postmortem examination of her brain confirmed that she had AD. Sister Emma, who was fifteen months older, had received a perfect score on her test and, at the time of Sister Helen's death, was still mentally sharp.[61] In fact, some of the sisters enrolled in the study would maintain high levels of cognitive functioning into their nineties and beyond, even though autopsies of their brains detected the plaques and tangles typical of AD.[62] Such findings demonstrate the protective factors of cognitive reserve that we discussed in the first chapter. By 2016, only 8 of the 678 women enrolled in the Nun Study were still alive, with the youngest being one hundred.[63] It truly is remarkable that these women who dedicated their lives to teaching continue to instruct and inspire long after their deaths.

Fiction Is Stronger Than Truth

> Fiction is the lie through which we tell the truth.
> —attributed to Albert Camus (1913–1960)

> Good fiction's job [is] to comfort the disturbed and disturb the comfortable.
> —David Foster Wallace (1962–2008), in an interview with
>   Larry McCaffery

No one would claim that reading isn't good for you; after all, it's one of the best ways that people have for finding out about the world. The amount of information that we acquire through the written word is simply enormous. Not only that, but certain types of reading might confer psychological benefits that go far beyond a knowledge of history or the news of the day. Specifically, reading fiction might make us better human beings.

At first, this claim may seem far-fetched. How could novels or short stories tell us greater truths than nonfiction descriptions of events or ideas? What makes fiction special is that it exposes us to the psychological depths that exist in everyone. By reading about fictional characters, we develop a better understanding of the perspectives of other people, which in turn makes readers of fiction more socially perceptive.[64] It's been argued that reading fiction increases the empathy that we feel toward other people. In addition, reading fiction may also enhance what psychologists call one's theory of mind (ToM). This refers to a person's ability to understand the intentions, beliefs, and desires of other people. By mentally engaging with the complex motivations and actions of characters in fictional works, we may hone our abilities to see the world from points of view that differ from our own.

To test the supposed benefits of reading fiction, researchers have had to find ways to quantify these constructs. There are several tests for measuring empathy and the components of ToM, but determining how much fiction someone has read can be tricky. Asking people directly about their reading habits is problematic, because a strong component of social desirability may influence the answer: everyone wants to be perceived as being well read. So psychologists who study reading have created an "exposure to print" measure, which asks participants to pick out the names of fiction and nonfiction authors from a list that also contains names of nonwriters.[65] Several studies have found positive associations between measures of empathy, ToM, and exposure to print. A recent reanalysis of these studies by the psychologists Micah Mumper and Richard Gerrig has confirmed this finding, although the effect was modest.[66] These findings are also in line with research by Zazie Todd, who recruited participants to read novels and discuss them as a group. In the discussions, a common theme was expressions of sympathy and empathy for the fictional characters.[67]

If cumulative exposure to the written word has measurable effects on more global cognitive and social processes, then we might expect to see other specific advantages for reading, and we do. Changes in the connectivity of the brain have been observed as research participants read a work of historical fiction over a period of three weeks. These beneficial changes were observed in the short term, during the study itself, and also in the days after the reading concluded.[68]

The psychologist Mei-Ching Lien and her colleagues compared the word recognition abilities of college students and a group of older adults in their sixties and seventies. The researchers asked the participants to identify words while simultaneously responding to competing visual and auditory tasks. Doing two things at once normally requires additional cognitive resources, which can be problematic for older adults. In this study, however, the older participants outperformed their younger counterparts on these competing tasks. The researchers suggest that a lifetime of exposure to print may lower the resources required to access words in memory—a facility that the college students have not yet acquired.[69] Other researchers have found additional advantages of exposure to print for older adults, such as reducing the limitations of working memory while reading. These are important findings, because they suggest that being an inveterate reader compensates for declines in other cognitive processes.[70] It is clear, therefore, that reading fiction can benefit adults in a wide variety of ways.

Amazingly, reading fiction has also been associated with a longer life. A large-scale study conducted by researchers at the Yale University School of Public Health found that book readers had a twenty-three-month "survival advantage" compared to non–book readers. Put another way, the study found a 20 percent lower mortality rate over a twelve-year period for book readers. The study was, by definition, correlational; after all, researchers cannot randomly assign people to book reading and non-book-reading conditions for years at a time. Therefore we cannot distinguish between the competing hypotheses that more reading leads to a longer life, or longer life leads to more reading. In addition, many factors are undoubtedly involved in this association, although the beneficial effect of reading persisted even after the researchers controlled for a host of potential moderators, such as age, gender, education, marital status, health, and affluence. The beneficial effect was driven primarily by the reading of books, as opposed to reading magazines and newspapers. And since most book readers read fiction, this ties into the other advantages mentioned earlier. In fact, the study showed that as little as thirty minutes a day spent reading books was beneficial. The authors of the study suggest that the greater cognitive engagement required for reading books—as opposed to periodicals—accounts for this longevity effect.[71]

Epilogue

If old age stops the hunter from going hunting, he must be content with telling his ancient exploits.

—proverb of the Bambara of West Africa

We began this book by discussing how aging affects language. Although we found that some specific linguistic abilities do decline in normal aging, most losses do not result from declines in language per se. Rather, they are largely caused by the slowing of cognitive processing, the constriction of working memory, the lessening of inhibitory control, and declines in hearing and vision.

In fact, even these declines may not be what they seem. As we have seen, although some older adults are more verbose and off topic, this may result from changes in their discourse goals. Verbal fluency and word-finding difficulties may be due to the fact that older adults simply have more knowledge than their younger counterparts.

We hope that our attempt to disentangle changes in memory, perception, and other cognitive processes from changes in language itself is not seen as an attempt to minimize the impact of age-related declines in functioning. These declines place real burdens on older adults and their families. Our point is that knowing the origin of changes in linguistic ability allows us to respond to them more effectively.

Likewise, it would be overly simplistic to draw any conclusions about aging by adding up cognitive gains and losses and then weighing the pluses against the minuses. The scales of justice might work like this, but as we all know, aging isn't just.

Nevertheless, we have seen that losses in some areas can be offset by gains in others. This can happen quite unconsciously, as when a larger vocabulary makes up for word-finding difficulties. But it can also occur as the result of a conscious decision, such as when a person sets meaningful goals for himself, optimizes his personal capabilities, and finds ways to compensate.[1]

In the book's final chapters, where we explored how language affects aging, we found plenty of good news to report. Just as your doctor might advise you to "keep moving," we advise you to keep talking, keep listening, keep reading, and keep writing. It turns out that exercising our linguistic abilities is an excellent way to optimize cognitive function and combat cognitive decline. Perhaps Megan Lenehan and her colleagues put it best: "Sending your grandparents to university increases cognitive reserve."[2]

When we are young, we use language to learn about the world around us and to understand who we are and how we fit into that world. Language gives us a window into our inner lives and a mirror that reflects the self. Without language, how could we make friends, be entertained, or fall in love? Why should any of this change with age? As we have seen, it certainly doesn't have to.

Notes

Prologue

1. A journey: Thomas R. Cole, *The Journey of Life: A Cultural History of Aging in America* (Cambridge: Cambridge University Press, 1992).

2. "Stable across the lifespan": e.g., Meredith A. Shafto and Lorraine K. Tyler, "Language in the Aging Brain: The Network Dynamics of Cognitive Decline and Preservation," *Science* 346, no. 6209 (2014): 583.

3. The loss of memory: David Sterrett et al., "Perceptions of Aging during Each Decade of Life after 30," West Health Institute/NORC Survey on Aging in America, 2017.

1 Setting the Stage

1. Had done so: Camille L. Ryan and Kurt Bauman, "Educational Attainment in the United States," United States Census, March 2016, https://www.census.gov/content/dam/Census/library/publications/2016/demo/p20-578.pdf.

2. Part of their lives: Marc Prensky, "Digital Natives, Digital Immigrants, Part 1," *On the Horizon* 9, no. 2 (2001): 1–6.

3. Lisa H. Trahan et al., "The Flynn Effect: A Meta-analysis," *Psychological Bulletin* 140, no. 5 (2014): 1332–1360.

4. James R. Flynn, "The Mean IQ of Americans: Massive Gains 1932 to 1978," *Psychological Bulletin* 95, no. 1 (1984): 29–51.

5. A dozen other countries: James R. Flynn, "Massive IQ Gains in 14 Nations: What IQ Tests Really Measure," *Psychological Bulletin* 101, no. 2 (1987): 171–191.

6. All play a role: Tamara C. Daley et al., "IQ on the Rise: The Flynn Effect in Rural Kenyan Children," *Psychological Science* 14, no. 3 (2003): 215–219.

7. Effect is continuing: Jon Martin Sundet, Dag G. Barlaug, and Tore M. Torjussen, "The End of the Flynn Effect? A Study of Secular Trends in Mean Intelligence Test Scores of Norwegian Conscripts during Half a Century," *Intelligence* 32, no. 4 (2004): 349–362.

8. Or even reversing: Thomas W. Teasdale and David R. Owen, "Secular Declines in Cognitive Test Scores: A Reversal of the Flynn Effect," *Intelligence* 36, no. 2 (2008): 121–126.

9. Cognitive decline: Wendy Johnson, Matt McGue, and Ian J. Deary, "Normative Cognitive Aging," in *Behavior Genetics of Cognition across the Lifespan*, ed. Deborah Finkel and Chandra A. Reynolds (New York: Springer, 2014), 135–167.

10. Nonthreatening conditions: Claude M. Steele and Joshua Aronson, "Stereotype Threat and the Intellectual Test Performance of African Americans," *Journal of Personality and Social Psychology* 69, no. 5 (1995): 797–811.

11. Than younger participants: Alison L. Chasteen et al., "How Feelings of Stereotype Threat Influence Older Adults' Memory Performance," *Experimental Aging Research* 31, no. 3 (2005): 235–260.

12. With more education: Thomas M. Hess, Joey T. Hinson, and Elizabeth A. Hodges, "Moderators of and Mechanisms Underlying Stereotype Threat Effects on Older Adults' Memory Performance," *Experimental Aging Research* 35, no. 2 (2009): 153–177.

13. Decline in processing speed: Timothy A. Salthouse, "The Processing-Speed Theory of Adult Age Differences in Cognition," *Psychological Review* 103, no. 3 (1996): 403–428.

14. Comparing two pictures: Lori L. Veiel, Martha Storandt, and Richard A. Abrams, "Visual Search for Change in Older Adults," *Psychology and Aging* 21, no. 4 (2006): 754–762.

15. Age-related declines: Kara L. Bopp and Paul Verhaeghen, "Aging and Verbal Memory Span: A Meta-analysis," *Journals of Gerontology Series B: Psychological Sciences and Social Sciences* 60, no. 5 (2005): P223–P233.

16. And they do: Robert West and Claude Alain, "Age-Related Decline in Inhibitory Control Contributes to the Increased Stroop Effect Observed in Older Adults," *Psychophysiology* 37, no. 2 (2000): 179–189.

17. Those who are younger: Jutta Kray and Ulman Lindenberger, "Adult Age Differences in Task Switching," *Psychology and Aging* 15, no. 1 (2000): 126–147.

18. Hardly at all: David F. Hultsch et al., *Memory Change in the Aged* (Cambridge: Cambridge University Press, 1998).

19. After age seventy-five: Brent J. Small, Roger A. Dixon, and John J. McArdle, "Tracking Cognition-Health Changes from 55 to 95 Years of Age," *Journals of Gerontology Series B: Psychological Sciences and Social Sciences* 66, suppl. 1 (2011): i153–i161.

20. And proper nutrition: Kristine N. Williams and Susan Kemper, "Interventions to Reduce Cognitive Decline in Aging," *Journal of Psychosocial Nursing and Mental Health Services* 48, no. 5 (2010): 42–51; Pamela Greenwood and Raja Parasuraman, *Nurturing the Older Brain and Mind* (Cambridge, MA: MIT Press, 2012).

21. Confer some benefits: Barbara Carretti et al., "Gains in Language Comprehension Relating to Working Memory Training in Healthy Older Adults," *International Journal of Geriatric Psychiatry* 28, no. 5 (2013): 539–546.

22. Something more serious: Rónán O'Caoimh, Suzanne Timmons, and D. William Molloy, "Screening for Mild Cognitive Impairment: Comparison of 'MCI Specific' Screening Instruments," *Journal of Alzheimer's Disease* 51, no. 2 (2016): 619–629.

23. Different leisure activities: Yaakov Stern, "Cognitive Reserve in Ageing and Alzheimer's Disease," *Lancet Neurology* 11, no. 11 (2012): 1006–1012.

24. Parkinson's disease: John V. Hindle et al., "The Effects of Cognitive Reserve and Lifestyle on Cognition and Dementia in Parkinson's Disease—a Longitudinal Cohort Study," *International Journal of Geriatric Psychiatry* 31, no. 1 (2016): 13–23.

25. Stroke is reduced: Eric B. Larson, Kristine Yaffe, and Kenneth M. Langa, "New Insights into the Dementia Epidemic," *New England Journal of Medicine* 369, no. 24 (2013): 2275–2277.

26. Are elder orphans: Christina Ianzito, "Elder Orphans: How to Plan for Aging without a Family Caregiver," AARP, 2017, https://www.aarp.org/caregiving/basics/info-2017/tips-aging-alone.html.

27. Designated surrogate or caregiver: Maria T. Carney et al., "Elder Orphans Hiding in Plain Sight: A Growing Vulnerable Population," *Current Gerontology and Geriatrics Research,* article ID 4723250 (2016): 1; italics in original.

28. These solo agers: Sara Z. Geber, "Are You Ready for Solo Agers and Elder Orphans?" American Society on Aging, December 27, 2017, http://www.asaging.org/blog/are-you-ready-solo-agers-and-elder-orphans.

29. Elder abuse: Jed Montayre, Jasmine Montayre, and Sandra Thaggard, "The Elder Orphan in Healthcare Settings: An Integrative Review," *Journal of Population Ageing* (2018), https://doi.org/10.1007/s12062-018-9222-x.

30. Constraints in old age: Paul B. Baltes and Margret M. Baltes, "Psychological Perspectives on Successful Aging: The Model of Selective Optimization with Compensation," in *Successful Aging: Perspectives from the Behavioral Sciences*, ed. Paul Baltes and Margret Baltes (Cambridge: Cambridge University Press, 1990), 27.

31. Increasing vulnerabilities: Margret M. Baltes and Laura L. Carstensen, "The Process of Successful Ageing," *Ageing and Society* 16, no. 4 (1996): 405.

32. In this area: Deb Amlen, "How to Solve the *New York Times* Crossword," https://www.nytimes.com/guides/crosswords/how-to-solve-a-cross word-puzzle.

33. Called into question: Stephen Katz and Toni Calasanti, "Critical Perspectives on Successful Aging: Does It 'Appeal More Than It Illuminates'?" *Gerontologist* 55, no. 1 (2014): 26–33.

34. The same way: Theodore D. Cosco et al., "Operational Definitions of Successful Aging: A Systematic Review," *International Psychogeriatrics* 26, no. 3 (2014): 373–381.

2 The Language of Sight and Sound

1. "Pink and Stripy": Alex Russell, Richard J. Stevenson, and Anina N. Rich, "Chocolate Smells Pink and Stripy: Exploring Olfactory-Visual Synesthesia," *Cognitive Neuroscience* 6, nos. 2–3 (2015): 77.

2. Kinds of synesthesia: Julia Simner, "Defining Synaesthesia," *British Journal of Psychology* 103, no. 1 (2012): 1–15.

3. Four percent of the population: Julia Simner et al., "Synaesthesia: The Prevalence of Atypical Cross-Modal Experiences," *Perception* 35, no. 8 (2006): 1024–1033.

4. "With an olive sheen": Vladimir Nabokov, *Speak, Memory: An Autobiography Revisited* (New York: Putnam, 1966), 55.

5. A linguistic phenomenon: Julia Simner, "Beyond Perception: Synaesthesia as a Psycholinguistic Phenomenon," *Trends in Cognitive Sciences* 11, no. 1 (2007): 23–29; Simner, "Defining Synaesthesia."

6. Words, letters, or numbers: Simner, "Beyond Perception,"23.

7. Its written counterpart: Joanna Atkinson et al., "Synesthesia for Manual Alphabet Letters and Numeral Signs in Second-Language Users of Signed Languages," *Neurocase* 22, no. 4 (2016): 379–386.

8. Higher rates of synesthesia: Marcus R. Watson et al., "The Prevalence of Synaesthesia Depends on Early Language Learning," *Consciousness and Cognition* 48 (2017): 212–231.

9. Wide range of tasks: Marcus R. Watson et al., "Synesthesia and Learning: A Critical Review and Novel Theory," *Frontiers in Human Neuroscience* 8, no. 98 (2014): 1–15.

10. The visual system: Julia Simner et al., "Does Synaesthesia Age? Changes in the Quality and Consistency of Synaesthetic Associations," *Neuropsychologia* 106 (2017): 407–416.

11. "Are qualitatively distinct": Watson et al., "Synesthesia and Learning," 6, italics in original; see also Daniel Bor et al., "Adults Can Be Trained to Acquire Synesthetic Experiences," *Scientific Reports* 4, no. 7089 (2014): 1–8.

12. Low-vision adults: Patricia Grant and Rich Hogle, *Safety and Efficacy of the BrainPort V100 Device in Individuals Blinded by Traumatic Injury* (Middleton, WI: WICAB Inc., 2017); Amy C. Nau et al., "Acquisition of Visual Perception in Blind Adults Using the BrainPort Artificial Vision Device," *American Journal of Occupational Therapy* 69, no. 1 (2015): 1–8.

13. Pretty much alike: Joan T. Erber and Lenore T. Szuchman, *Great Myths of Aging* (Malden, MA: Wiley, 2015).

14. Heart disease: Qi Huang and Jianguo Tang, "Age-Related Hearing Loss or Presbycusis," *European Archives of Oto-rhino-laryngology* 267, no. 8 (2010): 1179–1191.

15. Reduces the risk: Sharon G. Curhan et al., "Body Mass Index, Waist Circumference, Physical Activity, and Risk of Hearing Loss in Women," *American Journal of Medicine* 126, no. 12 (2013): 1142.e1–1142.e8.

16. Taken into account: Karen J. Cruickshanks et al., "Prevalence of Hearing Loss in Older Adults in Beaver Dam, Wisconsin: The Epidemiology of Hearing Loss Study," *American Journal of Epidemiology* 148, no. 9 (1998): 879–886.

17. Sent to the brain: Richard A. Schmiedt, "The Physiology of Cochlear Presbycusis," in *The Aging Auditory System*, ed. Sandra Gordon-Salant et al. (New York: Springer, 2010), 9–38.

18. Of limited use: Susan L. Phillips et al., "Frequency and Temporal Resolution in Elderly Listeners with Good and Poor Word Recognition," *Journal of Speech, Language, and Hearing Research* 43, no. 1 (2000): 217–228.

19. Hearing they do have: M. Kathleen Pichora-Fuller and Harry Levitt, "Speech Comprehension Training and Auditory and Cognitive Processing in Older Adults," *American Journal of Audiology* 21, no. 2 (2012): 351–357.

20. Available for memory: M. Kathleen Pichora-Fuller, Bruce A. Schneider, and Meredyth Daneman, "How Young and Old Adults Listen to and Remember Speech in Noise," *Journal of the Acoustical Society of America* 97, no. 1 (1995): 593–608.

21. Worst of both worlds: David M. Baguley, "Hyperacusis," *Journal of the Royal Society of Medicine* 96, no. 12 (2003): 582–585.

22. Significant sensory problem: Katherine Bouton, *Shouting Won't Help: Why I—and 50 Million Other Americans—Can't Hear You* (New York: Farrar, Straus and Giroux, 2013).

23. Quality of life: Andrea Ciorba et al., "The Impact of Hearing Loss on the Quality of Life of Elderly Adults," *Clinical Interventions in Aging* 7, no. 6 (2012): 159–163.

24. Their parents' generation: Weihai Zhan et al., "Generational Differences in the Prevalence of Hearing Impairment in Older Adults," *American Journal of Epidemiology* 171, no. 2 (2009): 260–266.

25. At high volume: Ineke Vogel et al., "Adolescents and MP3 Players: Too Many Risks, Too Few Precautions," *Pediatrics* 123, no. 6 (2009): e953–e958.

26. His right ear: "How Reagan Copes with 1930s Ear Injury," *Chicago Tribune*, November 9, 1987, sec. 1, 16.

27. Treasury engraving plates: Leonard Maltin, *Leonard Maltin's Classic Movie Guide: From the Silent Era through 1965*, 2nd ed. (New York: Random House, 2010).

28. Ringing of a telephone: Harvard Health Publishing, "Tinnitus: Ringing in the Ears and What to Do about It," August 16, 2017, http:// www.health.harvard.edu/diseases-and-conditions/tinnitus-ringing-in -the-ears-and-what-to-do-about-it.

29. Such as aspirin: Karen Klinka, "High-Pitched Ringing in Ears May Be Wake-Up Call," *Oklahoman*, August 9, 1994, http://newsok.com/article /2474010.

30. Severe and debilitating: David M. Nondahl et al., "Prevalence and 5-Year Incidence of Tinnitus among Older Adults: The Epidemiology of Hearing Loss Study," *Journal of the American Academy of Audiology* 13, no. 6 (2002): 323–331.

31. Librarians, for example: Howard J. Hoffman and George W. Reed, "Epidemiology of Tinnitus," in *Tinnitus: Theory and Management*, ed. James B. Snow (Hamilton, Ontario: B. C. Decker, 2004), 16–41.

32. Improvised explosive devices: Sarah M. Theodoroff et al., "Hearing Impairment and Tinnitus: Prevalence, Risk Factors, and Outcomes in US Service Members and Veterans Deployed to the Iraq and Afghanistan Wars," *Epidemiologic Reviews* 37, no. 1 (2015): 71–85.

33. Industrial-grade sound amplification: Chrissy Hughes, "Celebrities with Tinnitus," Restored Hearing, July 1, 2015, https://restoredhearing .com/2015/07/01/celebrities-with-tinnitus.

34. She turned twenty-seven: Chris Harnick, "Liza Minnelli on 'Cabaret' Memories, 'Arrested Development' Return and More," *Huffpost*, January 29, 2013, http://www.huffingtonpost.com/2013/01/28/liza-minnelli -cabaret-arrested development_n_2566747.html.

35. He was experiencing: I. Kaufman Arenberg et al., "Van Gogh Had Meniere's Disease and Not Epilepsy," *JAMA* 264, no. 4 (1990): 491–493.

36. At age forty-seven: Lawrence K. Altman, "A Tube Implant Corrected Shepard's Ear Disease, *New York Times*, February 2, 1971, https://www .nytimes.com/1971/02/02/archives/a-tube-implant-corrected-shepards -ear-disease.html.

37. *Star Trek* television series: Hearing Solution Centers, "Tinnitus and Star Trek," 2015, https://www.heartulsa.com/blog/tinnitus-star-trek.

38. "Or you go insane": STR Staff, "Fame Won't Stop the Ringing—20 Celebrities with Tinnitus," January 28, 2018, http://www.stoptheringing .org/fame-wont-stop-the-ringing-20-celebrities-with-tinnitus.

39. Awareness of bodily pain: David M. Nondahl et al., "The Impact of Tinnitus on Quality of Life in Older Adults," *Journal of the American Academy of Audiology* 18, no. 3 (2007): 257–266.

40. Women who consume less: Jordan T. Glicksman, Sharon G. Curhan, and Gary C. Curhan, "A Prospective Study of Caffeine Intake and Risk of Incident Tinnitus," *American Journal of Medicine* 127, no. 8 (2014): 739–743.

41. Hearing aid in public: Steven R. Weisman, "Reagan Begins to Wear a Hearing Aid in Public," *New York Times*, September 8, 1983, http:// www.nytimes.com/1983/09/08/us/reagan-begins-to-wear-a-hearing-aid -in-public.html.

42. Adult male voice: Sarah Evans et al., "The Relationship between Testosterone and Vocal Frequencies in Human Males," *Physiology and Behavior* 93, no. 4 (2008): 783–788.

43. Older voices: Donna S. Lundy et al., "Cause of Hoarseness in Elderly Patients," *Otolaryngology—Head and Neck Surgery* 118, no. 4 (1998): 481–485.

44. The aging voice: Koichi Omori et al., "Influence of Size and Etiology of Glottal Gap in Glottic Incompetence Dysphonia," *Laryngoscope* 108, no. 4 (1998): 514–518.

45. Lived in rural areas: Chang Hwan Ryu et al., "Voice Changes in Elderly Adults: Prevalence and the Effect of Social, Behavioral, and Health Status on Voice Quality," *Journal of the American Geriatrics Society* 63, no. 8: (2015): 1608–1614.

46. Emerge as culprits: Ryu et al., "Voice Changes."

47. Normal pitch over time: Irma M. Verdonck–de Leeuw and Hans F. Mahieu, "Vocal Aging and the Impact on Daily Life: A Longitudinal Study," *Journal of Voice* 18, no. 2 (2004): 193–202.

48. Such as emphysema: Daniel R. Boone et al., *The Voice and Voice Therapy* (New York: Allyn & Bacon, 2005).

49. Decrease with age: Regina Helena Garcia Martins et al., "Aging Voice: Presbyphonia," *Aging Clinical and Experimental Research* 26, no. 1 (2014): 1–5.

50. Older adults themselves: Peter B. Mueller, "Voice Ageism," *Contemporary Issues in Communication Science and Disorders* 25 (1998): 62–64.

51. Events like large parties: Verdonck–de Leeuw et al., "Vocal Aging."

52. Treatment for voice disorders: Nicole M. Etter, Joseph C. Stemple, and Dana M. Howell, "Defining the Lived Experience of Older Adults with Voice Disorders," *Journal of Voice* 27, no. 1 (2013): 61–67.

53. Consequences for older adults: Nicholas R. Nicholson, "A Review of Social Isolation: An Important but Underassessed Condition in Older Adults," *Journal of Primary Prevention* 33, nos. 2–3 (2012): 137–152.

54. For the vocal folds: Joseph P. Bradley, Edie Hapner, and Michael M. Johns, "What Is the Optimal Treatment for Presbyphonia?" *Laryngoscope* 124, no. 11 (2014): 2439–2440.

55. Not to undergo therapy: Eric E. Berg et al., "Voice Therapy Improves Quality of Life in Age-Related Dysphonia: A Case-Control Study," *Journal of Voice* 22, no. 1 (2008): 70–74.

56. Throughout the world: Gullapalli N. Rao, Rohit Khanna, and Abhishek Payal, "The Global Burden of Cataract," *Current Opinion in Ophthalmology* 22, no. 1 (2011): 4–9.

57. A bad sunburn: Mikhail Linetsky et al., "UVA Light-Excited Kynurenines Oxidize Ascorbate and Modify Lens Proteins through the Formation of Advanced Glycation End Products: Implications for Human Lens Aging and Cataract Formation," *Journal of Biological Chemistry* 289, no. 24 (2014): 17111–17123.

58. Through an incision: F. J. Ascaso and V. Huerva, "The History of Cataract Surgery," in *Cataract Surgery*, ed. Farhan Zaidi (Rijeka, Croatia: InTech, 2013), 75–90.

59. Age of eighty: Sonia Mehta, "Age-Related Macular Degeneration," *Primary Care: Clinics in Office Practice* 42, no. 3 (2015): 377–391.

60. Lasers, medication, and surgery: Gordon J. Johnson et al., *The Epidemiology of Eye Disease, 2nd ed.* (London: Taylor & Francis, 2003).

61. Could read it: "Fewer Blind Americans Learning to Use Braille," NBC News, March 26, 2009.

62. Any office environment: Andy Brown et al., "The Uptake of Web 2.0 Technologies, and Its Impact on Visually Disabled Users," *Universal Access in the Information Society* 11, no. 2 (2012): 185–199.

63. Play a role as well: Susan A. Strenk, Lawrence M. Strenk, and Jane F. Koretz, "The Mechanism of Presbyopia," *Progress in Retinal and Eye Research* 24, no. 3 (2005): 379–393.

64. In the lens over time: Roger J. W. Truscott and Xiangjia Zhu, "Presbyopia and Cataract: A Question of Heat and Time," *Progress in Retinal and Eye Research* 29, no. 6 (2010): 487–499.

65. Coping with this problem: W. Neil Charman, "Developments in the Correction of Presbyopia I: Spectacle and Contact Lenses," *Ophthalmic and Physiological Optics* 34, no. 1 (2014): 8–29.

66. "Double spectacles": They may have been independently developed by others as well; see John R. Levene, "Benjamin Franklin, FRS, Sir Joshua Reynolds, FRS, PRA, Benjamin West, PRA, and the Invention of Bifocals," *Notes and Records of the Royal Society of London* 27, no. 1 (1972): 141–163.

67. Wearable contact lenses: Tony Adams, "Multiple Presbyopic Corrections across Multiple Centuries," *Optometry and Vision Science* 90, no. 5 (2013): 409–410.

68. Have also been devised: J. Kevin Belville and Ronald J. Smith, eds., *Presbyopia Surgery: Pearls and Pitfalls* (Thorofare, NJ: Slack, 2006).

69. Declines with age: Cynthia Owsley, Robert Sekuler, and Dennis Siemsen, "Contrast Sensitivity throughout Adulthood," *Vision Research* 23, no. 7 (1983): 689–699.

70. Younger adults before training: Denton J. DeLoss, Takeo Watanabe, and George J. Andersen, "Improving Vision among Older Adults: Behavioral Training to Improve Sight," *Psychological Science* 26, no. 4 (2015): 456–466.

71. Images that are blurred: Uri Polat et al., "Training the Brain to Overcome the Effect of Aging on the Human Eye," *Scientific Reports* 2 (2012): 1–6.

72. Control (comparison) subjects: Daniel J. Simons et al., "Do 'Brain-Training' Programs Work?" *Psychological Science in the Public Interest* 17, no. 3 (2016): 103–186.

73. Online app stores: Austin Frakt, "Training Your Brain So That You Don't Need Reading Glasses," *New York Times*, March 27, 2017, https://nyti.ms/2nEi3iR.

74. Identify them accurately: Carmen María Sarabia-Cobo et al., "Skilful Communication: Emotional Facial Expressions Recognition in Very Old Adults," *International Journal of Nursing Studies* 54 (2016): 104–111.

75. Worse at identifying deceit: Jennifer Tehan Stanley and Fredda Blanchard-Fields, "Challenges Older Adults Face in Detecting Deceit: The Role of Emotion Recognition," *Psychology and Aging* 23, no. 1 (2008): 24–32.

76. Sixty to seventy-six years: Naomi Cocks, Gary Morgan, and Sotaro Kita, "Iconic Gesture and Speech Integration in Younger and Older Adults," *Gesture* 11, no. 1 (2011): 24–39.

77. Being emotionally neutral: Joann Montepare et al., "The Use of Body Movements and Gestures as Cues to Emotions in Younger and Older Adults," *Journal of Nonverbal Behavior* 23, no. 2 (1999): 133–152.

78. Taken into account: César F. Lima et al., "In the Ear of the Beholder: How Age Shapes Emotion Processing in Nonverbal Vocalizations," *Emotion* 14, no. 1 (2014): 145–160.

79. Mitigate this effect: Kate Dupuis and M. Kathleen Pichora-Fuller, "Use of Affective Prosody by Young and Older Adults," *Psychology and Aging* 25, no. 1 (2010): 16–29.

80. Struggle with as well: Louise H. Phillips et al., "Older Adults Have Difficulty in Decoding Sarcasm," *Developmental Psychology* 51, no. 12 (2015): 1840–1852.

81. Different basic emotions: Ted Ruffman et al., "A Meta-analytic Review of Emotion Recognition and Aging: Implications for Neuropsychological Models of Aging," *Neuroscience and Biobehavioral Reviews* 32, no. 4 (2008): 863–881.

82. Positive than negative information: Andrew E. Reed, Larry Chan, and Joseph A. Mikels, "Meta-analysis of the Age-Related Positivity Effect: Age Differences in Preferences for Positive over Negative Information," *Psychology and Aging* 29, no. 1 (2014): 1–15.

83. Sad or angry faces: Mara Mather and Laura L. Carstensen, "Aging and Attentional Biases for Emotional Faces," *Psychological Science* 14, no. 5 (2003): 409–415.

84. Facial displays of sadness: Atsunobu Suzuki et al., "Decline or Improvement? Age-Related Differences in Facial Expression Recognition," *Biological Psychology* 74, no. 1 (2007): 75–84.

85. Emotional intelligence: Peter Salovey and John D. Mayer, "Emotional Intelligence," *Imagination, Cognition and Personality* 9, no. 3 (1990): 185–211.

86. Who were aging healthily: Romola S. Bucks and Shirley A. Radford, "Emotion Processing in Alzheimer's Disease," *Aging and Mental Health* 8, no. 3 (2004): 222–232.

87. Effects of these declines: Baltes and Baltes, *Successful Aging*.

3 The Story of Speech

1. Names of objects: Deborah M. Burke and Meredith A. Shafto, "Aging and Language Production," *Current Directions in Psychological Science* 13, no. 1 (2004): 21–24.

2. Annoyances of aging: Deborah M. Burke and Meredith A. Shafto, "Language and Aging," in *The Handbook of Aging and Cognition, 3rd ed.*, ed. Fergus I. Craik and Timothy A. Salthouse (New York: Psychology Press, 2008), 373–443.

3. As college students: Marilyn K. Heine, Beth A. Ober, and Gregory K. Shenaut, "Naturally Occurring and Experimentally Induced Tip-of-the-Tongue Experiences in Three Adult Age Groups," *Psychology and Aging* 14, no. 3 (1999): 445–457.

4. More than 90 percent: Bennett L. Schwartz, *Tip-of-the-Tongue States: Phenomenology, Mechanism, and Lexical Retrieval* (Mahwah, NJ: Erlbaum, 2002).

5. That are not resolved: Alan S. Brown, *The Tip of the Tongue State* (New York: Psychology Press, 2012).

6. Stars at sea: Roger Brown and David McNeill, "The 'Tip of the Tongue' Phenomenon," *Journal of Verbal Learning and Verbal Behavior* 5, no. 4 (1966): 333.

7. Less available for them: Alan S. Brown and Lori A. Nix, "Age-Related Changes in the Tip-of-the-Tongue Experience," *American Journal of Psychology* 109, no. 1 (1996): 79–91.

8. Long-term memory: Bennett L. Schwartz and Leslie D. Frazier, "Tip-of-the-Tongue States and Aging: Contrasting Psycholinguistic and Meta-cognitive Perspectives," *Journal of General Psychology* 132, no. 4 (2005): 377–391.

9. Experience more TOT states: Donna J. Dahlgren, "Impact of Knowledge and Age on Tip-of-the-Tongue Rates," *Experimental Aging Research* 24, no. 2 (1998): 139–153.

10. Ultimately lead to success: Bennett L. Schwartz and Janet Metcalfe, "Tip-of-the-Tongue (TOT) States: Retrieval, Behavior, and Experience," *Memory and Cognition* 39, no. 5 (2011): 737–749.

11. Valuable sources of information: Anne M. Cleary and Alexander B. Claxton, "The Tip-of-the-Tongue Heuristic: How Tip-of-the-Tongue

States Confer Perceptibility on Inaccessible Words," *Journal of Experimental Psychology: Learning, Memory, and Cognition* 41, no. 5 (2015): 1533–1539.

12. Maintain your aerobic fitness: Katrien Segaert et al., "Higher Physical Fitness Levels Are Associated with Less Language Decline in Healthy Ageing," *Scientific Reports* 8, 6715 (2018): 1–10.

13. Drawing of a protractor: Edith Kaplan, Harold Goodglass, and Sandra Weintraub, *Boston Naming Test* (Philadelphia: Lea & Febiger, 1983).

14. Health status of the participants: Pierre Goulet, Bernadette Ska, and Helen J. Kahn, "Is There a Decline in Picture Naming with Advancing Age?" *Journal of Speech, Language, and Hearing Research* 37, no. 3 (1994): 629–644.

15. After age seventy: Pierre Feyereisen, "A Meta-analytic Procedure Shows an Age-Related Decline in Picture Naming: Comments on Goulet, Ska, and Kahn (1994)," *Journal of Speech, Language, and Hearing Research* 40, no. 6 (1997): 1328–1333.

16. Two percent per decade: Lisa Tabor Connor et al., "Change in Object Naming Ability during Adulthood," *Journals of Gerontology Series B: Psychological Sciences and Social Sciences* 59, no. 5 (2004): P203–P209.

17. "Ocopus" for octopus: Rhoda Au et al., "Naming Ability across the Adult Life Span," *Aging, Neuropsychology, and Cognition* 2, no. 4 (1995): 303.

18. Long-term memory: Linda Mortensen, Antje S. Meyer, and Glyn W. Humphreys, "Age-Related Effects on Speech Production: A Review," *Language and Cognitive Processes* 21, nos. 1–3 (2006): 238–290.

19. Found in other studies: Christopher Randolph et al., "Determinants of Confrontation Naming Performance," *Archives of Clinical Neuropsychology* 14, no. 6 (1999): 489–496; Ronald F. Zec et al., "A Cross-Sectional Study of the Effects of Age, Education, and Gender on the Boston Naming Test," *Clinical Neuropsychologist* 21, no. 4 (2007): 587–616.

20. Familiarity the with the test items: Randolph et al., "Determinants of Confrontation."

21. "Trellis" and "abacus": Maureen Schmitter-Edgecombe, M. Vesneski, and D. W. R. Jones, "Aging and Word-Finding: A Comparison of Spontaneous and Constrained Naming Tests," *Archives of Clinical Neuropsychology* 15, no. 6 (2000): 479–493.

22. Word retrieval difficulties: Martin L. Albert et al., "Effects of Health Status on Word Finding in Aging," *Journal of the American Geriatrics Society* 57, no. 12 (2009): 2300–2305.

23. In the following section: Victoria Tumanova et al., "Speech Disfluencies of Preschool-Age Children Who Do and Do Not Stutter," *Journal of Communication Disorders* 49 (2014): 25–41.

24. Lecturers in the humanities: Stanley Schachter et al., "Speech Disfluency and the Structure of Knowledge," *Journal of Personality and Social Psychology* 60, no. 3 (1991): 362–367.

25. "A white shirt": Heather Bortfeld et al., "Disfluency Rates in Conversation: Effects of Age, Relationship, Topic, Role, and Gender," *Language and Speech* 44, no. 2 (2001): 123–147.

26. Lacking in confidence: David Zielinski, ed., *Master Presenter: Lessons from the World's Top Experts on Becoming a More Influential Speaker* (San Francisco: Wiley, 2013).

27. Varying degrees of success: Jean E. Fox Tree, "Folk Notions of *Um* and *Uh, You Know,* and *Like,*" *Text and Talk* 27, no. 3 (2007): 297–314.

28. Following pause was longer: Herbert H. Clark and Jean E. Fox Tree, "Using *Uh* and *Um* in Spontaneous Speaking," *Cognition* 84, no. 1 (2002): 73–111.

29. Men employing "uh": Eric K. Acton, "On Gender Differences in the Distribution of Um and Uh," *University of Pennsylvania Working Papers in Linguistics* 17, no. 2 (2011): 1–9.

30. Decreases with age: Mark Liberman, "Language Log: Young Men Talk like Old Women," November 6, 2005, http://itre.cis.upenn.edu/~myl/languagelog/archives/002629.html.

31. No differences have been found: Patricia V. Cooper, "Discourse Production and Normal Aging: Performance on Oral Picture Description Tasks," *Journal of Gerontology* 45, no. 5 (1990): 210–214; Sandra W. Duchin and Edward D. Mysak, "Disfluency and Rate Characteristics of Young Adult, Middle-Aged, and Older Males," *Journal of Communication Disorders* 20, no. 3 (1987): 245–257.

32. Pictures with negative content: Nichol Castro and Lori E. James, "Differences between Young and Older Adults' Spoken Language Production in Descriptions of Negative versus Neutral Pictures," *Aging, Neuropsychology, and Cognition* 21, no. 2 (2014): 222–238.

33. "Shorter and less complex": Barbara B. Shadden, "Discourse Behaviors in Older Adults," *Seminars in Speech and Language* 18, no. 2 (1997): 143–157.

34. Seventies, eighties, and nineties: Jeffrey P. Searl, Rodney M. Gabel, and J. Steven Fulks, "Speech Disfluency in Centenarians," *Journal of Communication Disorders* 35, no. 5 (2002): 383–392.

35. Without cognitive impairment: Frederique Gayraud, Hye-Ran Lee, and Melissa Barkat-Defradas, "Syntactic and Lexical Context of Pauses and Hesitations in the Discourse of Alzheimer Patients and Healthy Elderly Subjects," *Clinical Linguistics and Phonetics* 25, no. 3 (2011): 198–209.

36. Novel way of expressing something: Allison Wray, *Formulaic Language and the Lexicon* (Cambridge: Cambridge University Press, 2002).

37. "Have a nice day": Diana Van Lancker-Sidtis and Gail Rallon, "Tracking the Incidence of Formulaic Expressions in Everyday Speech: Methods for Classification and Verification," *Language and Communication* 24, no. 3 (2004): 207–240.

38. On such phrases: Kelly Ann Bridges and Diana Van Lancker Sidtis, "Formulaic Language in Alzheimer's Disease," *Aphasiology* 27, no. 7 (2013): 799–810.

39. Use formulaic language appropriately: Boyd H. Davis and Margaret Maclagan, "Pauses, Fillers, Placeholders, and Formulaicity in Alzheimer's Discourse," in *Fillers, Pauses and Placeholders*, ed. Nino Amiridze, Boyd

H. Davis, and Margaret Maclagan (Amsterdam: John Benjamins, 2010), 189–216.

40. Historical events: Steve Luxemberg, "'The King's Speech': Brilliant Filmmaking, Less-than-Brilliant History," *Washington Post*, January 28, 2011.

41. Mentally challenged: Jeffrey K. Johnson, "The Visualization of the Twisted Tongue: Portrayals of Stuttering in Film, Television, and Comic Books," *Journal of Popular Culture* 41, no. 2 (2008): 245–261.

42. Dennis McLellan, "Stutter Group Pickets over 'Wanda' Role," *Los Angeles Times*, March 29, 1989, http://articles.latimes.com/1989-03-29 /entertainment/ca-716_1_wanda-insults-people.

43. One percent of adults: Carlos Frigerio-Domingues and Dennis Drayna, "Genetic Contributions to Stuttering: The Current Evidence," *Molecular Genetics and Genomic Medicine* 5, no. 2 (2017): 95–102.

44. Than those who don't stutter: Ashley Craig and Yvonne Tran, "Trait and Social Anxiety in Adults with Chronic Stuttering: Conclusions following Meta-analysis," *Journal of Fluency Disorders* 40 (2014): 35–43.

45. Half of their genes: Corrado Fagnani et al., "Heritability and Environmental Effects for Self-Reported Periods with Stuttering: A Twin Study from Denmark," *Logopedics Phoniatrics Vocology* 36, no. 3 (2011): 114–120.

46. Translated into specific treatments: Roger J. Ingham et al., "Stuttering Treatment and Brain Research in Adults: A Still Unfolding Relationship," *Journal of Fluency Disorders* 55 (2018): 106–119.

47. When they are putting: David Owens, "The Yips: What's behind the Condition That Every Golfer Dreads?" *New Yorker*, May 26, 2014, https://www.newyorker.com/magazine/2014/05/26/the-yips.

48. Action dystonias: G. Kiziltan and M. A. Akalin, "Stuttering May Be a Type of Action Dystonia," *Movement Disorders* 11, no. 3 (1996): 278–282.

49. About to stammer: Eric S. Jackson et al., "Responses of Adults Who Stutter to the Anticipation of Stuttering," *Journal of Fluency Disorders* 45 (2015): 38–51.

50. Severity of a person's stammer: Christopher D. Constantino et al., "A Preliminary Investigation of Daily Variability of Stuttering in Adults," *Journal of Communication Disorders* 60 (2016): 39–50.

51. Their promotion chances: Michelle Klompas and Eleanor Ross, "Life Experiences of People Who Stutter, and the Perceived Impact of Stuttering on Quality of Life: Personal Accounts of South African Individuals," *Journal of Fluency Disorders* 29, no. 4 (2004): 275–305.

52. Younger and unmarried: Debora Freud et al., "The Relationship between the Experience of Stuttering and Demographic Characteristics of Adults Who Stutter," *Journal of Fluency Disorders* 52 (2017): 53–63.

53. Interacting with store clerks: Travis M. Andrews, "Annie Glenn: 'When I Called John, He Cried. People Just Couldn't Believe That I Could Really Talk.'" *Washington Post*, December 9, 2016, https://www.washington post.com/news/morning-mix/wp/2016/12/09/to-john-glenn-the-real -hero-was-his-wife-annie-conqueror-of-disability/?noredirect=on&utm _term=.c02f21305c42.

54. Controlling breathing and speech rate: The Stuttering Foundation, "Annie Glenn," June 17, 2015, https://www.stutteringhelp.org/content /annie-glenn.

55. Person that they had become: Klompas and Ross, "Life Experiences of People Who Stutter."

56. Than when they were younger: Walther H. Manning, Deborah Dailey, and Sue Wallace, "Attitude and Personality Characteristics of Older Stutterers," *Journal of Fluency Disorders* 9 (1984): 213.

57. Health and finance: Geraldine Bricker-Katz, Michelle Lincoln, and Patricia McCabe, "A Life-Time of Stuttering: How Emotional Reactions to Stuttering Impact Activities and Participation in Older People," *Disability and Rehabilitation* 31, no. 21 (2009): 1742–1752.

58. Picture of a tricycle: Jonathan D. Rohrer, Martin N. Rossor, and Jason D. Warren, "Neologistic Jargon Aphasia and Agraphia in Primary Progressive Aphasia," *Journal of the Neurological Sciences* 277, no. 1 (2009): 155–159.

59. Host of other conditions: Zac Lane et al., "Differentiating Psychosis versus Fluent Aphasia," *Clinical Schizophrenia and Related Psychoses* 4, no. 4 (2010): 258–261.

60. His normal function: Maarten G. Lansberg, Erich Bluhmki, and Vincent N. Thijs, "Efficacy and Safety of Tissue Plasminogen Activator 3 to 4.5 Hours after Acute Ischemic Stroke: A Meta-analysis," *Stroke* 40, no. 7 (2009): 2438–2441.

61. "Gesture salad": Ruth Campbell, Mairéad MacSweeney, and Dafydd Waters, "Sign Language and the Brain: A Review," *Journal of Deaf Studies and Deaf Education* 13, no. 1 (2008): 3–20.

62. Comprehend the written word poorly: Norman Geschwind, "The Organization of Language and the Brain," *Science* 170, no. 3961 (1970): 940–944.

63. Cognitively intact individuals: Randi Starrfelt and Marlene Behrmann, "Number Reading in Pure Alexia—a Review," *Neuropsychologia* 49, no. 9 (2011): 2283–2298.

64. When words are long: E. H. Lacey et al., "Transcranial Direct Current Stimulation for Pure Alexia: Effects on Brain and Behavior," *Brain Stimulation: Basic, Translational, and Clinical Research in Neuromodulation* 8, no. 2 (2015): 305–307.

65. Family support: M. M. Watila and S. A. Balarabe, "Factors Predicting Post-stroke Aphasia Recovery," *Journal of the Neurological Sciences* 352, no. 1 (2015): 12–18.

66. Extended period: Marian C. Brady et al., "Speech and Language Therapy for Aphasia following Stroke," *Cochrane Database of Systematic Reviews*, no. 6, article number CD000425 (2016).

67. Changing brain function: Andrea Gomez Palacio Schjetnan et al., "Transcranial Direct Current Stimulation in Stroke Rehabilitation: A Review of Recent Advancements," *Stroke Research and Treatment*, article ID 170256 (2013).

68. Are also being developed: Michael Pugliese et al., "Mobile Tablet-Based Therapies following Stroke: A Systematic Scoping Review of

Administrative Methods and Patient Experiences," *PloS One* 13, no. 1 (2018): e0191566; Sarel Van Vuuren and Leora R. Cherney, "A Virtual Therapist for Speech and Language Therapy," in *Intelligent Virtual Agents*, ed. T. Bickmore, S. Marsella, and C. Sidner (New York: Springer, 2014), 438–448.

69. Numbers, mathematics, and calculation: Anna J. Wilson et al., "Dyscalculia and Dyslexia in Adults: Cognitive Bases of Comorbidity," *Learning and Individual Differences* 37 (2015): 118–132.

70. Figure is 7 percent: Robin L. Peterson and Bruce F. Pennington, "Developmental Dyslexia," *Annual Review of Clinical Psychology* 11 (2015): 283–307.

71. Play an important role: Suzanne C. Swagerman et al., "Genetic Transmission of Reading Ability," *Brain and Language* 172 (2015): 3–8.

72. Spelling and sound: Johannes C. Ziegler et al., "Developmental Dyslexia in Different Languages: Language-Specific or Universal?" *Journal of Experimental Child Psychology* 86, no. 3 (2003): 169–193.

73. Shame or fear: Kathleen Tanner, "Adult Dyslexia and the 'Conundrum of Failure,'" *Disability and Society* 24, no. 6 (2009): 785–797.

74. Bush had dyslexia: Gail Sheehy, "The Accidental Candidate," *Vanity Fair*, October 2000.

75. For the condition: Andrew Cohen, "Bush's Mangling of Language Points to Dyslexia: Writer," *Globe and Mail*, September 13, 2000.

76. Might have dyslexia: Trude Nergård-Nilssen and Charles Hulme, "Developmental Dyslexia in Adults: Behavioural Manifestations and Cognitive Correlates," *Dyslexia* 20, no. 3 (2014): 191–207.

77. Those without dyslexia: James H. Smith-Spark, Adam P. Zięcik, and Christopher Sterling, "Self-Reports of Increased Prospective and Retrospective Memory Problems in Adults with Developmental Dyslexia," *Dyslexia* 22, no. 3 (2016): 245–262.

78. Inappropriate treatment options: Claudia Metzler-Baddeley, Amanda Salter, and Roy W. Jones, "The Significance of Dyslexia Screening for the

Assessment of Dementia in Older People," *International Journal of Geriatric Psychiatry* 23, no. 7 (2008): 766–768.

79. Than their peers: Eddy Cavalli et al., "Vocabulary Skills Are Well Developed in University Students with Dyslexia: Evidence from Multiple Case Studies," *Research in Developmental Disabilities* 51 (2016): 89–102.

80. Times New Roman: Jessica J. Wery and Jennifer A. Diliberto, "The Effect of a Specialized Dyslexia Font, OpenDyslexic, on Reading Rate and Accuracy," *Annals of Dyslexia* 67, no. 2 (2017): 114–127.

81. No differences in reading speed: Eva Marinus et al., "A Special Font for People with Dyslexia: Does It Work and, If So, Why?" *Dyslexia* 22, no. 3 (2016): 233–244.

82. Computer graphics and architecture: Brock L. Eide and Fernette F. Eide, *The Dyslexic Advantage: Unlocking the Hidden Potential of the Dyslexic Brain* (New York: Plume, 2012).

83. Interacted with foreigners: Georg Herman Monrad-Krohn, "Dysprosody or Altered 'Melody of Language,'" *Brain* 70 (1947): 405–415; J. Ryalls and I. Reinvang, "Some Further Notes on Monrad-Krohn's Case Study of Foreign Accent Syndrome," *Folia Phoniatrica et Logopaedica* 37, nos. 3–4 (1985): 160–162.

84. "Alsatian" accent: Inger Moen, "Monrad-Krohn's Foreign Accent Syndrome Case," in *Classic Cases in Neuropsychology*, ed. Chris Code et al. (Hove, UK: Psychology Press, 1996), 145–156.

85. West Country accent: Ryan Jaslow, "George Michael Wakes from Coma with New Accent: What's Foreign Accent Syndrome?" *CBS News*, July 19, 2012, https://www.cbsnews.com/news/george-michael-wakes-from-coma-with-new-accent-whats-foreign-accent-syndrome.

86. Motor planning problem: Sheila E. Blumstein and Kathleen Kurowski, "The Foreign Accent Syndrome: A Perspective," *Journal of Neurolinguistics* 19, no. 5 (2006): 346–355.

87. Foreign accent persisted: Stefanie Keulen et al., "Foreign Accent Syndrome as a Psychogenic Disorder: A Review," *Frontiers in Human Neuroscience* 10, no. 168 (2016).

88. And the United States: Barbara Bradford, "Upspeak in British English," *English Today* 13, no. 3 (1997): 29–36.

89. As a second language: Moen, "Monrad-Krohn's Foreign Accent Syndrome."

90. How speech is perceived: BBC News, "Stroke Gives Woman a Foreign Accent," July 4, 2006, http://news.bbc.co.uk/2/hi/uk_news/england/tyne /5144300.stm.

91. Scottish, English, Irish, or American: Cinzia Di Dio, Joerg Schulz, and Jennifer Gurd, "Foreign Accent Syndrome: In the Ear of the Beholder?" *Aphasiology* 20, no. 9 (2006): 951–962.

92. Not totally foreign either: Jo Verhoeven et al., "Accent Attribution in Speakers with Foreign Accent Syndrome," *Journal of Communication Disorders* 46, no. 2 (2013): 156–168.

93. "I don't like it": BBC News, July 4, 2006.

94. "Someone who sounded like me": Anthony DiLollo, Julie Scherz, and Robert A. Neimeyer, "Psychosocial Implications of Foreign Accent Syndrome: Two Case Examples," *Journal of Constructivist Psychology 27*, no. 1 (2014): 24.

4   Word Domination

1. Boundaries in ambiguous sentences: Margaret M. Kjelgaard, Debra A. Titone, and Arthur Wingfield, "The Influence of Prosodic Structure on the Interpretation of Temporary Syntactic Ambiguity by Young and Elderly Listeners," *Experimental Aging Research* 25, no. 3 (1999): 187–207.

2. To make their decisions: Ken J. Hoyte, Hiram Brownell, and Arthur Wingfield, "Components of Speech Prosody and Their Use in Detection of Syntactic Structure by Older Adults," *Experimental Aging Research* 35, no. 1 (2009): 129–151.

3. Some nonnative speakers: Angela N. Burda et al., "Age and Understanding Speakers with Spanish or Taiwanese Accents," *Perceptual and Motor Skills* 97, no. 1 (2003): 11–20.

4. Older adults with normal hearing: Sandra Gordon-Salant et al., "Perception of Contrastive Bi-syllabic Lexical Stress in Unaccented and Accented Words by Younger and Older Listeners," *Journal of the Acoustical Society of America* 139, no. 3 (2016): 1132–1148.

5. Both younger and older adults: Alejandrina Cristia et al., "Linguistic Processing of Accented Speech across the Lifespan," *Frontiers in Psychology* 3, no. 479 (2012): 1–15.

6. To understand them: Alexandra Jesse and Esther Janse, "Audiovisual Benefit for Recognition of Speech Presented with Single-Talker Noise in Older Listeners," *Language and Cognitive Processes* 27, nos. 7–8 (2012): 1167–1191.

7. "Remarkably poor": Raymond S. Nickerson and Marilyn Jager Adams, "Long-Term Memory for a Common Object," *Cognitive Psychology* 11, no. 3 (1979): 288.

8. Characters on keyboard: Alan D. Castel, Meenely Nazarian, and Adam B. Blake, "Attention and Incidental Memory in Everyday Settings," in *The Handbook of Attention*, ed. Jonathan M. Fawcett, Evan F. Risko, and Alan Kingstone (Cambridge, MA: MIT Press), 463–483.

9. Impaired their spelling ability: Larry L. Jacoby and Ann Hollingshead, "Reading Student Essays May Be Hazardous to Your Spelling: Effects of Reading Incorrectly and Correctly Spelled Words," *Canadian Journal of Psychology* 44, no. 3 (1990): 345–358.

10. Spelling ability also declined: Larry L. Jacoby, "Memory Observed and Memory Unobserved," in *Remembering Reconsidered: Ecological and Traditional Approaches to the Study of Memory*, ed. Ulric Neisser and Eugene Winograd (Cambridge: Cambridge University Press, 1988), 145–192.

11. "Hazardous to your spelling": Jacoby and Hollingshead, "Reading Student Essays May Be Hazardous."

12. On par with college-aged students: Donald G. MacKay, Lise Abrams, and Manissa J. Pedroza, "Aging on the Input versus Output Side: Theoretical Implications of Age-Linked Asymmetries between Detecting

versus Retrieving Orthographic Information," *Psychology and Aging* 14, no. 1 (1999): 3–17.

13. Participants in their sixties: Lise Abrams, Meagan T. Farrell, and Sara J. Margolin, "Older Adults' Detection of Misspellings during Reading," *Journals of Gerontology Series B: Psychological Sciences and Social Sciences* 65B, no. 6 (2010): 680–683.

14. "Anathema" and "obsequious": Francis T. Durso and Wendelyn J. Shore, "Partial Knowledge of Word Meanings," *Journal of Experimental Psychology: General* 120, no. 2 (1991): 190–202.

15. Speaker of English: Robin Goulden, Paul Nation, and John Read, "How Large Can a Receptive Vocabulary Be?" *Applied Linguistics* 11, no. 4 (1990): 356.

16. Via online sources: Kathryn Zickuhr et al., "Younger Americans' Reading and Library Habits," *Pew Internet and American Life Project*, October 23, 2012, http://libraries.pewinternet.org/2012/10/23/younger -americans-reading-and-library-habits.

17. Younger and older participants: Ryan P. Bowles and Timothy A. Salthouse, "Vocabulary Test Format and Differential Relations to Age," *Psychology and Aging* 23, no. 2 (2008): 366–376.

18. Over 21,000 words: Eugene B. Zechmeister et al., "Growth of a Functionally Important Lexicon," *Journal of Reading Behavior* 27, no. 2 (1995): 201–212.

19. "Lifetime of word usage": Gitit Kavé and Vered Halamish, "Doubly Blessed: Older Adults Know More Vocabulary and Know Better What They Know," *Psychology and Aging* 30, no. 1 (2015): 72.

20. Short-term and working memory: Joshua K. Hartshorne and Laura T. Germine, "When Does Cognitive Functioning Peak? The Asynchronous Rise and Fall of Different Cognitive Abilities across the Life Span," *Psychological Science* 26, no. 4 (2015): 433–443.

21. Word-finding difficulties: Meredith A. Shafto et al., "Age-Related Increases in Verbal Knowledge Are Not Associated with Word Finding

Problems in the Cam-CAN Cohort: What You Know Won't Hurt You," *Journals of Gerontology Series B: Psychological Sciences and Social Sciences* 72, no. 1 (2018): 100–106.

22. No such compensation was necessary: Eiji Aramaki et al., "Vocabulary Size in Speech May Be an Early Indicator of Cognitive Impairment," *PloS One* 11, no. 5 (2016): 1–13.

23. In sixty seconds: Tom N. Tombaugh, Jean Kozak, and Laura Rees, "Normative Data Stratified by Age and Education for Two Measures of Verbal Fluency: FAS and Animal Naming," *Archives of Clinical Neuropsychology* 14, no. 2 (1999): 167–177.

24. "I've already said it": Janet Patterson, "Verbal Fluency," in *Encyclopedia of Clinical Neuropsychology,* vol. 4, ed. Jeffrey S. Kreutzer, John DeLuca, and Bruce Caplan (New York: Springer, 2011), 2603–2605.

25. Planning and search strategies: Julie D. Henry and John R. Crawford, "A Meta-analytic Review of Verbal Fluency Performance following Focal Cortical Lesions," *Neuropsychology* 18, no. 2 (2004): 284–295.

26. Tied to processing speed: Joan McDowd et al., "Understanding Verbal Fluency in Healthy Aging, Alzheimer's Disease, and Parkinson's Disease," *Neuropsychology* 25, no. 2 (2011): 210–225.

27. Measure of language processing: Douglas M. Whiteside et al., "Verbal Fluency: Language or Executive Function Measure?" *Applied Neuropsychology: Adult* 23, no. 1 (2016): 29–34.

28. Predictors of high performance: Tombaugh et al., "Normative Data Stratified by Age."

29. But not for age: Karen I. Bolla et al., "Predictors of Verbal Fluency (FAS) in the Healthy Elderly," *Journal of Clinical Psychology* 46, no. 5 (1990): 623–628.

30. But not for education: Adam M. Brickman et al., "Category and Letter Verbal Fluency across the Adult Lifespan: Relationship to EEG Theta Power," *Archives of Clinical Neuropsychology* 20, no. 5 (2005): 561–573.

31. Outperformed younger adults: Sara J. Czaja et al., "Examining Age Differences in Performance of a Complex Information Search and Retrieval Task," *Psychology and Aging* 16, no. 4 (2001): 564–579.

32. Perform better than older: Danielle Barry, Marsha E. Bates, and Erich Labouvie, "FAS and CFL Forms of Verbal Fluency Differ in Difficulty: A Meta-analytic Study," *Applied Neuropsychology* 15, no. 2 (2008): 97–106.

33. On the two tasks: Brickman et al., "Category and letter Verbal Fluency.".

34. No better than their peers: Ian S. Hargreaves et al., "How a Hobby Can Shape Cognition: Visual Word Recognition in Competitive Scrabble Players," *Memory and Cognition* 40, no. 1 (2012): 1–7.

35. Higher levels of knowledge: Michael Ramscar et al., "The Myth of Cognitive Decline: Non-linear Dynamics of Lifelong Learning," *Topics in Cognitive Science* 6, no. 1 (2014): 5–42.

36. The more complex the grammar: Susan Kemper and Aaron Sumner, "The Structure of Verbal Abilities in Young and Older Adults," *Psychology and Aging* 16, no. 2 (2001): 312–322.

37. Limitation for the older participants: Susan Kemper, Ruth E. Herman, and Chiung-Ju Liu, "Sentence Production by Young and Older Adults in Controlled Contexts," *Journals of Gerontology Series B: Psychological Sciences and Social Sciences* 59, no. 5 (2004): P220–P224.

38. Declines continuing over time: Susan Kemper, Marilyn Thompson, and Janet Marquis, "Longitudinal Change in Language Production: Effects of Aging and Dementia on Grammatical Complexity and Semantic Content," *Psychology and Aging* 16, no. 4 (2001): 600–614.

39. Declined for all groups: Marilyn A. Nippold, Paige M. Cramond, and Christine Hayward-Mayhew, "Spoken Language Production in Adults: Examining Age-Related Differences in Syntactic Complexity," *Clinical Linguistics and Phonetics* 28, no. 3 (2014): 195–207.

40. Only sixty-seven: Fermín Moscoso del Prado Martín, "Vocabulary, Grammar, Sex, and Aging," *Cognitive Science* 41, no. 4 (2017): 950–975.

41. And by executive function: Susan Kemper, "Memory and Executive Function: Language Production in Late Life," in *Language Development: The Lifespan Perspective*, ed. Annette Gerstenberg and Anja Voeste (Amsterdam: John Benjamins, 2015), 59–76.

42. Abilities of the participants: Moscoso del Prado Martín, "Vocabulary, Grammar, Sex."

43. Alzheimer's disease (AD): Alan D. Baddeley et al., "The Decline of Working Memory in Alzheimer's Disease: A Longitudinal Study," *Brain* 114, no. 6 (1991): 2521–2542.

44. And we do: Kemper et al., "Longitudinal Change.".

45. Remain fairly grammatical: Kelly Lyons et al., "Oral Language and Alzheimer's Disease: A Reduction in Syntactic Complexity," *Aging, Neuropsychology, and Cognition* 1, no. 4 (1994): 271–281.

46. Suspected of having AD: Susan Kemper et al., "On the Preservation of Syntax in Alzheimer's Disease: Evidence from Written Sentences," *Archives of Neurology* 50, no. 1 (1993): 81–86.

47. Working memory and executive function: Kemper, "Memory and Executive Function," 63.

48. Dolores Gold et al., "Measurement and Correlates of Verbosity in Elderly People," *Journal of Gerontology: Psychological Sciences* 43, no. 2 (1988): 27.

49. But not talkativeness: Dolores Pushkar Gold et al., "Off-Target Verbosity and Talkativeness in Elderly People," *Canadian Journal on Aging* 12, no. 1 (1993): 67–77.

50. Lexical mistakes: Guila Glosser and Toni Deser, "A Comparison of Changes in Macrolinguistic and Microlinguistic Aspects of Discourse Production in Normal Aging," *Journal of Gerontology* 47, no. 4 (1992): 266–272.

51. Over longer periods: Dolores Pushkar Gold and Tannis Y. Arbuckle, "A Longitudinal Study of Off-Target Verbosity," *Journals of Gerontology Series B: Psychological Sciences and Social Sciences* 50, no. 6 (1995): 307–315.

52. Their thoughts and speech: Tannis Y. Arbuckle and Dolores Pushkar Gold, "Aging, Inhibition, and Verbosity," *Journal of Gerontology* 48, no. 5 (1993): 225–232.

53. Their younger counterparts: Lori E. James et al., "Production and Perception of 'Verbosity' in Younger and Older Adults," *Psychology and Aging* 13, no. 3 (1998): 355–367.

54. As equally credible: C. A. Brimacombe et al., "Perceptions of Older Adult Eyewitnesses: Will You Believe Me When I'm 64?" *Law and Human Behavior* 27, no. 5 (2003): 507–522.

55. To be less believable: C. A. Brimacombe et al., "Is Age Irrelevant? Perceptions of Young and Old Adult Eyewitnesses," *Law and Human Behavior* 21, no. 6 (1997): 619–634; Sheree T. Kwong See, Hunter G. Hoffman, and Tammy L. Wood, "Perceptions of an Old Female Eyewitness: Is the Older Eyewitness Believable?" *Psychology and Aging* 16, no. 2 (2001): 346–350.

56. James et al., "Production and Perception," 355.

57. About a different topic: Elizabeth A. L. Stine-Morrow, Matthew C. Shake, and Soo Rim Noh, "Language and Communication," in *Aging in America, vol. 1,* ed. John C. Cavanaugh and Christine K. Cavanaugh (Santa Barbara, CA: Praeger Perspectives, 2010), 56–78.

58. Diverse expressive styles: Dunja L. Trunk and Lise Abrams, "Do Younger and Older Adults' Communicative Goals Influence Off-Topic Speech in Autobiographical Narratives?" *Psychology and Aging* 24, no. 2 (2009): 324–377.

59. Older adults with dementia: Katinka Dijkstra et al., "Conversational Coherence: Discourse Analysis of Older Adults with and without Dementia," *Journal of Neurolinguistics* 17, no. 4 (2004): 276.

60. Stereotypes about the elderly: Janet B. Ruscher and Megan M. Hurley, "Off-Target Verbosity Evokes Negative Stereotypes of Older Adults," *Journal of Language and Social Psychology* 19, no. 1 (2000): 141–149.

61. Ear of the beholder: Richard M. Roberts and Roger J. Kreuz, "Nonstandard Discourse and Its Coherence," *Discourse Processes* 16, no. 4 (1993): 451–464.

62. Susan Kemper et al., "Telling Stories: The Structure of Adults' Narratives," *European Journal of Cognitive Psychology* 2, no. 3 (1991): 208.

63. Tale they were telling: Kemper et al., "Telling Stories."

64. Told by the undergraduates: Cynthia Adams et al., "Adult Age Group Differences in Story Recall Style," *Journal of Gerontology* 45, no. 1 (1990): P17–P27.

65. Similar degrees of accuracy: Danielle K. Davis, Nicole Alea, and Susan Bluck, "The Difference between Right and Wrong: Accuracy of Older and Younger Adults' Story Recall," *International Journal of Environmental Research and Public Health* 12, no. 9 (2015): 10861–10885.

66. Understanding of story quality: Jacqueline M. Baron and Susan Bluck, "That Was a Good Story! Preliminary Construction of the Perceived Story Quality Index," *Discourse Processes* 48, no. 2 (2011): 93–118.

67. Ages eighteen to twenty-eight: Susan Kemper et al., "Life-Span Changes to Adults' Language: Effects of Memory and Genre," *Applied Psycholinguistics* 10, no. 1 (1989): 49–66.

68. Productions of younger subjects: Michael W. Pratt and Susan L. Robins, "That's the Way It Was: Age Differences in the Structure and Quality of Adults' Personal Narratives," *Discourse Processes* 14, no. 1 (1991): 73–85.

69. "More effective oral transmission": Nancy L. Mergler, Marion Faust, and Michael D. Goldstein, "Storytelling as an Age-Dependent Skill: Oral Recall of Orally Presented Stories," *International Journal of Aging and Human Development* 20, no. 3 (1985): 205.

70. What they are saying: Arthur A. Wingfield and Elizabeth A. L. Stine-Morrow, "Language and Speech," in *Handbook of Cognitive Aging*, 2nd ed., ed. Fergus I. M. Craik and Timothy A. Salthouse (Mahwah, NJ: Erlbaum, 2000), 359–416.

71. Being objectively accurate: Roger A. Dixon and Odette N. Gould, "Adults Telling and Retelling Stories Collaboratively," in *Interactive Minds: Life-Span Perspectives on the Social Foundation of Cognition*, ed. Paul

B. Baltes and Ursula M. Staudinger (Cambridge: Cambridge University Press, 1996), 221–241.

72. With new acquaintances: Odette N. Gould et al., "Collaborative Recall in Married and Unacquainted Dyads," *International Journal of Behavioral Development* 26, no. 1 (2002): 36–44.

73. All parts of the story together: Odette N. Gould and Roger A. Dixon, "How We Spent Our Vacation: Collaborative Storytelling by Young and Old Adults," *Psychology and Aging* 8, no. 1 (1993): 10–17.

74. Collaborative problem solving: Cynthia A. Berg et al., "Task Control and Cognitive Abilities of Self and Spouse in Collaboration in Middle-Aged and Older Couples," *Psychology and Aging* 22, no. 3 (2007): 420–427.

75. Declines in cognitive ability: Dixon and Gould, "Adults Telling and Retelling Stories"; Gould and Dixon, "How We Spent Our Vacation"; Gould, Osborn, et al., "Collaborative Recall."

5 Using Language

1. Wants of others: Roger Kreuz and Richard Roberts, *Getting Through: The Pleasures and Perils of Cross-Cultural Communication* (Cambridge, MA: MIT Press, 2017).

2. The listener as much: Louise Schubotz, Judith Holler, and Asli Özyürek, "Age-Related Differences in Multi-modal Audience Design: Young, but Not Old Speakers, Adapt Speech and Gestures to Their Addressee's Knowledge," in *Proceedings of the 4th GESPIN—Gesture and Speech in Interaction* (Nantes, France, September 2015), 211–216.

3. Than it is cognitive: Dana R. Murphy, Meredyth Daneman, and Bruce A. Schneider, "Why Do Older Adults Have Difficulty Following Conversations?" *Psychology and Aging* 21, no. 1 (2006): 49–61.

4. More pronounced for males: Alfredo Ardila and Monica Rosselli, "Spontaneous Language Production and Aging: Sex and Educational Effects," *International Journal of Neuroscience* 87, nos. 1–2 (1996): 71–78.

5. Important social cue: Gillian Slessor, Louise H. Phillips, and Rebecca Bull, "Age-Related Declines in Basic Social Perception: Evidence from Tasks Assessing Eye-Gaze Processing," *Psychology and Aging* 23, no. 4 (2008): 812–842.

6. Make appropriate requests: Thomas Holtgraves and Patrick McNamara, "Parkinson's Disease and Politeness," *Journal of Language and Social Psychology* 29, no. 2 (2010): 178–193.

7. To a conversational partner: Antonio Carotenuto et al., "Communication in Multiple Sclerosis: Pragmatic Deficit and Its Relation with Cognition and Social Cognition," *Archives of Clinical Neuropsychology* 33, no. 2 (2018): 1–12.

8. Amyotrophic lateral sclerosis: Valentina Bambini et al., "Communication and Pragmatic Breakdowns in Amyotrophic Lateral Sclerosis Patients," *Brain and Language* 153 (2016): 1–12.

9. Multiparty conversation: Rachel H. Messer, "Pragmatic Language Changes during Normal Aging: Implications for Health Care," *Healthy Aging and Clinical Care in the Elderly* 7 (2015): 1–7.

10. To provoke thought: Richard M. Roberts and Roger J. Kreuz, "Why Do People Use Figurative Language?" *Psychological Science* 5, no. 3 (1994): 159–163.

11. Interpretation of such sentences: Isabella Morrone et al., "Aging and Inhibition Processes: The Case of Metaphor Treatment," *Psychology and Aging* 25, no. 3 (2010): 697–701.

12. As their younger counterparts: Mary R. Newsome and Sam Glucksberg, "Older Adults Filter Irrelevant Information during Metaphor Comprehension," *Experimental Aging Research* 28, no. 3 (2002): 253–267.

13. Those in their twenties: Pei-Fang Hung and Marilyn A. Nippold, "Idiom Understanding in Adulthood: Examining Age-Related Differences," *Clinical Linguistics and Phonetics* 28, no. 3 (2014): 208–221.

14. Literal meaning of idioms: Chris Westbury and Debra Titone, "Idiom Literality Judgments in Younger and Older Adults: Age-Related Effects in

Resolving Semantic Interference," *Psychology and Aging* 26, no. 2 (2011): 467–474.

15. Nonliteral intent of the speaker: Phillips et al., "Older Adults Have Difficulty."

16. In such tasks: G. Gaudreau et al., "Mental State Inferences Abilities Contribution to Verbal Irony Comprehension in Older Adults with Mild Cognitive Impairment," *Behavioural Neurology,* article ID 685613 (2015).

17. Decline in the seventies: Marilyn A. Nippold, Linda D. Uhden, and Ilsa E. Schwarz, "Proverb Explanation through the Lifespan: A Developmental Study of Adolescents and Adults," *Journal of Speech, Language, and Hearing Research* 40, no. 2 (1997): 245–253.

18. Summarizing or interpreting proverbs: Hanna K. Ulatowska et al., "Discourse in Healthy Old-Elderly Adults: A Longitudinal Study," *Aphasiology* 12, nos. 7–8 (1998): 619–633.

19. Why such a decline occurs: Jennifer Uekermann, Patrizia Thoma, and Irene Daum, "Proverb Interpretation Changes in Aging," *Brain and Cognition* 67, no. 1 (2008): 51–57.

20. Trends in literature over time: Olivier Morin and Alberto Acerbi, "Birth of the Cool: A Two-Centuries Decline in Emotional Expression in Anglophone Fiction," *Cognition and Emotion* 31, no. 8 (2017): 1663–1675.

21. Particular word categories: James W. Pennebaker and Lori D. Stone, "Words of Wisdom: Language Use over the Life Span," *Journal of Personality and Social Psychology* 85, no. 2 (2003): 291–301.

22. Differences in language use: Margaret L. Kern et al., "From 'Sooo Excited!!!' to 'So Proud': Using Language to Study Development," *Developmental Psychology* 50, no. 1 (2013): 178–188.

23. Society undergoes significant shifts: Gillian Sankoff, "Language Change across the Lifespan," *Annual Review of Linguistics* 4 (2018): 297–316.

24. A major role as well: Judith Rich Harris, *The Nurture Assumption: Why Children Turn Out the Way They Do* (New York: Free Press, 1998).

25. As young as twenty months: Caroline Floccia et al., "Parent or Community: Where Do 20-Month-Olds Exposed to Two Accents Acquire Their Representation of Words?" *Cognition* 124, no. 1 (2012): 95–100.

26. Out of touch: Angie Williams and Howard Giles, "Intergenerational Conversations: Young Adults' Retrospective Accounts," *Human Communication Research* 23, no. 2 (1996): 220–250.

27. As the culture changes: Anne White et al., "Mind the Generation Gap: Differences between Young and Old in Everyday Lexical Categories," *Journal of Memory and Language* 98 (2018): 12–25.

28. In nursing homes in 1981: Linnda R. Caporael, "The Paralanguage of Caregiving: Baby Talk to the Institutionalized Aged," *Journal of Personality and Social Psychology* 40, no. 5 (1981): 876–884.

29. Dubbed "elderspeak": Gillian Cohen and Dorothy Faulkner, "Does 'Elderspeak' Work? The Effect of Intonation and Stress on Comprehension and Recall of Spoken Discourse in Old Age," *Language and Communication* 6, nos. 1–2 (1986): 91–98.

30. By their conversational partners: Nikolas Coupland et al., "Accommodating the Elderly: Invoking and Extending a Theory," *Language in Society* 17, no. 1 (1988): 1–41.

31. Perceived as patronizing: Helen Edwards and Patricia Noller, "Perceptions of Overaccommodation Used by Nurses in Communication with the Elderly," *Journal of Language and Social Psychology* 12, no. 3 (1993): 207–223.

32. Paraphrases are also common: Sik Hung Ng, "Power: An Essay in Honour of Henri Tajfel," in *Social Groups and Identities: Developing the Legacy of Henri Tajfel*, ed. W. Peter Robinson (Oxford: Butterworth-Heinemann, 1996), 191–214.

33. Swooping up and down: Anna I. Corwin, "Overcoming Elderspeak: A Qualitative Study of Three Alternatives," *Gerontologist* 58, no. 4 (2018): 724–729.

34. In a hospital setting: Mary Lee Hummert et al., "Communication with Older Adults: The Influence of Age Stereotypes, Context, and Communicator Age," *Human Communication Research* 25, no. 1 (1988): 124–151.

35. Such problematic behaviors: Kristine N. Williams et al., "Elderspeak Communication: Impact on Dementia Care," *American Journal of Alzheimer's Disease and Other Dementias* 24, no. 1 (2009): 11–20.

36. But not with them: John Leland, "In 'Sweetie' and 'Dear,' a Hurt for the Elderly," *New York Times*, October 6, 2008, http://www.nytimes.com/2008/10/07/us/07aging.html.

37. More negative self-perceptions: Becca R. Levy, "Mind Matters: Cognitive and Physical Effects of Aging Self-Stereotypes," *Journals of Gerontology Series B: Psychological Sciences and Social Sciences* 58, no. 4 (2003): P203–P211; Becca R. Levy et al., "Longevity Increased by Positive Self-Perceptions of Aging," *Journal of Personality and Social Psychology* 83, no. 2 (2002): 261–270.

38. Patronizing and disrespectful: Odette N. Gould, Cybil Saum, and Jennifer Belter, "Recall and Subjective Reactions to Speaking Styles: Does Age Matter?" *Experimental Aging Research* 28, no. 2 (2002): 199–213.

39. Created communication problems: Susan Kemper and Tamara Harden, "Experimentally Disentangling What's Beneficial about Elderspeak from What's Not," *Psychology and Aging* 14, no. 4 (1999): 656–670.

40. Or was pushy: Williams and Giles, "Intergenerational Conversations.".

41. One-hour training sessions: Kristine Williams, Susan Kemper, and Mary L. Hummert, "Improving Nursing Home Communication: An Intervention to Reduce Elderspeak," *Gerontologist* 43, no. 2 (2003): 242–247.

42. Other than English at home: US Census Bureau, "Table 53: Languages Spoken at Home by Language, 2008," *Statistical Abstract of the United States*, https://www2.census.gov/library/publications/2010/compendia/statab/130ed/tables/11s0053.pdf.

43. May persist for decades: Harry P. Bahrick, "Semantic Memory Content in Permastore: Fifty Years of Memory for Spanish Learned in

School," *Journal of Experimental Psychology: General* 113, no. 1 (1984): 1–29.

44. Not employed recently: Michael Erard, *Babel No More: The Search for the World's Most Extraordinary Language Learners* (New York: Free Press, 2012).

45. Their monolingual peers: Stephanie M. Carlson and Andrew N. Meltzoff, "Bilingual Experience and Executive Functioning in Young Children," *Developmental Science* 11, no. 2 (2008): 282–298.

46. Vocabulary development is slower: D. Kimbrough Oller and Rebecca E. Eilers, eds., *Language and Literacy in Bilingual Children,* vol. 2 (Clevedon, UK: Multilingual Matters, 2002).

47. Not cognitively impaired: Becca L. Stilwell et al., "Language Changes in Bilingual Individuals with Alzheimer's Disease," *International Journal of Language and Communication Disorders* 51, no. 2 (2016): 113–127.

48. Deterioration in both languages: Marco Calabria et al., "Language Deterioration in Bilingual Alzheimer's Disease Patients: A Longitudinal Study," *Journal of Neurolinguistics* 43 (2017): 59–74.

49. Not been supported: See also Barbara Lust et al., "Reversing Ribot: Does Regression Hold in Language of Prodromal Alzheimer's Disease?" *Brain and Language* 143 (2015): 1–10.

50. "More harsh [and] businesslike": François Grosjean, *Life with Two Languages: An Introduction to Bilingualism* (Cambridge, MA: Harvard University Press, 1982), 279.

51. Level of education: J. Bruce Morton and Sarah N. Harper, "What Did Simon Say? Revisiting the Bilingual Advantage," *Developmental Science* 10, no. 6 (2007): 719–726.

52. Which cognitive processes: Kenneth R. Paap, Hunter A. Johnson, and Oliver Sawi, "Bilingual Advantages in Executive Functioning Either Do Not Exist or Are Restricted to Very Specific and Undetermined Circumstances," *Cortex* 69 (2015): 265–278.

53. Bilinguals over monolinguals: Kenneth R. Paap and Zachary I. Greenberg, "There Is No Coherent Evidence for a Bilingual Advantage in Executive Processing," *Cognitive Psychology* 66, no. 2 (2013): 232–258.

54. Younger or older adults: Shanna Kousaie and Natalie A. Phillips, "Ageing and Bilingualism: Absence of a 'Bilingual Advantage' in Stroop Interference in a Nonimmigrant Sample," *Quarterly Journal of Experimental Psychology* 65, no. 2 (2012): 356–369.

55. Result of publication bias: Angela De Bruin, Barbara Treccani, and Sergio Della Sala, "Cognitive Advantage in Bilingualism: An Example of Publication Bias?" *Psychological Science* 26, no. 1 (2015): 99–107.

56. Called this conclusion into question: Ellen Bialystok et al., "Publication Bias and the Validity of Evidence: What's the Connection?" *Psychological Science* 26, no. 6 (2015): 944–946.

57. Comprehension and language production: Brooke N. Macnamara and Andrew R. A. Conway, "Novel Evidence in Support of the Bilingual Advantage: Influences of Task Demands and Experience on Cognitive Control and Working Memory," *Psychonomic Bulletin and Review* 21, no. 2 (2014): 520–525.

58. Better than monolinguals: Margarita Kaushanskaya and Viorica Marian, "The Bilingual Advantage in Novel Word Learning," *Psychonomic Bulletin and Review* 16, no. 4 (2009): 705–710.

59. Cognitive performance in general: Simons et al., "Do 'Brain-Training' Programs Work?".

60. Both of their languages: Ellen Bialystok, "Reshaping the Mind: The Benefits of Bilingualism," *Canadian Journal of Experimental Psychology* 65, no. 4 (2011): 229–235.

61. Very successful at it: Richard Roberts and Roger Kreuz, *Becoming Fluent: How Cognitive Science Can Help Adults Learn a Foreign Language* (Cambridge, MA: MIT Press, 2015).

62. Increase career opportunities: Rebecca M. Callahan and Patricia C. Gándara, eds., *The Bilingual Advantage: Language, Literacy and the US Labor Market* (Bristol, UK: Multilingual Matters, 2014).

63. Make people more empathic: Samantha P. Fan et al., "The Exposure Advantage: Early Exposure to a Multilingual Environment Promotes Effective Communication," *Psychological Science* 26, no. 7 (2015): 1090–1097.

6 The Write Stuff

1. Cellular immune function: James W. Pennebaker, Janice K. Kiecolt-Glaser, and Ronald Glaser, "Disclosure of Traumas and Immune Function: Health Implications for Psychotherapy," *Journal of Consulting and Clinical Psychology* 56, no. 2 (1988): 239–245.

2. Have been reported: James W. Pennebaker, "Writing about Emotional Experiences as a Therapeutic Process," *Psychological Science* 8, no. 3 (1997): 162–166.

3. Arthritis and asthma: Joshua M. Smyth et al., "Effects of Writing about Stressful Experiences on Symptom Reduction in Patients with Asthma or Rheumatoid Arthritis: A Randomized Trial," *JAMA* 281, no. 14 (1999): 1304–1309.

4. Year after the interviews: James W. Pennebaker, *Opening Up: The Healing Power of Expressing Emotions*, 2nd ed. (New York: Guilford Press, 1997); James W. Pennebaker, Steven D. Barger, and John Tiebout, "Disclosure of Traumas and Health among Holocaust Survivors," *Psychosomatic Medicine* 51, no. 5 (1989): 577–589.

5. But not psychological health: James W. Pennebaker, Tracy J. Mayne, and Martha E. Francis, "Linguistic Predictors of Adaptive Bereavement," *Journal of Personality and Social Psychology* 72, no. 4 (1997): 863–871.

6. A fragmented list: Joshua Smyth, Nicole True, and Joy Souto, "Effects of Writing about Traumatic Experiences: The Necessity for Narrative Structuring," *Journal of Social and Clinical Psychology* 20, no. 2 (2001): 161–172.

7. Echoed by others as well: Timothy D. Wilson, *Strangers to Ourselves: Discovering the Adaptive Unconscious* (Cambridge, MA: Belknap Press, 2002).

8. Depressive symptoms: James W. Pennebaker, *The Secret Life of Pronouns: What Our Words Say about Us* (New York: Bloomsbury Press, 2011).

9. Steve Jobs quote: Stanford News, "'You've Got to Find What You Love,' Jobs Says," June 14, 2005, https://news.stanford.edu/2005/06/14/jobs-061505.

10. Make sense of it all: note that some researchers have challenged this assumption; see Sharan B. Merriam, "Butler's Life Review: How Universal Is It?" *International Journal of Aging and Human Development* 37, no. 3 (1993): 163–175.

11. "The growing personality": Erik H. Erikson, "The Problem of Ego Identity," in *Identity and the Life Cycle,* by Erik H. Erikson (New York: Norton, 1959/1980), 57; italics in original.

12. The next generation: Erikson, in Daniel Goleman, "Erikson, in His Own Old Age, Expands His View of Life," *New York Times,* June 14, 1988, C1–C14.

13. Life review therapy: Robert N. Butler, "The Life Review: An Interpretation of Reminiscence in the Aged," *Psychiatry* 26, no. 1 (1963): 65–76.

14. Life satisfaction: Ernst Bohlmeijer et al., "The Effects of Reminiscence on Psychological Well-Being in Older Adults: A Meta-analysis," *Aging and Mental Health* 11, no. 3 (2007): 291–300.

15. And empowerment: Graham J. McDougall, Carol E. Blixen, and Lee-Jen Suen, "The Process and Outcome of Life Review Psychotherapy with Depressed Homebound Older Adults," *Nursing Research* 46, no. 5 (1997): 277–283.

16. In a group setting: James E. Birren and Betty A. Birren, "Autobiography: Exploring the Self and Encouraging Development," in *Aging and Biography: Explorations in Adult Development*, ed. James E. Birren et al. (New York: Springer, 1996), 283–299.

17. "In the future": Gary T. Reker, James E. Birren, and Cheryl Svensson, "Self-Aspect Reconstruction through Guided Autobiography: Exploring

Underlying Processes," *International Journal of Reminiscence and Life Review* 2, no. 1 (2014): 10.

18. Taxonomy of reminiscence: Lisa M. Watt and Paul T. Wong, "A Taxonomy of Reminiscence and Therapeutic Implications," *Journal of Gerontological Social Work* 16, nos. 1–2 (1991): 37–57; Paul T. Wong and Lisa M. Watt, "What Types of Reminiscence Are Associated with Successful Aging?" *Psychology and Aging* 6, no. 2 (1991): 272–279.

19. Types of reminiscence: see Gerben J. Westerhof, Ernst Bohlmeijer, and Jeffrey Dean Webster, "Reminiscence and Mental Health: A Review of Recent Progress in Theory, Research and Interventions," *Ageing and Society* 30, no. 4 (2010): 697–721.

20. "Contribute to successful aging": Watt and Wong, "A Taxonomy of Reminiscence," 44.

21. "If left unresolved": Watt and Wong, "A Taxonomy of Reminiscence,", 51.

22. Into the realm of transcendence: Erik H. Erikson and Joan M. Erikson, *The Life Cycle Completed (Extended Version)* (New York: Norton, 1997).

23. First-time published authors was forty-two: Debra P. Kong, "How Old Are Traditionally Published First-Time Authors?" The Write Type: Multi-author Musings, December 5, 2010, http://writetype.blogspot .com/2010/12/how-old-are-traditionally-published.html.

24. Years of deliberate practice: Anders Ericsson and Robert Pool, *Peak: Secrets from the New Science of Expertise* (Boston: Houghton Mifflin Harcourt, 2016).

25. Published his first story: LitRejections, "Best-Sellers Initially Rejected," http://www.litrejections.com/best-sellers-initially-rejected.

26. Pirate radio station: Michael Johnson, "Ted Allbeury: Respected Spy Writer Who Had Served as a Secret Agent in the War and the Cold War," *Guardian*, January 2, 2006, https://www.theguardian.com/news/2006 /jan/03/guardianobituaries.booksobituaries.

27. "Superego need for punishment": Salman Akhtar, *Comprehensive Dictionary of Psychoanalysis* (London: Karnac Books, 2009), 310.

28. "Frustration": Helen Sword, *Air and Light and Time and Space: How Successful Academics Write* (Cambridge, MA: Harvard University Press, 2017).

29. Genius of his early years: "Blocked: Why Do Writers Stop Writing?" *New Yorker*, June 14, 2004.

30. *In Cold Blood*: Azeen Ghorayshi, "A Trip around the Writer's Block," *Full Stop*, May 29, 2012, http://www.full-stop.net/2012/05/29/blog/azeen/a-trip-around-the-writers-block.

31. Anything of significance: Thomas Kunkel, "What Exactly Was Joseph Mitchell Doing All Those Years at the *New Yorker*?" *Publishers Weekly*, April 3, 2015, http://www.publishersweekly.com/pw/by-topic/industry-news/tip-sheet/article/66086-what-exactly-was-joseph-mitchell-doing-all-those-years-at-the-new-yorker.html; Ben Lazarus, "Why Joseph Mitchell Stopped Writing," *New Republic*, May 1, 2015, https://newrepublic.com/article/121690/thomas-kunkels-man-profile-joseph-mitchell-new-yorker.

32. Read by anyone but him: Maria Konnikova, "How to Beat Writer's Block," *New Yorker*, March 11, 2016.

33. Treat depression and anxiety: Alice W. Flaherty, *The Midnight Disease: The Drive to Write, Writer's Block, and the Creative Brain* (Boston: Houghton Mifflin, 2004).

34. Repair pipes and run wires: Harry Bruce, *Page Fright: Foibles and Fetishes of Famous Writers* (Toronto: McClelland & Stewart, 2009).

35. Creative practices with researchers: Mihaly Csikszentmihalyi, "Review of 'The Midnight Disease,'" *Perspectives in Biology and Medicine* 48, no. 1 (2005): 148–150.

36. Self-fulfilling prophecy: Andra L. Cole, "Writer's Block, Procrastination, and the Creative Process: It's All a Matter of Perspective," in *The Art of Writing Inquiry*, ed. Lorri Neilsen, Ardra L. Cole, and J. Gary Knowles (Halifax, Nova Scotia: Backalong Books, 2001), 292–301.

37. For later investigations: Mike Rose, *Writer's Block: The Cognitive Dimension* (Carbondale: Southern Illinois University Press, 1984).

38. Improvement in writing quality: Peter Salovey and Matthew D. Haar, "The Efficacy of Cognitive-Behavior Therapy and Writing Process Training for Alleviating Writing Anxiety," *Cognitive Therapy and Research* 14, no. 5 (1990): 515–528.

39. "Can be fruitful forever": Charles McGrath, "No Longer Writing, Philip Roth Still Has Plenty to Say," *New York Times*, January 16, 2018.

40. Iris Murdoch, *Jackson's Dilemma* (London: Penguin Books, 1995), 58.

41. "Writing is a mess": Brad Leithauser, "The Good Servant," *New York Times*, January 7, 1996, http://www.nytimes.com/books/98/12/20/specials/murdoch-dilemma.html.

42. Age of seventy-nine: Richard Nichols, "Iris Murdoch, Novelist and Philosopher, Is Dead," *New York Times*, February 9, 1999, http://www.nytimes.com/learning/general/onthisday/bday/0715.html.

43. Judi Dench: Adrienne Day, "Alzheimer's Early Tell: The Language of Authors Who Suffered from Dementia Has a Story for the Rest of Us," *Nautilus*, September 29, 2016, http://nautil.us/issue/40/learning/alzheimers-early-tell.

44. More common: Peter Garrard et al., "The Effects of Very Early Alzheimer's Disease on the Characteristics of Writing by a Renowned Author," *Brain* 128, no. 2 (2005): 250–260.

45. Twenty years before she died: Xuan Le et al., "Longitudinal Detection of Dementia through Lexical and Syntactic Changes in Writing: A Case Study of Three British Novelists," *Literary and Linguistic Computing* 26, no. 4 (2011): 435–461.

46. Were statistically significant: Le et al., "Longitudinal Detection of Dementia.".

47. Shrinking vocabulary size: Ian Lancashire, "Vocabulary and Dementia in Six Novelists," in *Language Development: The Lifespan Perspective,*

ed. Annette Gerstenberg and Anja Voeste (Amsterdam: John Benjamins, 2015), 77–107.

48. *Jackson's Dilemma* was published: Joanna Coles, "Duet in Perfect Harmony," *Guardian*, September 21, 1996, https://www.theguardian.com/books/1996/sep/21/fiction.joannacoles.

49. "The haze of Alzheimer's": Martin Robinson, "'The Moment I Died': Discworld Author Terry Pratchett Revealed His Struggles with a 'Haze of Alzheimer's' in His Unfinished Autobiography," *Daily Mail*, February 3, 2017, http://www.dailymail.co.uk/news/article-4187146/Terry-Pratchett-reveals-struggles-haze-Alzheimer-s.html.

50. Bush's press conference remarks: Visar Berisha et al., "Tracking Discourse Complexity Preceding Alzheimer's Disease Diagnosis: A Case Study Comparing the Press Conferences of Presidents Ronald Reagan and George Herbert Walker Bush," *Journal of Alzheimer's Disease* 45, no. 3 (2015): 959–963.

51. Vascular dementia: Kristine Williams et al., "Written Language Clues to Cognitive Changes of Aging: An Analysis of the Letters of King James VI/I," *Journals of Gerontology Series B: Psychological Sciences and Social Sciences* 58, no. 1 (2003): P42–P44.

52. "When the talent dies": quoted in Camilla Long, "Martin Amis and the Sex War," *Sunday Times*, January 24, 2010.

53. "St. James Church": David Snowdon, *Aging with Grace: What the Nun Study Teaches Us about Leading Longer, Healthier, and More Meaningful Lives* (New York: Bantam Books, 2001), 110.

54. "Otto Schmitt": Snowdon, *Aging with Grace*, 110.

55. In the present: Michael D. Lemonick and Alice Park, "The Nun Study: How One Scientist and 678 Sisters Are Helping Unlock the Secrets of Alzheimer's," *Time*, May 14, 2001, 54–59, 62, 64.

56. Although not as strongly: David A. Snowdon et al., "Linguistic Ability in Early Life and Cognitive Function and Alzheimer's Disease in Late Life: Findings from the Nun Study," *JAMA* 275, no. 7 (1996): 528–532.

57. Diagnosis of AD postmortem: David A. Snowdon, Lydia H. Greiner, and William R. Markesbery, "Linguistic Ability in Early Life and the Neuropathology of Alzheimer's Disease and Cerebrovascular Disease: Findings from the Nun Study," *Annals of the New York Academy of Sciences* 903, no. 1 (2000): 34–38.

58. In old age: Kathryn P. Riley et al., "Early Life Linguistic Ability, Late Life Cognitive Function, and Neuropathology: Findings from the Nun Study," *Neurobiology of Aging* 26, no. 3 (2005): 341–347.

59. Who used the fewest: Deborah D. Danner, David A. Snowdon, and Wallace V. Friesen, "Positive Emotions in Early Life and Longevity: Findings from the Nun Study," *Journal of Personality and Social Psychology* 80, no. 5 (2001): 804–813.

60. Diagnosed with AD: Jessica J. Weyerman, Cassidy Rose, and Maria C. Norton, "Personal Journal Keeping and Linguistic Complexity Predict Late-Life Dementia Risk: The Cache County Journal Pilot Study," *Journals of Gerontology Series B: Psychological Sciences and Social Sciences* 72, no. 6 (2017): 991–995.

61. Still mentally sharp: Snowdon *Aging with Grace.*

62. Typical of AD: David A. Snowdon, "Aging and Alzheimer's Disease: Lessons from the Nun Study," *Gerontologist* 37, no. 2 (1997): 150–156.

63. Youngest being one hundred: Natalie Zarrelli, "The Neurologists Who Fought Alzheimer's by Studying Nuns' Brains," *Atlas Obscura*, March 24, 2016, http://www.atlasobscura.com/articles/the-neurologists -who-fought-alzheimers-by-studying-nuns-brains.

64. More socially perceptive: Raymond A. Mar and Keith Oatley, "The Function of Fiction Is the Abstraction and Simulation of Social Experience," *Perspectives on Psychological Science* 3, no. 3 (2008): 173–192.

65. Names of nonwriters: Raymond A. Mar et al., "Bookworms versus Nerds: Exposure to Fiction versus Non-fiction, Divergent Associations with Social Ability, and the Simulation of Fictional Social Worlds," *Journal of Research in Personality* 40, no. 5 (2006): 694–712.

66. Effect was modest: Micah L. Mumper and Richard J. Gerrig, "Leisure Reading and Social Cognition: A Meta-analysis," *Psychology of Aesthetics, Creativity, and the Arts* 11, no. 1 (2017): 109–120.

67. Empathy for the fictional characters: Zazie Todd, "Talking about Books: A Reading Group Study," *Psychology of Aesthetics, Creativity, and the Arts* 2, no. 4 (2008): 256–263.

68. After the reading concluded: Gregory S. Berns et al., "Short- and Long-Term Effects of a Novel on Connectivity in the Brain," *Brain Connectivity* 3, no. 6 (2013): 590–600.

69. Have not yet acquired: Mei-Ching Lien et al., "Visual Word Recognition without Central Attention: Evidence for Greater Automaticity with Advancing Age," *Psychology and Aging* 21, no. 3 (2006): 431–447.

70. Other cognitive processes: Brennan R. Payne et al., "The Effects of Print Exposure on Sentence Processing and Memory in Older Adults: Evidence for Efficiency and Reserve," *Aging, Neuropsychology, and Cognition* 19, nos. 1–2 (2012): 122–149.

71. This longevity effect: Avni Bavishi, Martin D. Slade, and Becca R. Levy, "A Chapter a Day: Association of Book Reading with Longevity," *Social Science and Medicine* 164 (2016): 44–48.

Epilogue

1. Finds ways to compensate: Baltes and Baltes, "Psychological Perspectives on Successful Aging."

2. Megan E. Lenehan et al., "Sending Your Grandparents to University Increases Cognitive Reserve: The Tasmanian Healthy Brain Project," *Neuropsychology* 30, no. 5 (2016): 525.

References

Abrams, Lise, Meagan T. Farrell, and Sara J. Margolin. 2010. Older adults' detection of misspellings during reading. *Journals of Gerontology Series B: Psychological Sciences and Social Sciences* 65B (6): 680–683.

Acton, Eric K. 2011. On gender differences in the distribution of um and uh. *University of Pennsylvania Working Papers in Linguistics* 17 (2): 1–9.

Adams, Cynthia, Gisela Labouvie-Vief, Cathy J. Hobart, and Mary Dorosz. 1990. Adult age group differences in story recall style. *Journal of Gerontology* 45 (1): P17–P27.

Adams, Tony. 2013. Multiple presbyopic corrections across multiple centuries. *Optometry and Vision Science* 90 (5): 409–410.

Akhtar, Salman. 2009. *Comprehensive Dictionary of Psychoanalysis*. London: Karnac Books.

Albert, Martin L., Avron Spiro, Keely J. Sayers, Jason A. Cohen, Christopher B. Brady, Mira Goral, and Loraine K. Obler. 2009. Effects of health status on word finding in aging. *Journal of the American Geriatrics Society* 57 (12): 2300–2305.

Altman, Lawrence K. 1971. A tube implant corrected Shepard's ear disease. *New York Times*, February 2, 1971. https://www.nytimes.com/1971/02/02/archives/a-tube-implant-corrected-shepards-ear-disease.html.

Amlen, Deb. n.d. How to solve the *New York Times* crossword. *New York Times*. https://www.nytimes.com/guides/crosswords/how-to-solve-a-crossword-puzzle.

Andrews, Travis M. 2016. Annie Glenn: "When I called John, he cried. People just couldn't believe that I could really talk." *Washington Post*, December 9, 2016. https://www.washingtonpost.com/news/morning -mix/wp/2016/12/09/to-john-glenn-the-real-hero-was-his-wife-annie -conqueror-of-disability/?noredirect=on&utm_term=.c02f21305c42.

Aramaki, Eiji, Shuko Shikata, Mai Miyabe, and Ayae Kinoshita. 2016. Vocabulary size in speech may be an early indicator of cognitive impairment. *PloS One* 11 (5): 1–13.

Arbuckle, Tannis Y., and Dolores Pushkar Gold. 1993. Aging, inhibition, and verbosity. *Journal of Gerontology* 48 (5): 225–232.

Ardila, Alfredo, and Monica Rosselli. 1996. Spontaneous language production and aging: Sex and educational effects. *International Journal of Neuroscience* 87 (1–2): 71–78.

Arenberg, I. Kaufman, Lynn Flieger Countryman, Lawrence H. Bernstein, and George E. Shambaugh. 1990. Van Gogh had Meniere's disease and not epilepsy. *JAMA* 264 (4): 491–493.

Ascaso, F. J., and V. Huerva. 2013. The history of cataract surgery. In *Cataract Surgery*, ed. Farhan Zaidi, 75–90. Rijeka, Croatia: InTech.

Atkinson, Joanna, Tanya Lyons, David Eagleman, Bencie Woll, and Jamie Ward. 2016. Synesthesia for manual alphabet letters and numeral signs in second-language users of signed languages. *Neurocase* 22 (4): 379–386.

Au, Rhoda, Philip Joung, Marjorie Nicholas, Loraine K. Obler, Robin Kass, and Martin L. Albert. 1995. Naming ability across the adult life span. *Aging, Neuropsychology, and Cognition* 2 (4): 300–311.

Baddeley, A. D., S. Bressi, Sergio Della Sala, Robert Logie, and H. Spinnler. 1991. The decline of working memory in Alzheimer's disease: A longitudinal study. *Brain* 114 (6): 2521–2542.

Baguley, David M. 2003. Hyperacusis. *Journal of the Royal Society of Medicine* 96 (12): 582–585.

Bahrick, Harry P. 1984. Semantic memory content in permastore: Fifty years of memory for Spanish learned in school. *Journal of Experimental Psychology: General* 113 (1): 1–29.

Baltes, Margret M., and Laura L. Carstensen. 1996. The process of successful ageing. *Ageing and Society* 16 (4): 397–422.

Baltes, Paul B., and Margret M. Baltes. 1990. Psychological perspectives on successful aging: The model of selective optimization with compensation. In *Successful Aging: Perspectives from the Behavioral Sciences*, ed. Paul Baltes and Margret Baltes, 1–34. Cambridge: Cambridge University Press.

Bambini, Valentina, Giorgio Arcara, Ilaria Martinelli, Sara Bernini, Elena Alvisi, Andrea Moro, Stefano F. Cappa, and Mauro Ceroni. 2016. Communication and pragmatic breakdowns in amyotrophic lateral sclerosis patients. *Brain and Language* 153:1–12.

Baron, Jacqueline M., and Susan Bluck. 2011. That was a good story! Preliminary construction of the perceived story quality index. *Discourse Processes* 48 (2): 93–118.

Barry, Danielle, Marsha E. Bates, and Erich Labouvie. 2008. FAS and CFL forms of verbal fluency differ in difficulty: A meta-analytic study. *Applied Neuropsychology* 15 (2): 97–106.

Bavishi, Avni, Martin D. Slade, and Becca R. Levy. 2016. A chapter a day: Association of book reading with longevity. *Social Science and Medicine* 164:44–48.

BBC News. 2006. Stroke gives woman a foreign accent. July 4, 2006. http://news.bbc.co.uk/2/hi/uk_news/england/tyne/5144300.stm.

Belville, J. Kevin, and Ronald J. Smith, eds. 2006. *Presbyopia Surgery: Pearls and Pitfalls*. Thorofare, NJ: Slack.

Berg, Cynthia A., Timothy W. Smith, Kelly J. Ko, Nancy J. M. Henry, Paul Florsheim, Gale Pearce, Bert N. Uchino, et al. 2007. Task control and cognitive abilities of self and spouse in collaboration in middle-aged and older couples. *Psychology and Aging* 22 (3): 420–427.

Berg, Eric E., Edie Hapner, Adam Klein, and Michael M. Johns. 2008. Voice therapy improves quality of life in age-related dysphonia: A case-control study. *Journal of Voice* 22 (1): 70–74.

Berisha, Visar, Shuai Wang, Amy LaCross, and Julie Liss. 2015. Tracking discourse complexity preceding Alzheimer's disease diagnosis: A case study comparing the press conferences of presidents Ronald Reagan and George Herbert Walker Bush. *Journal of Alzheimer's Disease* 45 (3): 959–963.

Berns, Gregory S., Kristina Blaine, Michael J. Prietula, and Brandon E. Pye. 2013. Short- and long-term effects of a novel on connectivity in the brain. *Brain Connectivity* 3 (6): 590–600.

Bialystok, Ellen. 2011. Reshaping the mind: The benefits of bilingualism. *Canadian Journal of Experimental Psychology* 65 (4): 229–235.

Bialystok, Ellen, Judith F. Kroll, David W. Green, Brian MacWhinney, and Fergus I. M. Craik. 2015. Publication bias and the validity of evidence: What's the connection? *Psychological Science* 26 (6): 944–946.

Birren, James E., and Birren, Betty A. 1996. Autobiography: Exploring the self and encouraging development. In *Aging and Biography: Explorations in Adult Development*, ed. James E. Birren, Gary M. Kenyon, Jan-Erik Ruth, Johannes J. F. Schroots, and Torbjorn Svensson, 283–299. New York: Springer.

Blumstein, Sheila E., and Kathleen Kurowski. 2006. The foreign accent syndrome: A perspective. *Journal of Neurolinguistics* 19 (5): 346–355.

Bohlmeijer, Ernst, Marte Roemer, Pim Cuijpers, and Filip Smit. 2007. The effects of reminiscence on psychological well-being in older adults: A meta-analysis. *Aging and Mental Health* 11 (3): 291–300.

Bolla, Karen I., Karen N. Lindgren, Cathy Bonaccorsy, and Margit L. Bleecker. 1990. Predictors of verbal fluency (FAS) in the healthy elderly. *Journal of Clinical Psychology* 46 (5): 623–628.

Boone, Daniel R., Stephen C. McFarlane, Shelley L. Von Berg, and Richard I. Zraick. 2005. *The Voice and Voice Therapy*. New York: Allyn & Bacon.

Bopp, Kara L., and Paul Verhaeghen. Aging and verbal memory span: A meta-analysis. 2005. *Journals of Gerontology Series B: Psychological Sciences and Social Sciences* 60 (5): P223–P233.

Bor, Daniel, Nicolas Rothen, David J. Schwartzman, Stephanie Clayton, and Anil K. Seth. 2014. Adults can be trained to acquire synesthetic experiences. *Scientific Reports* 4 (7089): 1–8.

Bortfeld, Heather, Silvia D. Leon, Jonathan E. Bloom, Michael F. Schober, and Susan E. Brennan. 2001. Disfluency rates in conversation: Effects of age, relationship, topic, role, and gender. *Language and Speech* 44 (2): 123–147.

Bouton, Katherine. 2013. *Shouting Won't Help: Why I—and 50 Million Other Americans—Can't Hear You.* New York: Farrar, Straus and Giroux.

Bowles, Ryan P., and Timothy A. Salthouse. 2008. Vocabulary test format and differential relations to age. *Psychology and Aging* 23 (2): 366–376.

Bradford, Barbara. 1997. Upspeak in British English. *English Today* 13 (3): 29–36.

Bradley, Joseph P., Edie Hapner, and Michael M. Johns. 2014. What is the optimal treatment for presbyphonia? *Laryngoscope* 124 (11): 2439–2440.

Brady, Marian C., Helen Kelly, Jon Godwin, Pam Enderby, and Pauline Campbell. 2016. Speech and language therapy for aphasia following stroke. *Cochrane Database of Systematic Reviews* 6 (CD000425).

Bricker-Katz, Geraldine, Michelle Lincoln, and Patricia McCabe. 2009. A life-time of stuttering: How emotional reactions to stuttering impact activities and participation in older people. *Disability and Rehabilitation* 31 (21): 1742–1752.

Brickman, Adam M., Robert H. Paul, Ronald A. Cohen, Leanne M. Williams, Kristin L. MacGregor, Angela L. Jefferson, David F. Tate, John Gunstad, and Evian Gordon. 2005. Category and letter verbal fluency across the adult lifespan: relationship to EEG theta power. *Archives of Clinical Neuropsychology* 20 (5): 561–573.

Bridges, Kelly Ann, and Diana Van Lancker Sidtis. 2013. Formulaic language in Alzheimer's disease. *Aphasiology* 27 (7): 799–810.

Brimacombe, C. A., Sandy Jung, Lynn Garrioch, and Meredith Allison. 2003. Perceptions of older adult eyewitnesses: Will you believe me when I'm 64? *Law and Human Behavior* 27 (5): 507–522.

Brimacombe, C. A., Nyla Quinton, Natalie Nance, and Lynn Garrioch. 1997. Is age irrelevant? Perceptions of young and old adult eyewitnesses. *Law and Human Behavior* 21 (6): 619–634.

Brown, Alan S. 2012. *The Tip of the Tongue State*. New York: Psychology Press.

Brown, Alan S., and Lori A. Nix. 1996. Age-related changes in the tip-of-the-tongue experience. *American Journal of Psychology* 109 (1): 79–91.

Brown, Andy, Caroline Jay, Alex Q. Chen, and Simon Harper. 2012. The uptake of Web 2.0 technologies, and its impact on visually disabled users. *Universal Access in the Information Society* 11 (2): 185–199.

Brown, Roger, and David McNeill. 1966. The "tip of the tongue" phenomenon. *Journal of Verbal Learning and Verbal Behavior* 5 (4): 325–337.

Bruce, Harry. 2009. *Page Fright: Foibles and Fetishes of Famous Writers*. Toronto: McClelland & Stewart.

Bucks, Romola S., and Shirley A. Radford. 2004. Emotion processing in Alzheimer's disease. *Aging and Mental Health* 8 (3): 222–232.

Burda, Angela N., Carlin F. Hageman, Julie A. Scherz, and Harold T. Edwards. 2003. Age and understanding speakers with Spanish or Taiwanese accents. *Perceptual and Motor Skills* 97 (1): 11–20.

Burke, Deborah M., and Meredith A. Shafto. 2004. Aging and language production. *Current Directions in Psychological Science* 13 (1): 21–24.

Burke, Deborah M., and Meredith A. Shafto. 2008. Language and aging. In *The Handbook of Aging and Cognition*, 3rd ed., ed. Fergus I. Craik and Timothy A. Salthouse, 373–443. New York: Psychology Press.

Butler, Robert N. 1963. The life review: An interpretation of reminiscence in the aged. *Psychiatry* 26 (1): 65–76.

Calabria, Marco, Gabriele Cattaneo, Paula Marne, Mireia Hernández, Montserrat Juncadella, Jordi Gascón-Bayarri, Isabel Sala, et al. 2017. Language deterioration in bilingual Alzheimer's disease patients: A longitudinal study. *Journal of Neurolinguistics* 43:59–74.

Callahan, Rebecca M., and Patricia C. Gándara, eds. 2014. *The Bilingual Advantage: Language, Literacy and the US Labor Market*. Bristol, UK: Multilingual Matters.

Campbell, Ruth, Mairéad MacSweeney, and Dafydd Waters. 2008. Sign language and the brain: A review. *Journal of Deaf Studies and Deaf Education* 13 (1): 3–20.

Caporael, Linnda R. 1981. The paralanguage of caregiving: Baby talk to the institutionalized aged. *Journal of Personality and Social Psychology* 40 (5): 876–884.

Carlson, Stephanie M., and Andrew N. Meltzoff. 2008. Bilingual experience and executive functioning in young children. *Developmental Science* 11 (2): 282–298.

Carney, Maria T., Janice Fujiwara, Brian E. Emmert, Tara A. Liberman, and Barbara Paris. 2016. Elder orphans hiding in plain sight: A growing vulnerable population. *Current Gerontology and Geriatrics Research*, article ID 4723250.

Carotenuto, Antonio, Giorgio Arcara, Giuseppe Orefice, Ilaria Cerillo, Valentina Giannino, Mario Rasulo, Rosa Iodice, and Valentina Bambini. 2018. Communication in multiple sclerosis: Pragmatic deficit and its relation with cognition and social cognition. *Archives of Clinical Neuropsychology* 33 (2): 1–12.

Carretti, Barbara, Erika Borella, Michela Zavagnin, and Rossana Beni. 2013. Gains in language comprehension relating to working memory training in healthy older adults. *International Journal of Geriatric Psychiatry* 28 (5): 539–546.

Castel, Alan D., Meenely Nazarian, and Adam B. Blake. 2015. Attention and incidental memory in everyday settings. In *The Handbook of Attention*, ed. Jonathan M. Fawcett, Evan F. Risko, and Alan Kingstone, 463–483. Cambridge, MA: MIT Press.

Castro, Nichol, and Lori E. James. 2014. Differences between young and older adults' spoken language production in descriptions of negative versus neutral pictures. *Aging, Neuropsychology, and Cognition* 21 (2): 222–238.

Cavalli, Eddy, Séverine Casalis, Abdessadek El Ahmadi, Melody Zira, Florence Poracchia-George, and Pascale Cole. 2016. Vocabulary skills are well developed in university students with dyslexia: Evidence from multiple case studies. *Research in Developmental Disabilities* 51:89–102.

Charman, W. Neil. 2014. Developments in the correction of presbyopia I: Spectacle and contact lenses. *Ophthalmic and Physiological Optics* 34 (1): 8–29.

Chasteen, Alison L., Sudipa Bhattacharyya, Michelle Horhota, Raymond Tam, and Lynn Hasher. 2005. How feelings of stereotype threat influence older adults' memory performance. *Experimental Aging Research* 31 (3): 235–260.

Chicago Tribune. 1987. How Reagan copes with 1930s ear injury. November 9, 1987, sec. 1, 16.

Ciorba, Andrea, Chiara Bianchini, Stefano Pelucchi, and Antonio Pastore. 2012. The impact of hearing loss on the quality of life of elderly adults. *Clinical Interventions in Aging* 7 (6): 159–163.

Clark, Herbert H., and Jean E. Fox Tree. 2002. Using *uh* and *um* in spontaneous speaking. *Cognition* 84 (1): 73–111.

Cleary, Anne M., and Alexander B. Claxton. 2015. The tip-of-the-tongue heuristic: How tip-of-the-tongue states confer perceptibility on inaccessible words. *Journal of Experimental Psychology: Learning, Memory, and Cognition* 41 (5): 1533–1539.

Cocks, Naomi, Gary Morgan, and Sotaro Kita. 2011. Iconic gesture and speech integration in younger and older adults. *Gesture* 11 (1): 24–39.

Cohen, Andrew. 2000. Bush's mangling of language points to dyslexia: Writer. *Globe and Mail*, September 13, 2000.

Cohen, Gillian, and Dorothy Faulkner. 1986. Does "elderspeak" work? The effect of intonation and stress on comprehension and recall of spoken discourse in old age. *Language and Communication* 6 (1–2): 91–98.

Cole, Ardra L. 2001. Writer's block, procrastination, and the creative process: It's all a matter of perspective. In *The Art of Writing Inquiry*, ed. Lorri Neilsen, Ardra L. Cole, and J. Gary Knowles, 292–301. Halifax, Nova Scotia: Backalong Books.

Cole, Thomas R. 1992. *The Journey of Life: A Cultural History of Aging in America*. Cambridge: Cambridge University Press.

Coles, Joanna. 1996. Duet in perfect harmony. *Guardian*, September 21, 1996. https://www.theguardian.com/books/1996/sep/21/fiction .joannacoles.

Connor, Lisa Tabor, Avron Spiro III, Loraine K. Obler, and Martin L. Albert. 2004. Change in object naming ability during adulthood. *Journals of Gerontology Series B: Psychological Sciences and Social Sciences* 59 (5): P203–P209.

Constantino, Christopher D., Paula Leslie, Robert W. Quesal, and J. Scott Yaruss. 2016. A preliminary investigation of daily variability of stuttering in adults. *Journal of Communication Disorders* 60:39–50.

Cooper, Patricia V. 1990. Discourse production and normal aging: Performance on oral picture description tasks. *Journal of Gerontology* 45 (5): 210–214.

Corwin, Anna I. 2018. Overcoming elderspeak: A qualitative study of three alternatives. *Gerontologist* 58 (4): 724–729.

Cosco, Theodore D., A. Matthew Prina, Jaime Perales, Blossom C. M. Stephan, and Carol Brayne. 2014. Operational definitions of successful aging: A systematic review. *International Psychogeriatrics* 26 (3): 373–381.

Coupland, Nikolas, Justine Coupland, Howard Giles, and Karen Henwood. 1988. Accommodating the elderly: Invoking and extending a theory. *Language in Society* 17 (1): 1–41.

Craig, Ashley, and Yvonne Tran. 2014. Trait and social anxiety in adults with chronic stuttering: Conclusions following meta-analysis. *Journal of Fluency Disorders* 40:35–43.

Cristia, Alejandrina, Amanda Seidl, Charlotte Vaughn, Rachel Schmale, Ann Bradlow, and Caroline Floccia. 2012. Linguistic processing of accented speech across the lifespan. *Frontiers in Psychology* 3:479.

Cruickshanks, Karen J., Terry L. Wiley, Theodore S. Tweed, Barbara E. K. Klein, Ronald Klein, Julie A. Mares-Perlman, and David M. Nondahl.

1998. Prevalence of hearing loss in older adults in Beaver Dam, Wisconsin: The epidemiology of hearing loss study. *American Journal of Epidemiology* 148 (9): 879–886.

Csikszentmihalyi, Mihaly. 2005. Review of "The Midnight Disease." *Perspectives in Biology and Medicine* 48 (1): 148–150.

Curhan, Sharon G., Roland Eavey, Molin Wang, Meir J. Stampfer, and Gary C. Curhan. 2013. Body mass index, waist circumference, physical activity, and risk of hearing loss in women. *American Journal of Medicine* 126 (12): 1142.e1–1142.e8.

Czaja, Sara J., Joseph Sharit, Raymond Ownby, David L. Roth, and Sankaran Nair. 2001. Examining age differences in performance of a complex information search and retrieval task. *Psychology and Aging* 16 (4): 564–579.

Dahlgren, Donna J. 1998. Impact of knowledge and age on tip-of-the-tongue rates. *Experimental Aging Research* 24 (2): 139–153.

Daley, Tamara C., Shannon E. Whaley, Marian D. Sigman, Michael P. Espinosa, and Charlotte Neumann. 2003. IQ on the rise: The Flynn effect in rural Kenyan children. *Psychological Science* 14 (3): 215–219.

Danner, Deborah D., David A. Snowdon, and Wallace V. Friesen. 2001. Positive emotions in early life and longevity: Findings from the Nun Study. *Journal of Personality and Social Psychology* 80 (5): 804–813.

Davis, Boyd H., and Margaret Maclagan. 2010. Pauses, fillers, placeholders, and formulaicity in Alzheimer's discourse. In *Fillers, Pauses and Placeholders*, ed. Nino Amiridze, Boyd H. Davis, and Margaret Maclagan, 189–216. Amsterdam: John Benjamins.

Davis, Danielle K., Nicole Alea, and Susan Bluck. 2015. The difference between right and wrong: Accuracy of older and younger adults' story recall. *International Journal of Environmental Research and Public Health* 12 (9): 10861–10885.

Day, Adrienne. 2016. Alzheimer's early tell: The language of authors who suffered from dementia has a story for the rest of us. *Nautilus*, September 29, 2016. http://nautil.us/issue/40/learning/alzheimers-early-tell.

De Bruin, Angela, Barbara Treccani, and Sergio Della Sala. 2015. Cognitive advantage in bilingualism: An example of publication bias? *Psychological Science* 26 (1): 99–107.

DeLoss, Denton J., Takeo Watanabe, and George J. Andersen. 2015. Improving vision among older adults: Behavioral training to improve sight. *Psychological Science* 26 (4): 456–466.

Di Dio, Cinzia, Joerg Schulz, and Jennifer Gurd. 2006. Foreign accent syndrome: In the ear of the beholder? *Aphasiology* 20 (9): 951–962.

Dijkstra, Katinka, Michelle S. Bourgeois, Rebecca S. Allen, and Louis D. Burgio. 2004. Conversational coherence: Discourse analysis of older adults with and without dementia. *Journal of Neurolinguistics* 17 (4): 263–283.

DiLollo, Anthony, Julie Scherz, and Robert A. Neimeyer. 2014. Psychosocial implications of foreign accent syndrome: Two case examples. *Journal of Constructivist Psychology* 27 (1): 14–30.

Dixon, Roger A., and Odette N. Gould. 1996. Adults telling and retelling stories collaboratively. In *Interactive Minds: Life-Span Perspectives on the Social Foundation of Cognition*, ed. Paul B. Baltes and Ursula M. Staudinger, 221–241. Cambridge: Cambridge University Press.

Duchin, Sandra W., and Edward D. Mysak. 1987. Disfluency and rate characteristics of young adult, middle-aged, and older males. *Journal of Communication Disorders* 20 (3): 245–257.

Dupuis, Kate, and M. Kathleen Pichora-Fuller. 2010. Use of affective prosody by young and older adults. *Psychology and Aging* 25 (1): 16–29.

Durso, Francis T., and Wendelyn J. Shore. 1991. Partial knowledge of word meanings. *Journal of Experimental Psychology: General* 120 (2): 190–202.

Edwards, Helen, and Patricia Noller. 1993. Perceptions of overaccommodation used by nurses in communication with the elderly. *Journal of Language and Social Psychology* 12 (3): 207–223.

Eide, Brock L., and Fernette F. Eide. 2012. *The Dyslexic Advantage: Unlocking the Hidden Potential of the Dyslexic Brain*. New York: Plume.

Erard, Michael. 2012. *Babel No More: The Search for the World's Most Extraordinary Language Learners*. New York: Free Press.

Erber, Joan T., and Lenore T. Szuchman. 2015. *Great Myths of Aging*. Malden, MA: John Wiley & Sons.

Ericsson, Anders, and Robert Pool. 2016. *Peak: Secrets from the New Science of Expertise*. Boston: Houghton Mifflin Harcourt.

Erikson, Erik H. 1959/1980. The problem of ego identity. In *Identity and the Life Cycle*, by Erik H. Erikson. New York: Norton.

Erikson, Erik H., and Joan M. Erikson. 1997. *The Life Cycle Completed (Extended Version)*. New York: Norton.

Etter, Nicole M., Joseph C. Stemple, and Dana M. Howell. 2013. Defining the lived experience of older adults with voice disorders. *Journal of Voice* 27 (1): 61–67.

Evans, Sarah, Nick Neave, Delia Wakelin, and Colin Hamilton. 2008. The relationship between testosterone and vocal frequencies in human males. *Physiology and Behavior* 93 (4): 783–788.

Fagnani, Corrado, Steen Fibiger, Axel Skytthe, and Jacob V. B. Hjelmborg. 2011. Heritability and environmental effects for self-reported periods with stuttering: A twin study from Denmark. *Logopedics Phoniatrics Vocology* 36 (3): 114–120.

Fan, Samantha P., Zoe Liberman, Boaz Keysar, and Katherine D. Kinzler. 2015. The exposure advantage: Early exposure to a multilingual environment promotes effective communication. *Psychological Science* 26 (7): 1090–1097.

Feyereisen, Pierre. 1997. A meta-analytic procedure shows an age-related decline in picture naming: Comments on Goulet, Ska, and Kahn (1994). *Journal of Speech, Language, and Hearing Research* 40 (6): 1328–1333.

Flaherty, Alice W. 2004. *The Midnight Disease: The Drive to Write, Writer's Block, and the Creative Brain*. Boston: Houghton Mifflin.

Floccia, Caroline, Claire Delle Luche, Samantha Durrant, Joseph Butler, and Jeremy Goslin. 2012. Parent or community: Where do 20-month-olds exposed to two accents acquire their representation of words? *Cognition* 124 (1): 95–100.

Flynn, James R. 1984. The mean IQ of Americans: Massive gains 1932 to 1978. *Psychological Bulletin* 95 (1): 29–51.

Flynn, James R. 1987. Massive IQ gains in 14 nations: What IQ tests really measure. *Psychological Bulletin* 101 (2): 171–191.

Fox Tree, Jean E. 2007. Folk notions of *um* and *uh, you know,* and *like. Text and Talk* 27 (3): 297–314.

Frakt, Austin. 2017. Training your brain so that you don't need reading glasses. *New York Times*, March 27, 2017. https://nyti.ms/2nEi3iR.

Freud, Debora, Marina Kichin-Brin, Ruth Ezrati-Vinacour, Ilan Roziner, and Ofer Amir. 2017. The relationship between the experience of stuttering and demographic characteristics of adults who stutter. *Journal of Fluency Disorders* 52:53–63.

Frigerio-Domingues, Carlos, and Dennis Drayna. 2017. Genetic contributions to stuttering: The current evidence. *Molecular Genetics and Genomic Medicine* 5 (2): 95–102.

Gardner, Howard. 1975. *The Shattered Mind: The Person after Brain Damage.* New York: Knopf.

Garrard, Peter, Lisa M. Maloney, John R. Hodges, and Karalyn Patterson. 2005. The effects of very early Alzheimer's disease on the characteristics of writing by a renowned author. *Brain* 128 (2): 250–260.

Gaudreau, G., L. Monetta, J. Macoir, S. Poulin, R. Laforce Jr., and C. Hudon. 2015. Mental state inferences abilities contribution to verbal irony comprehension in older adults with mild cognitive impairment. *Behavioural Neurology*, article ID 685613.

Gayraud, Frederique, Hye-Ran Lee, and Melissa Barkat-Defradas. 2011. Syntactic and lexical context of pauses and hesitations in the discourse of Alzheimer patients and healthy elderly subjects. *Clinical Linguistics and Phonetics* 25 (3): 198–209.

Geber, Sara Z. 2017. Are you ready for solo agers and elder orphans? *American Society on Aging*, December 27, 2017. http://www.asaging.org /blog/are-you-ready-solo-agers-and-elder-orphans.

Geschwind, Norman. 1970. The organization of language and the brain. *Science* 170 (3961): 940–944.

Ghorayshi, Azeen. 2012. A trip around the writer's block. *Full Stop*, May 29, 2012. http://www.full-stop.net/2012/05/29/blog/azeen/a-trip -around-the-writers-block.

Glicksman, Jordan T., Sharon G. Curhan, and Gary C. Curhan. 2014. A prospective study of caffeine intake and risk of incident tinnitus. *American Journal of Medicine* 127 (8): 739–743.

Glosser, Guila, and Toni Deser. 1992. A comparison of changes in macrolinguistic and microlinguistic aspects of discourse production in normal aging. *Journal of Gerontology* 47 (4): 266–272.

Gold, Dolores, David Andres, Tannis Arbuckle, and Alex Schwartzman. 1988. Measurement and correlates of verbosity in elderly people. *Journal of Gerontology: Psychological Sciences* 43 (2): 27–33.

Goleman, Daniel. 1988. Erikson, in his own old age, expands his view of life. *New York Times*, June 14, 1988, C1, C14.

Gordon-Salant, Sandra, Grace H. Yeni-Komshian, Erin J. Pickett, and Peter J. Fitzgibbons. 2016. Perception of contrastive bi-syllabic lexical stress in unaccented and accented words by younger and older listeners. *Journal of the Acoustical Society of America* 139 (3): 1132–1148.

Gould, Odette N., and Roger A. Dixon. 1993. How we spent our vacation: Collaborative storytelling by young and old adults. *Psychology and Aging* 8 (1): 10–17.

Gould, Odette N., Christopher Osborn, Heather Krein, and Michelle Mortenson. 2002. Collaborative recall in married and unacquainted dyads. *International Journal of Behavioral Development* 26 (1): 36–44.

Gould, Odette N., Cybil Saum, and Jennifer Belter. 2002. Recall and subjective reactions to speaking styles: Does age matter? *Experimental Aging Research* 28 (2): 199–213.

Goulden, Robin, Paul Nation, and John Read. 1990. How large can a receptive vocabulary be? *Applied Linguistics* 11 (4): 341–363.

Goulet, Pierre, Bernadette Ska, and Helen J. Kahn. 1994. Is there a decline in picture naming with advancing age? *Journal of Speech, Language, and Hearing Research* 37 (3): 629–644.

Grant, Patricia, and Rich Hogle. 2017. *Safety and Efficacy of the BrainPort V100 Device in Individuals Blinded by Traumatic Injury*. December 2017. Middleton, WI: WICAB, Inc.

Greenwood, Pamela, and Raja Parasuraman. 2012. *Nurturing the Older Brain and Mind*. Cambridge, MA: MIT Press.

Grosjean, François. 1982. *Life with Two Languages: An Introduction to Bilingualism*. Cambridge, MA: Harvard University Press.

Hargreaves, Ian S., Penny M. Pexman, Lenka Zdrazilova, and Peter Sargious. 2012. How a hobby can shape cognition: Visual word recognition in competitive Scrabble players. *Memory and Cognition* 40 (1): 1–7.

Harnick, Chris. 2013. Liza Minnelli on *Cabaret* memories, *Arrested Development* return and more. *Huffpost*, January 29, 2013. http://www.huffingtonpost.com/2013/01/28/liza-minnelli-cabaret-arrested-development_n_2566747.html.

Harris, Judith Rich. 1998. *The Nurture Assumption: Why Children Turn Out the Way They Do*. New York: Free Press.

Hartshorne, Joshua K., and Laura T. Germine. 2015. When does cognitive functioning peak? The asynchronous rise and fall of different cognitive abilities across the life span. *Psychological Science* 26 (4): 433–443.

Harvard Health Publishing. 2017. Tinnitus: Ringing in the ears and what to do about it. August 16, 2017. http://www.health.harvard.edu/diseases-and-conditions/tinnitus-ringing-in-the-ears-and-what-to-do-about-it.

Hearing Solution Centers. 2015. Tinnitus and *Star Trek*. https://www
.heartulsa.com/blog/tinnitus-star-trek.

Heine, Marilyn K., Beth A. Ober, and Gregory K. Shenaut. 1999. Naturally occurring and experimentally induced tip-of-the-tongue experiences in three adult age groups. *Psychology and Aging* 14 (3): 445–457.

Henry, Julie D., and John R. Crawford. 2004. A meta-analytic review of verbal fluency performance following focal cortical lesions. *Neuropsychology* 18 (2): 284–295.

Hess, Thomas M., Joey T. Hinson, and Elizabeth A. Hodges. 2009. Moderators of and mechanisms underlying stereotype threat effects on older adults' memory performance. *Experimental Aging Research* 35 (2): 153–177.

Hindle, John V., Catherine S. Hurt, David J. Burn, Richard G. Brown, Mike Samuel, Kenneth C. Wilson, and Linda Clare. 2016. The effects of cognitive reserve and lifestyle on cognition and dementia in Parkinson's disease—a longitudinal cohort study. *International Journal of Geriatric Psychiatry* 31 (1): 13–23.

Hoffman, Howard J., and George W. Reed. 2004. Epidemiology of tinnitus. In *Tinnitus: Theory and Management*, ed. James B. Snow, 16–41. Hamilton, Ontario: B. C. Decker.

Holtgraves, Thomas, and Patrick McNamara. 2010. Parkinson's disease and politeness. *Journal of Language and Social Psychology* 29 (2): 178–193.

Hoyte, Ken J., Hiram Brownell, and Arthur Wingfield. 2009. Components of speech prosody and their use in detection of syntactic structure by older adults. *Experimental Aging Research* 35 (1): 129–151.

Huang, Qi, and Jianguo Tang. 2010. Age-related hearing loss or presbycusis. *European Archives of Oto-rhino-laryngology* 267 (8): 1179–1191.

Hughes, Chrissy. 2015. Celebrities with tinnitus. Restored hearing, July 1, 2015. https://restoredhearing.com/2015/07/01/celebrities-with-tinnitus.

Hultsch, David F., Christopher Hertzog, Roger A. Dixon, and Brent J. Small. 1998. *Memory Change in the Aged.* Cambridge: Cambridge University Press.

Hummert, Mary Lee, Jaye L. Shaner, Teri A. Garstka, and Clark Henry. 1988. Communication with older adults: The influence of age stereotypes, context, and communicator age. *Human Communication Research* 25 (1): 124–151.

Hung, Pei-Fang, and Marilyn A. Nippold. 2014. Idiom understanding in adulthood: Examining age-related differences. *Clinical Linguistics and Phonetics* 28 (3): 208–221.

Ianzito, Christina. n.d. Elder orphans: How to plan for aging without a family caregiver. AARP. https://www.aarp.org/caregiving/basics/info-2017 /tips-aging-alone.html.

Ingham, Roger J., Janis C. Ingham, Harald A. Euler, and Katrin Neumann. 2018. Stuttering treatment and brain research in adults: A still unfolding relationship. *Journal of Fluency Disorders* 55:106–119.

Jackson, Eric S., J. Scott Yaruss, Robert W. Quesal, Valerie Terranova, and D. H. Whalen. 2015. Responses of adults who stutter to the anticipation of stuttering. *Journal of Fluency Disorders* 45:38–51.

Jacoby, Larry L. 1988. Memory observed and memory unobserved. In *Remembering Reconsidered: Ecological and Traditional Approaches to the Study of Memory*, ed. Ulric Neisser and Eugene Winograd, 145–192. Cambridge: Cambridge University Press.

Jacoby, Larry L., and Ann Hollingshead. 1990. Reading student essays may be hazardous to your spelling: Effects of reading incorrectly and correctly spelled words. *Canadian Journal of Psychology* 44 (3): 345–358.

James, Lori E., Deborah M. Burke, Ayda Austin, and Erika Hulme. 1998. Production and perception of "verbosity" in younger and older adults. *Psychology and Aging* 13 (3): 355–367.

Jaslow, Ryan. 2012. George Michael wakes from coma with new accent: What's foreign accent syndrome? CBS News, July 19, 2012. https://

www.cbsnews.com/news/george-michael-wakes-from-coma-with-new
-accent-whats-foreign-accent-syndrome.

Jesse, Alexandra, and Esther Janse. 2012. Audiovisual benefit for recognition of speech presented with single-talker noise in older listeners. *Language and Cognitive Processes* 27 (7–8): 1167–1191.

Johnson, Gordon J., Darwin C. Minassian, Robert Alexander Weale, and Sheila K. West. 2003. *The Epidemiology of Eye Disease*. 2nd ed. London: Taylor & Francis.

Johnson, Jeffrey K. 2008. The visualization of the twisted tongue: Portrayals of stuttering in film, television, and comic books. *Journal of Popular Culture* 41 (2): 245–261.

Johnson, Michael. 2006. Ted Allbeury: Respected spy writer who had served as a secret agent in the war and the cold war. *Guardian*, January 2, 2006. https://www.theguardian.com/news/2006/jan/03/guardianobituar ies.booksobituaries.

Johnson, Wendy, Matt McGue, and Ian J. Deary. 2014. Normative cognitive aging. In *Behavior Genetics of Cognition across the Lifespan*, ed. Deborah Finkel and Chandra A. Reynolds, 135–167. New York: Springer.

Kaplan, Edith, Harold Goodglass, and Sandra Weintraub. 1983. *Boston Naming Test*. Philadelphia: Lea & Febiger.

Katz, Stephen, and Toni Calasanti. 2014. Critical perspectives on successful aging: Does it "appeal more than it illuminates"? *Gerontologist* 55 (1): 26–33.

Kaushanskaya, Margarita, and Viorica Marian. 2009. The bilingual advantage in novel word learning. *Psychonomic Bulletin and Review* 16 (4): 705–710.

Kavé, Gitit, and Vered Halamish. 2015. Doubly blessed: Older adults know more vocabulary and know better what they know. *Psychology and Aging* 30 (1): 68–73.

Kemper, Susan. 2015. Memory and executive function: Language production in late life. In *Language Development: The Lifespan Perspective*, ed. Annette Gerstenberg and Anja Voeste, 59–76. Amsterdam: John Benjamins.

Kemper, Susan, and Tamara Harden. 1999. Experimentally disentangling what's beneficial about elderspeak from what's not. *Psychology and Aging* 14 (4): 656–670.

Kemper, Susan, Ruth E. Herman, and Chiung-Ju Liu. 2004. Sentence production by young and older adults in controlled contexts. *Journals of Gerontology Series B: Psychological Sciences and Social Sciences* 59 (5): P220–P224.

Kemper, Susan, Donna Kynette, Shannon Rash, Kevin O'Brien, and Richard Sprott. 1989. Life-span changes to adults' language: Effects of memory and genre. *Applied Psycholinguistics* 10 (1): 49–66.

Kemper, Susan, Emily LaBarge, F. Richard Ferraro, Hintat Cheung, Him Cheung, and Martha Storandt. 1993. On the preservation of syntax in Alzheimer's disease: Evidence from written sentences. *Archives of Neurology* 50 (1): 81–86.

Kemper, Susan, Shannon Rash, Donna Kynette, and Suzanne Norman. 1991. Telling stories: The structure of adults' narratives. *European Journal of Cognitive Psychology* 2 (3): 205–228.

Kemper, Susan, and Aaron Sumner. 2001. The structure of verbal abilities in young and older adults. *Psychology and Aging* 16 (2): 312–322.

Kemper, Susan, Marilyn Thompson, and Janet Marquis. 2001. Longitudinal change in language production: Effects of aging and dementia on grammatical complexity and semantic content. *Psychology and Aging* 16 (4): 600–614.

Kern, Margaret L., Johannes C. Eichstaedt, H. Andrew Schwartz, Gregory Park, Lyle H. Ungar, David J. Stillwell, Michal Kosinski, Lukasz Dziurzynski, and Martin E. P. Seligman. 2013. From "Sooo excited!!!" to "So proud": Using language to study development. *Developmental Psychology* 50 (1): 178–188.

Keulen, Stefanie, Jo Verhoeven, Elke De Witte, Louis De Page, Roelien Bastiaanse, and Peter Mariën. 2016. Foreign accent syndrome as a psychogenic disorder: A review. *Frontiers in Human Neuroscience* 10 (168).

Kiziltan, G., and M. A. Akalin. 1996. Stuttering may be a type of action dystonia. *Movement Disorders* 11 (3): 278–282.

Kjelgaard, Margaret M., Debra A. Titone, and Arthur Wingfield. 1999. The influence of prosodic structure on the interpretation of temporary syntactic ambiguity by young and elderly listeners. *Experimental Aging Research* 25 (3): 187–207.

Klinka, Karen. 1994. High-pitched ringing in ears may be wake-up call. *Oklahoman*, August 9, 1994. http://newsok.com/article/2474010.

Klompas, Michelle, and Eleanor Ross. 2004. Life experiences of people who stutter, and the perceived impact of stuttering on quality of life: Personal accounts of South African individuals. *Journal of Fluency Disorders* 29 (4): 275–305.

Kong, Debra P. 2010. How old are traditionally published first-time authors? *The Write Type: Multi-author Musings*, December 5, 2010. http://writetype.blogspot.com/2010/12/how-old-are-traditionally-published.html.

Konnikova, Maria. 2016. How to beat writer's block. *New Yorker*, March 11, 2016.

Kousaie, Shanna, and Natalie A. Phillips. 2012. Ageing and bilingualism: Absence of a "bilingual advantage" in Stroop interference in a nonimmigrant sample. *Quarterly Journal of Experimental Psychology* 65 (2): 356–369.

Kray, Jutta, and Ulman Lindenberger. Adult age differences in task switching. 2000. *Psychology and Aging* 15 (1): 126–147.

Kreuz, Roger, and Richard Roberts. 2017. *Getting Through: The Pleasures and Perils of Cross-Cultural Communication*. Cambridge, MA: MIT Press.

Kunkel, Thomas. 2015. What exactly was Joseph Mitchell doing all those years at the *New Yorker*? *Publishers Weekly*, April 3, 2015. http://www

.publishersweekly.com/pw/by-topic/industry-news/tip-sheet/article
/66086-what-exactly-was-joseph-mitchell-doing-all-those-years-at-the
-new-yorker.html.

Kwong See, Sheree T., Hunter G. Hoffman, and Tammy L. Wood. 2001. Perceptions of an old female eyewitness: Is the older eyewitness believable? *Psychology and Aging* 16 (2): 346–350.

Lacey, E. H., X. Jiang, R. B. Friedman, S. F. Snider, L. C. Parra, Y. Huang, and P. E. Turkeltaub. 2015. Transcranial direct current stimulation for pure alexia: Effects on brain and behavior. *Brain Stimulation: Basic, Translational, and Clinical Research in Neuromodulation* 8 (2): 305–307.

Lancashire, Ian. 2015. Vocabulary and dementia in six novelists. In *Language Development: The Lifespan Perspective*, ed. Annette Gerstenberg and Anja Voeste, 7–107. Amsterdam: John Benjamins.

Lane, Zac, Adam Singer, David Roffwarg, and Erick Messias. 2010. Differentiating psychosis versus fluent aphasia. *Clinical Schizophrenia and Related Psychoses* 4 (4): 258–261.

Lansberg, Maarten G., Erich Bluhmki, and Vincent N. Thijs. 2009. Efficacy and safety of tissue plasminogen activator 3 to 4.5 hours after acute ischemic stroke: A meta-analysis. *Stroke* 40 (7): 2438–2441.

Larson, Eric B., Kristine Yaffe, and Kenneth M. Langa. 2013. New insights into the dementia epidemic. *New England Journal of Medicine* 369 (24): 2275–2277.

Lazarus, Ben. 2015. Why Joseph Mitchell stopped writing. *New Republic*, May 1, 2015. https://newrepublic.com/article/121690/thomas-kunkels -man-profile-joseph-mitchell-new-yorker.

Le, Xuan, Ian Lancashire, Graeme Hirst, and Regina Jokel. 2011. Longitudinal detection of dementia through lexical and syntactic changes in writing: A case study of three British novelists. *Literary and Linguistic Computing* 26 (4): 435–461.

Leithauser, Brad. 1996. The good servant. *New York Times*, January 7, 1996. http://www.nytimes.com/books/98/12/20/specials/murdoch-dilemma .html.

Leland, John. 2008. In "Sweetie" and "Dear," a hurt for the elderly. *New York Times*, October 6, 2008. http://www.nytimes.com/2008/10/07/us /07aging.html.

Lemonick, Michael D., and Alice Park. 2001. The Nun Study: How one scientist and 678 sisters are helping unlock the secrets of Alzheimer's. *Time* 157 (19): 54–59, 62, 64.

Lenehan, Megan E., Mathew J. Summers, Nichole L. Saunders, Jeffery J. Summers, David D. Ward, Karen Ritchie, and James C. Vickers. 2016. Sending your grandparents to university increases cognitive reserve: The Tasmanian Healthy Brain Project. *Neuropsychology* 30 (5): 525–531.

Levene, John R. 1972. Benjamin Franklin, FRS, Sir Joshua Reynolds, FRS, PRA, Benjamin West, PRA, and the invention of bifocals. *Notes and Records of the Royal Society of London* 27 (1): 141–163.

Levy, Becca R. 2003. Mind matters: Cognitive and physical effects of aging self-stereotypes. *Journals of Gerontology Series B: Psychological Sciences and Social Sciences* 58 (4): P203–P211.

Levy, Becca R., Martin D. Slade, Suzanne R. Kunkel, and Stanislav V. Kasl. 2002. Longevity increased by positive self-perceptions of aging. *Journal of Personality and Social Psychology* 83 (2): 261–270.

Liberman, Mark. 2005. Young men talk like old women. *Language Log*, November 6, 2005. http://itre.cis.upenn.edu/~myl/languagelog/archives /002629.html.

Lien, Mei-Ching, Philip A. Allen, Eric Ruthruff, Jeremy Grabbe, Robert S. McCann, and Roger W. Remington. 2006. Visual word recognition without central attention: Evidence for greater automaticity with advancing age. *Psychology and Aging* 21 (3): 431–447.

Lima, César F., Tiago Alves, Sophie K. Scott, and São Luís Castro. 2014. In the ear of the beholder: How age shapes emotion processing in nonverbal vocalizations. *Emotion* 14 (1): 145–160.

Linetsky, Mikhail, Cibin T. Raghavan, Kaid Johar, Xingjun Fan, Vincent M. Monnier, Abhay R. Vasavada, and Ram H. Nagaraj. 2014. UVA light-excited kynurenines oxidize ascorbate and modify lens proteins through the formation of advanced glycation end products: Implications for human lens aging and cataract formation. *Journal of Biological Chemistry* 289 (24): 17111–17123.

LitRejections. n.d. Best-sellers initially rejected. http://www.litrejections .com/best-sellers-initially-rejected.

Long, Camilla. 2010. Martin Amis and the sex war. *Sunday Times*, January 24, 2010.

Lundy, Donna S., Carlos Silva, Roy R. Casiano, F. Ling Lu, and Jun Wu Xue. 1998. Cause of hoarseness in elderly patients. *Otolaryngology—Head and Neck Surgery* 118 (4): 481–485.

Lust, Barbara, Suzanne Flynn, Janet Cohen Sherman, James Gair, Charles R. Henderson, Claire Cordella, Jordan Whitlock, et al. 2015. Reversing Ribot: Does regression hold in language of prodromal Alzheimer's disease? *Brain and Language* 143:1–10.

Luxemberg, Steve. 2011. "The King's Speech": Brilliant filmmaking, less-than-brilliant history. *Washington Post*, January 28, 2011.

Lyons, Kelly, Susan Kemper, Emily LaBarge, F. Richard Ferraro, David Balota, and Martha Storandt. 1994. Oral language and Alzheimer's disease: A reduction in syntactic complexity. *Aging, Neuropsychology, and Cognition* 1 (4): 271–281.

MacKay, Donald G., Lise Abrams, and Manissa J. Pedroza. 1999. Aging on the input versus output side: Theoretical implications of age-linked asymmetries between detecting versus retrieving orthographic information. *Psychology and Aging* 14 (1): 3–17.

Macnamara, Brooke N., and Andrew R. A. Conway. 2014. Novel evidence in support of the bilingual advantage: Influences of task demands and experience on cognitive control and working memory. *Psychonomic Bulletin and Review* 21 (2): 520–525.

Maltin, Leonard. 2010. *Leonard Maltin's Classic Movie Guide: From the Silent Era through 1965*. 2nd ed. New York: Random House.

Manning, Walter H., Deborah Daily, and Sue Wallace. 1984. Attitude and personality characteristics of older stutterers. *Journal of Fluency Disorders* 9:207–215.

Mar, Raymond A., and Keith Oatley. 2008. The function of fiction is the abstraction and simulation of social experience. *Perspectives on Psychological Science* 3 (3): 173–192.

Mar, Raymond A., Keith Oatley, Jacob Hirsh, Jennifer dela Paz, and Jordan B. Peterson. 2006. Bookworms versus nerds: Exposure to fiction versus non-fiction, divergent associations with social ability, and the simulation of fictional social worlds. *Journal of Research in Personality* 40 (5): 694–712.

Marinus, Eva, Michelle Mostard, Eliane Segers, Teresa M. Schubert, Alison Madelaine, and Kevin Wheldall. 2016. A special font for people with dyslexia: Does it work and, if so, why? *Dyslexia* 22 (3): 233–244.

Martins, Regina Helena Garcia, Tatiana Maria Gonçalvez, Adriana Bueno Benito Pessin, and Anete Branco. 2014. Aging voice: Presbyphonia. *Aging Clinical and Experimental Research* 26 (1): 1–5.

Mather, Mara, and Laura L. Carstensen. 2003. Aging and attentional biases for emotional faces. *Psychological Science* 14 (5): 409–415.

McDougall, Graham J., Carol E. Blixen, and Lee-Jen Suen. 1997. The process and outcome of life review psychotherapy with depressed homebound older adults. *Nursing Research* 46 (5): 277–283.

McDowd, Joan, Lesa Hoffman, Ellen Rozek, Kelly E. Lyons, Rajesh Pahwa, Jeffrey Burns, and Susan Kemper. 2011. Understanding verbal fluency in healthy aging, Alzheimer's disease, and Parkinson's disease. *Neuropsychology* 25 (2): 210–225.

McGrath, Charles. 2018. No longer writing, Philip Roth still has plenty to say. *New York Times*, January 16, 2018.

McLellan, Dennis. 1989. Stutter group pickets over "Wanda" role. *Los Angeles Times*, March 29, 1989. http://articles.latimes.com/1989-03-29 /entertainment/ca-716_1_wanda-insults-people.

Mehta, Sonia. Age-related macular degeneration. 2015. *Primary Care: Clinics in Office Practice* 42 (3): 377–391.

Mergler, Nancy L., Marion Faust, and Michael D. Goldstein. 1985. Storytelling as an age-dependent skill: Oral recall of orally presented stories. *International Journal of Aging and Human Development* 20 (3): 205–228.

Merriam, Sharan B. 1993. Butler's life review: How universal is it? *International Journal of Aging and Human Development* 37 (3): 163–175.

Messer, Rachel H. 2015. Pragmatic language changes during normal aging: Implications for health care. *Healthy Aging and Clinical Care in the Elderly* 7:1–7.

Metzler-Baddeley, Claudia, Amanda Salter, and Roy W. Jones. 2008. The significance of dyslexia screening for the assessment of dementia in older people. *International Journal of Geriatric Psychiatry* 23 (7): 766–768.

Moen, Inger. 1996. Monrad-Krohn's foreign accent syndrome case. In *Classic Cases in Neuropsychology*, ed. Chris Code, Claus-W. Wallesch, Yves Joanette, and André Roch Lecours, 145–156. Hove, UK: Psychology Press.

Monrad-Krohn, Georg Herman. 1947. Dysprosody or altered "melody of language." *Brain* 70:405–415.

Montayre, Jed, Jasmine Montayre, and Sandra Thaggard. 2018. The elder orphan in healthcare settings: An integrative review. *Journal of Population Ageing.* https://doi.org/10.1007/s12062-018-9222-x.

Montepare, Joann, Elissa Koff, Deborah Zaitchik, and Marilyn Albert. 1999. The use of body movements and gestures as cues to emotions in younger and older adults. *Journal of Nonverbal Behavior* 23 (2): 133–152.

Morin, Olivier, and Alberto Acerbi. 2017. Birth of the cool: A two-centuries decline in emotional expression in Anglophone fiction. *Cognition and Emotion* 8:1663–1675.

Morrone, Isabella, Christelle Declercq, Jean-Luc Novella, and Chrystel Besche. 2010. Aging and inhibition processes: The case of metaphor treatment. *Psychology and Aging* 25 (3): 697–701.

Mortensen, Linda, Antje S. Meyer, and Glyn W. Humphreys. 2006. Age-related effects on speech production: A review. *Language and Cognitive Processes* 21 (1–3): 238–290.

Morton, J. Bruce, and Sarah N. Harper. 2007. What did Simon say? Revisiting the bilingual advantage. *Developmental Science* 10 (6): 719–726.

Moscoso del Prado Martín, Fermín. 2017. Vocabulary, grammar, sex, and aging. *Cognitive Science* 41 (4): 950–975.

Mueller, Peter B. 1998. Voice ageism. *Contemporary Issues in Communication Science and Disorders* 25:62–64.

Mumper, Micah L., and Richard J. Gerrig. 2017. Leisure reading and social cognition: A meta-analysis. *Psychology of Aesthetics, Creativity, and the Arts* 11 (1): 109–120.

Murdoch, Iris. 1995. *Jackson's Dilemma*. London: Penguin Books.

Murphy, Dana R., Meredyth Daneman, and Bruce A. Schneider. 2006. Why do older adults have difficulty following conversations? *Psychology and Aging* 21 (1): 49–61.

Nabokov, Vladimir. 1966. *Speak, Memory: An Autobiography Revisited*. New York: Putnam.

Nau, Amy C., Christine Pintar, Aimee Arnoldussen, and Christopher Fisher. 2015. Acquisition of visual perception in blind adults using the BrainPort artificial vision device. *American Journal of Occupational Therapy* 69 (1): 1–8.

NBC News. 2009. Fewer blind Americans learning to use Braille. March 26, 2009. http://www.nbcnews.com/id/29882719/ns/us_news-life/t/fewer-blind-americans-learning-use-braille/#.W0DZuC3GzOY.

Nergård-Nilssen, Trude, and Charles Hulme. 2014. Developmental dyslexia in adults: Behavioural manifestations and cognitive correlates. *Dyslexia* 20 (3): 191–207.

Newsome, Mary R., and Sam Glucksberg. 2002. Older adults filter irrelevant information during metaphor comprehension. *Experimental Aging Research* 28 (3): 253–267.

New Yorker. 2004. Blocked: Why do writers stop writing? June 14, 2004.

Ng, Sik Hung. 1996. Power: An essay in honour of Henri Tajfel. In *Social Groups and Identities: Developing the Legacy of Henri Tajfel*, ed. W. Peter Robinson, 191–214. Oxford: Butterworth-Heinemann.

Nichols, Richard. 1999. Iris Murdoch, novelist and philosopher, is dead. *New York Times*, February 9, 1999. http://www.nytimes.com/learning /general/onthisday/bday/0715.html.

Nicholson, Nicholas R. 2012. A review of social isolation: An important but underassessed condition in older adults. *Journal of Primary Prevention* 33 (2–3): 137–152.

Nickerson, Raymond S., and Marilyn Jager Adams. 1979. Long-term memory for a common object. *Cognitive Psychology* 11 (3): 287–307.

Nippold, Marilyn A., Paige M. Cramond, and Christine Hayward-Mayhew. 2014. Spoken language production in adults: Examining age-related differences in syntactic complexity. *Clinical Linguistics and Phonetics* 28 (3): 195–207.

Nippold, Marilyn A., Linda D. Uhden, and Ilsa E. Schwarz. 1997. Proverb explanation through the lifespan: A developmental study of adolescents and adults. *Journal of Speech, Language, and Hearing Research* 40 (2): 245–253.

Nondahl, David M., Karen J. Cruickshanks, Dayna S. Dalton, Barbara E. K. Klein, Ronald Klein, Carla R. Schubert, Ted S. Tweed, and Terry L. Wiley. 2007. The impact of tinnitus on quality of life in older adults. *Journal of the American Academy of Audiology* 18 (3): 257–266.

Nondahl, David M., Karen J. Cruickshanks, Terry L. Wiley, Ronald Klein, Barbara E. K. Klein, and Ted S. Tweed. 2002. Prevalence and 5-year incidence of tinnitus among older adults: The epidemiology of hearing loss study. *Journal of the American Academy of Audiology* 13 (6): 323–331.

O'Caoimh, Rónán, Suzanne Timmons, and D. William Molloy. 2016. Screening for mild cognitive impairment: Comparison of "MCI specific" screening instruments. *Journal of Alzheimer's Disease* 51 (2): 619–629.

Oller, D. Kimbrough, and Rebecca E. Eilers, eds. 2002. *Language and Literacy in Bilingual Children*. Vol. 2. Clevedon, UK: Multilingual Matters.

Omori, Koichi, David H. Slavit, Ashutosh Kacker, and Stanley M. Blaugrund. 1998. Influence of size and etiology of glottal gap in glottic incompetence dysphonia. *Laryngoscope* 108 (4): 514–518.

Owens, David. 2014. The yips: What's behind the condition that every golfer dreads? *New Yorker*, May 26, 2014. https://www.newyorker.com /magazine/2014/05/26/the-yips.

Owsley, Cynthia, Robert Sekuler, and Dennis Siemsen. 1983. Contrast sensitivity throughout adulthood. *Vision Research* 23 (7): 689–699.

Paap, Kenneth R., and Zachary I. Greenberg. 2013. There is no coherent evidence for a bilingual advantage in executive processing. *Cognitive Psychology* 66 (2): 232–258.

Paap, Kenneth R., Hunter A. Johnson, and Oliver Sawi. 2015. Bilingual advantages in executive functioning either do not exist or are restricted to very specific and undetermined circumstances. *Cortex* 69:265–278.

Patterson, Janet. 2011. Verbal fluency. In *Encyclopedia of Clinical Neuropsychology*, vol. 4, ed. Jeffrey S. Kreutzer, John DeLuca, and Bruce Caplan, 2603–2605. New York: Springer.

Payne, Brennan R., Xuefei Gao, Soo Rim Noh, Carolyn J. Anderson, and Elizabeth A. L. Stine-Morrow. 2012. The effects of print exposure on sentence processing and memory in older adults: Evidence for efficiency and reserve. *Aging, Neuropsychology, and Cognition* 19 (1–2): 122–149.

Pennebaker, James W. 1997a. *Opening Up: The Healing Power of Expressing Emotions*. 2nd ed. New York: Guilford Press.

Pennebaker, James W. 1997b. Writing about emotional experiences as a therapeutic process. *Psychological Science* 8 (3): 162–166.

Pennebaker, James W. 2011. *The Secret Life of Pronouns: What Our Words Say about Us*. New York: Bloomsbury Press.

Pennebaker, James W., Steven D. Barger, and John Tiebout. 1989. Disclosure of traumas and health among Holocaust survivors. *Psychosomatic Medicine* 51 (5): 577–589.

Pennebaker, James W., Janice K. Kiecolt-Glaser, and Ronald Glaser. 1988. Disclosure of traumas and immune function: Health implications for psychotherapy. *Journal of Consulting and Clinical Psychology* 56 (2): 239–245.

Pennebaker, James W., Tracy J. Mayne, and Martha E. Francis. 1997. Linguistic predictors of adaptive bereavement. *Journal of Personality and Social Psychology* 72 (4): 863–871.

Pennebaker, James W., and Lori D. Stone. 2003. Words of wisdom: Language use over the life span. *Journal of Personality and Social Psychology* 85 (2): 291–301.

Peterson, Robin L., and Bruce F. Pennington. 2015. Developmental dyslexia. *Annual Review of Clinical Psychology* 11:283–307.

Phillips, Louise H., Roy Allen, Rebecca Bull, Alexandra Hering, Matthias Kliegel, and Shelley Channon. 2015. Older adults have difficulty in decoding sarcasm. *Developmental Psychology* 51 (12): 1840–1852.

Phillips, Susan L., Sandra Gordon-Salant, Peter J. Fitzgibbons, and Grace Yeni-Komshian. 2000. Frequency and temporal resolution in elderly listeners with good and poor word recognition. *Journal of Speech, Language, and Hearing Research* 43 (1): 217–228.

Pichora-Fuller, M. Kathleen, and Harry Levitt. 2012. Speech comprehension training and auditory and cognitive processing in older adults. *American Journal of Audiology* 21 (2): 351–357.

Pichora-Fuller, M. Kathleen, Bruce A. Schneider, and Meredyth Daneman. 1995. How young and old adults listen to and remember speech in noise. *Journal of the Acoustical Society of America* 97 (1): 593–608.

Polat, Uri, Clifton Schor, Jian-Liang Tong, Ativ Zomet, Maria Lev, Oren Yehezkel, Anna Sterkin, and Dennis M. Levi. 2012. Training the brain to overcome the effect of aging on the human eye. *Scientific Reports* 2:1–6.

Pratt, Michael W., and Susan L. Robins. 1991. That's the way it was: Age differences in the structure and quality of adults' personal narratives. *Discourse Processes* 14 (1): 73–85.

Prensky, Marc. 2001. Digital natives, digital immigrants, part 1. *On the Horizon* 9 (5): 1–6.

Pugliese, Michael, Tim Ramsay, Dylan Johnson, and Dar Dowlatshahi. 2018. Mobile tablet-based therapies following stroke: A systematic scoping review of administrative methods and patient experiences. *PloS One* 13 (1): e0191566.

Pushkar Gold, Dolores, David Andres, Tannis Arbuckle, and Connie Zieren. 1993. Off-target verbosity and talkativeness in elderly people. *Canadian Journal on Aging* 12 (1): 67–77.

Pushkar Gold, Dolores, and Tannis Y. Arbuckle. 1995. A longitudinal study of off-target verbosity. *Journals of Gerontology Series B: Psychological Sciences and Social Sciences* 50 (6): 307–315.

Ramscar, Michael, Peter Hendrix, Cyrus Shaoul, Petar Milin, and Harald Baayen. 2014. The myth of cognitive decline: Non-linear dynamics of lifelong learning. *Topics in Cognitive Science* 6 (1): 5–42.

Randolph, Christopher, Amy E. Lansing, Robert J. Ivnik, C. Munro Cullum, and Bruce P. Hermann. 1999. Determinants of confrontation naming performance. *Archives of Clinical Neuropsychology* 14 (6): 489–496.

Rao, Gullapalli N., Rohit Khanna, and Abhishek Payal. 2011. The global burden of cataract. *Current Opinion in Ophthalmology* 22 (1): 4–9.

Reed, Andrew E., Larry Chan, and Joseph A. Mikels. 2014. Meta-analysis of the age-related positivity effect: Age differences in preferences for positive over negative information. *Psychology and Aging* 29 (1): 1–15.

Reker, Gary T., James E. Birren, and Cheryl Svensson. 2014. Self-aspect reconstruction through guided autobiography: Exploring underlying processes. *International Journal of Reminiscence and Life Review* 2 (1): 1–15.

Riley, Kathryn P., David A. Snowdon, Mark F. Desrosiers, and William R. Markesbery. 2005. Early life linguistic ability, late life cognitive function, and neuropathology: Findings from the Nun Study. *Neurobiology of Aging* 26 (3): 341–347.

Roberts, Richard M., and Roger J. Kreuz. 1993. Nonstandard discourse and its coherence. *Discourse Processes* 16 (4): 451–464.

Roberts, Richard M., and Roger J. Kreuz. 1994. Why do people use figurative language? *Psychological Science* 5 (3): 159–163.

Roberts, Richard, and Roger Kreuz. 2015. *Becoming Fluent: How Cognitive Science Can Help Adults Learn a Foreign Language*. Cambridge, MA: MIT Press.

Robinson, Martin. 2017. "The moment I died": Discworld author Terry Pratchett revealed his struggles with a "haze of Alzheimer's" in his unfinished autobiography. *Daily Mail*, February 3, 2017. http://www.dailymail.co.uk/news/article-4187146/Terry-Pratchett-reveals-struggles-haze-Alzheimer-s.html.

Rohrer, Jonathan D., Martin N. Rossor, and Jason D. Warren. 2009. Neologistic jargon aphasia and agraphia in primary progressive aphasia. *Journal of the Neurological Sciences* 277 (1): 155–159.

Rose, Mike. 1984. *Writer's Block: The Cognitive Dimension*. Carbondale, IL: Southern Illinois University Press.

Ruffman, Ted, Julie D. Henry, Vicki Livingstone, and Louise H. Phillips. 2008. A meta-analytic review of emotion recognition and aging: Implications for neuropsychological models of aging. *Neuroscience and Biobehavioral Reviews* 32 (4): 863–881.

Ruscher, Janet B., and Megan M. Hurley. 2000. Off-target verbosity evokes negative stereotypes of older adults. *Journal of Language and Social Psychology* 19 (1): 141–149.

Russell, Alex, Richard J. Stevenson, and Anina N. Rich. 2015. Chocolate smells pink and stripy: Exploring olfactory-visual synesthesia. *Cognitive Neuroscience* 6 (2–3): 77–88.

Ryalls, J., and I. Reinvang. 1985. Some further notes on Monrad-Krohn's case study of foreign accent syndrome. *Folia Phoniatrica et Logopaedica* 37 (3–4): 160–162.

Ryan, Camille L., and Kurt Bauman. 2016. Educational attainment in the United States: 2015. United States Census, Current Population Reports, March 2016. https://www.census.gov/content/dam/Census/library/pub lications/2016/demo/p20-578.pdf.

Ryu, Chang Hwan, Seungbong Han, Moo-Song Lee, Sang Yoon Kim, Soon Yuhl Nam, Jong-Lyel Roh, Junsun Ryu, Yuh-S. Jung, and Seung-Ho Choi. 2015. Voice changes in elderly adults: Prevalence and the effect of social, behavioral, and health status on voice quality. *Journal of the American Geriatrics Society* 63 (8): 1608–1614.

Salovey, Peter, and Matthew D. Haar. 1990. The efficacy of cognitive-behavior therapy and writing process training for alleviating writing anxiety. *Cognitive Therapy and Research* 14 (5): 515–528.

Salovey, Peter, and John D. Mayer. 1990. Emotional intelligence. *Imagination, Cognition and Personality* 9 (3): 185–211.

Salthouse, Timothy A. 1996. The processing-speed theory of adult age differences in cognition. *Psychological Review* 103 (3): 403–428.

Sankoff, Gillian. Language change across the lifespan. 2018. *Annual Review of Linguistics* 4 (1): 297–316.

Sarabia-Cobo, Carmen María, María José Navas, Heiner Ellgring, and Beatriz García-Rodríguez. 2016. Skilful communication: Emotional facial expressions recognition in very old adults. *International Journal of Nursing Studies* 54:104–111.

Schachter, Stanley, Nicholas Christenfeld, Bernard Ravina, and Frances Bilous. 1991. Speech disfluency and the structure of knowledge. *Journal of Personality and Social Psychology* 60 (3): 362–367.

Schjetnan, Andrea Gomez Palacio, Jamshid Faraji, Gerlinde A. Metz, Masami Tatsuno, and Artur Luczak. 2013. Transcranial direct current stimulation in stroke rehabilitation: A review of recent advancements. *Stroke Research and Treatment*, article ID 170256.

Schmiedt, Richard A. 2010. The physiology of cochlear presbycusis. In *The Aging Auditory System*, ed. Sandra Gordon-Salant, Robert D. Frisina, Arthur N. Popper, and Richard R. Fay, 9–38. New York: Springer.

Schmitter-Edgecombe, Maureen, M. Vesneski, and D. W. R. Jones. 2000. Aging and word-finding: A comparison of spontaneous and constrained naming tests. *Archives of Clinical Neuropsychology* 15 (6): 479–493.

Schubotz, Louise, Judith Holler, and Asli Özyürek. September 2015. Age-related differences in multi-modal audience design: Young, but not old speakers, adapt speech and gestures to their addressee's knowledge. In *Proceedings of the 4th GESPIN—Gesture and Speech in Interaction*, 211–216. Nantes, France.

Schwartz, Bennett L. 2002. *Tip-of-the-Tongue States: Phenomenology, Mechanism, and Lexical Retrieval*. Mahwah, NJ: Erlbaum.

Schwartz, Bennett L., and Leslie D. Frazier. 2005. Tip-of-the-tongue states and aging: Contrasting psycholinguistic and metacognitive perspectives. *Journal of General Psychology* 132 (4): 377–391.

Schwartz, Bennett L., and Janet Metcalfe. 2011. Tip-of-the-tongue (TOT) states: Retrieval, behavior, and experience. *Memory and Cognition* 39 (5): 737–749.

Searl, Jeffrey P., Rodney M. Gabel, and J. Steven Fulks. 2002. Speech disfluency in centenarians. *Journal of Communication Disorders* 35 (5): 383–392.

Segaert, Katrien, S. J. E. Lucas, C. V. Burley, Pieter Segaert, A. E. Milner, M. Ryan, and L. Wheeldon. 2018. Higher physical fitness levels are associated with less language decline in healthy ageing. *Scientific Reports* 8 (6715): 1–10.

Shadden, Barbara B. 1997. Discourse behaviors in older adults. *Seminars in Speech and Language* 18 (2): 143–157.

Shafto, Meredith A., Lori E. James, Lise Abrams, and Lorraine K. Tyler. 2018. Age-related increases in verbal knowledge are not associated with word finding problems in the Cam-CAN cohort: What you know won't hurt you. *Journals of Gerontology Series B: Psychological Sciences and Social Sciences* 72 (1): 100–106.

Shafto, Meredith A., and Lorraine K. Tyler. 2014. Language in the aging brain: The network dynamics of cognitive decline and preservation. *Science* 346 (6209): 583–587.

Sheehy, Gail. 2000. The accidental candidate. *Vanity Fair*, October 2000.

Simner, Julia. 2007. Beyond perception: Synaesthesia as a psycholinguistic phenomenon. *Trends in Cognitive Sciences* 11 (1): 23–29.

Simner, Julia. 2012. Defining synaesthesia. *British Journal of Psychology* 103 (1): 1–15.

Simner, Julia, Alberta Ipser, Rebecca Smees, and James Alvarez. 201). Does synaesthesia age? Changes in the quality and consistency of synaesthetic associations. *Neuropsychologia* 106:407–416.

Simner, Julia, Catherine Mulvenna, Noam Sagiv, Elias Tsakanikos, Sarah A. Witherby, Christine Fraser, Kirsten Scott, and Jamie Ward. 2006. Synaesthesia: The prevalence of atypical cross-modal experiences. *Perception* 35 (8): 1024–1033.

Simons, Daniel J., Walter R. Boot, Neil Charness, Susan E. Gathercole, Christopher F. Chabris, David Z. Hambrick, and Elizabeth A. L. Stine-Morrow. 2016. Do "brain-training" programs work? *Psychological Science in the Public Interest* 17 (3): 103–186.

Slessor, Gillian, Louise H. Phillips, and Rebecca Bull. 2008. Age-related declines in basic social perception: Evidence from tasks assessing eye-gaze processing. *Psychology and Aging* 23 (4): 812–842.

Small, Brent J., Roger A. Dixon, and John J. McArdle. 2011. Tracking cognition-health changes from 55 to 95 years of age. *Journals of Gerontology Series B: Psychological Sciences and Social Sciences* 66 (suppl. 1): i153–i161.

Smith-Spark, James H., Adam P. Ziecik, and Christopher Sterling. 2016. Self-reports of increased prospective and retrospective memory problems in adults with developmental dyslexia. *Dyslexia* 22 (3): 245–262.

Smyth, Joshua M., Arthur A. Stone, Adam Hurewitz, and Alan Kaell. 1999. Effects of writing about stressful experiences on symptom reduction in patients with asthma or rheumatoid arthritis: A randomized trial. *JAMA* 281 (14): 1304–1309.

Smyth, Joshua M., Nicole True, and Joy Souto. 2001. Effects of writing about traumatic experiences: The necessity for narrative structuring. *Journal of Social and Clinical Psychology* 20 (2): 161–172.

Snowdon, David A. 1997. Aging and Alzheimer's disease: Lessons from the Nun Study. *Gerontologist* 37 (2): 150–156.

Snowdon, David. 2001. *Aging with Grace: What the Nun Study Teaches Us about Leading Longer, Healthier, and More Meaningful Lives*. New York: Bantam Books.

Snowdon, David A., Lydia H. Greiner, and William R. Markesbery. 2000. Linguistic ability in early life and the neuropathology of Alzheimer's disease and cerebrovascular disease: Findings from the Nun Study. *Annals of the New York Academy of Sciences* 903 (1): 34–38.

Snowdon, David A., Susan J. Kemper, James A. Mortimer, Lydia H. Greiner, David R. Wekstein, and William R. Markesbery. 1996. Linguistic ability in early life and cognitive function and Alzheimer's disease in late life: Findings from the Nun Study. *JAMA* 275 (7): 528–532.

Stanford News. 2005. "You've got to find what you love," Jobs says. June 14, 2005. https://news.stanford.edu/2005/06/14/jobs-061505.

Stanley, Jennifer Tehan, and Fredda Blanchard-Fields. 2008. Challenges older adults face in detecting deceit: The role of emotion recognition. *Psychology and Aging* 23 (1): 24–32.

Starrfelt, Randi, and Marlene Behrmann. 2011. Number reading in pure alexia—a review. *Neuropsychologia* 49 (9): 2283–2298.

Steele, Claude M., and Joshua Aronson. 1995. Stereotype threat and the intellectual test performance of African Americans. *Journal of Personality and Social Psychology* 69 (5): 797–811.

Stern, Yaakov. 2012. Cognitive reserve in ageing and Alzheimer's disease. *Lancet Neurology* 11 (11): 1006–1012.

Sterrett, David, Jennifer Titus, Jennifer K. Benz, and Liz Kantor. 2017. Perceptions of aging during each decade of life after 30. West Health Institute/NORC Survey on Aging in America.

Stilwell, Becca L., Rebecca M. Dow, Carolien Lamers, and Robert T. Woods. 2016. Language changes in bilingual individuals with Alzheimer's disease. *International Journal of Language and Communication Disorders* 51 (2): 113–127.

Stine-Morrow, Elizabeth A. L., Matthew C. Shake, and Soo Rim Noh. 2010. Language and communication. In *Aging in America*, vol. 1, ed. John C. Cavanaugh and Christine K. Cavanaugh, 56–78. Santa Barbara, CA: Praeger Perspectives.

STR Staff. 2018. Fame won't stop the ringing—20 celebrities with tinnitus. January 28, 2018. http://www.stoptheringing.org/fame-wont-stop-the -ringing-20-celebrities-with-tinnitus.

Strenk, Susan A., Lawrence M. Strenk, and Jane F. Koretz. 2005. The mechanism of presbyopia. *Progress in Retinal and Eye Research* 24 (3): 379–393.

Stuttering Foundation. 2015. Annie Glenn. June 17, 2015. https://www .stutteringhelp.org/content/annie-glenn.

Sundet, Jon Martin, Dag G. Barlaug, and Tore M. Torjussen. 2004. The end of the Flynn effect? A study of secular trends in mean intelligence test scores of Norwegian conscripts during half a century. *Intelligence* 32 (4): 349–362.

Suzuki, Atsunobu, Takahiro Hoshino, Kazuo Shigemasu, and Mitsuru Kawamura. 2007. Decline or improvement? Age-related differences in facial expression recognition. *Biological Psychology* 74 (1): 75–84.

Swagerman, Suzanne C., Elsje Van Bergen, Conor Dolan, Eco J. C. de Geus, Marinka M. G. Koenis, Hilleke E. Hulshoff Pol, and Dorret I. Boomsma. 2015. Genetic transmission of reading ability. *Brain and Language* 172:3–8.

Sword, Helen. 2017. *Air and Light and Time and Space: How Successful Academics Write.* Cambridge, MA: Harvard University Press.

Tanner, Kathleen. 2009. Adult dyslexia and the "conundrum of failure." *Disability and Society* 24 (6): 785–797.

Teasdale, Thomas W., and David R. Owen. 2008. Secular declines in cognitive test scores: A reversal of the Flynn effect. *Intelligence* 36 (2): 121–126.

Theodoroff, Sarah M., M. Samantha Lewis, Robert L. Folmer, James A. Henry, and Kathleen F. Carlson. 2015. Hearing impairment and tinnitus: Prevalence, risk factors, and outcomes in US service members and veterans deployed to the Iraq and Afghanistan wars. *Epidemiologic Reviews* 37 (1): 71–85.

Todd, Zazie. 2008. Talking about books: A reading group study. *Psychology of Aesthetics, Creativity, and the Arts* 2 (4): 256–263.

Tombaugh, Tom N., Jean Kozak, and Laura Rees. 1999. Normative data stratified by age and education for two measures of verbal fluency: FAS and animal naming. *Archives of Clinical Neuropsychology* 14 (2): 167–177.

Trahan, Lisa H., Karla K. Stuebing, Jack M. Fletcher, and Merrill Hiscock. 2014. The Flynn effect: A meta-analysis. *Psychological Bulletin* 140 (5): 1332–1360.

Trunk, Dunja L., and Lise Abrams. 2009. Do younger and older adults' communicative goals influence off-topic speech in autobiographical narratives? *Psychology and Aging* 24 (2): 324–377.

Truscott, Roger J. W., and Xiangjia Zhu. 2010. Presbyopia and cataract: A question of heat and time. *Progress in Retinal and Eye Research* 29 (6): 487–499.

Tumanova, Victoria, Edward G. Conture, E. Warren Lambert, and Tedra A. Walden. 2014. Speech disfluencies of preschool-age children who do and do not stutter. *Journal of Communication Disorders* 49:25–41.

Uekermann, Jennifer, Patrizia Thoma, and Irene Daum. 2008. Proverb interpretation changes in aging. *Brain and Cognition* 67 (1): 51–57.

Ulatowska, Hanna K., Sandra Bond Chapman, Amy Peterson Highley, and Jacqueline Prince. 1998. Discourse in healthy old-elderly adults: A longitudinal study. *Aphasiology* 12 (7–8): 619–633.

US Census Bureau. 2011. *Statistical Abstract of the United States*. Table 53: Languages spoken at home by language, 2008. https://www2.census.gov /library/publications/2010/compendia/statab/130ed/tables/11s0053.pdf.

Van Lancker-Sidtis, Diana, and Gail Rallon. 2004. Tracking the incidence of formulaic expressions in everyday speech: Methods for classification and verification. *Language and Communication* 24 (3): 207–240.

Van Vuuren, Sarel, and Leora R. Cherney. 2014. A virtual therapist for speech and language therapy. In *Intelligent Virtual Agents*, ed. Timothy Bickmore, Stacy Marsella, and Candace Sidner, 438–448. New York: Springer.

Veiel, Lori L., Martha Storandt, and Richard A. Abrams. 2006. Visual search for change in older adults. *Psychology and Aging* 21 (4): 754–762.

Verdonck–de Leeuw, Irma M., and Hans F. Mahieu. 2004. Vocal aging and the impact on daily life: A longitudinal study. *Journal of Voice* 18 (2): 193–202.

Verhoeven, Jo, Guy De Pauw, Michèle Pettinato, Allen Hirson, John Van Borsel, and Peter Mariën. 2013. Accent attribution in speakers with foreign accent syndrome. *Journal of Communication Disorders* 46 (2): 156–168.

Vogel, Ineke, Hans Verschuure, Catharina P. B. van der Ploeg, Johannes Brug, and Hein Raat. 2009. Adolescents and MP3 players: Too many risks, too few precautions. *Pediatrics* 123 (6): e953–e958.

Watila, M. M., and S. A. Balarabe. 2015. Factors predicting post-stroke aphasia recovery. *Journal of the Neurological Sciences* 352 (1): 12–18.

Watson, Marcus R., Kathleen Akins, Chris Spiker, Lyle Crawford, and James T. Enns. 2014. Synesthesia and learning: A critical review and novel theory. *Frontiers in Human Neuroscience* 8 (98): 1–15.

Watson, Marcus R., Jan Chromý, Lyle Crawford, David M. Eagleman, James T. Enns, and Kathleen A. Akins. 2017. The prevalence of synaesthesia depends on early language learning. *Consciousness and Cognition* 48:212–231.

Watt, Lisa M., and Paul T. P. Wong. 1991. A taxonomy of reminiscence and therapeutic implications. *Journal of Gerontological Social Work* 16 (1–2): 37–57.

Weisman, Steven R. 1983. Reagan begins to wear a hearing aid in public. *New York Times*, September 8, 1983. http://www.nytimes.com/1983/09/08/us/reagan-begins-to-wear-a-hearing-aid-in-public.html.

Wery, Jessica J., and Jennifer A. Diliberto. 2017. The effect of a specialized dyslexia font, OpenDyslexic, on reading rate and accuracy. *Annals of Dyslexia* 67 (2): 114–127.

West, Robert, and Claude Alain. 2000. Age-related decline in inhibitory control contributes to the increased Stroop effect observed in older adults. *Psychophysiology* 37 (2): 179–189.

Westbury, Chris, and Debra Titone. 2011. Idiom literality judgments in younger and older adults: Age-related effects in resolving semantic interference. *Psychology and Aging* 26 (2): 467–474.

Westerhof, Gerben J., Ernst Bohlmeijer, and Jeffrey Dean Webster. 2010. Reminiscence and mental health: A review of recent progress in theory, research and interventions. *Ageing and Society* 30 (4): 697–721.

Weyerman, Jessica J., Cassidy Rose, and Maria C. Norton. 2017. Personal journal keeping and linguistic complexity predict late-life dementia risk: The Cache County journal pilot study. *Journals of Gerontology Series B: Psychological Sciences and Social Sciences* 72 (6): 991–995.

White, Anne, Gert Storms, Barbara C. Malt, and Steven Verheyen. 2018. Mind the generation gap: Differences between young and old in everyday lexical categories. *Journal of Memory and Language* 98:12–25.

Whiteside, Douglas M., Tammy Kealey, Matthew Semla, Hien Luu, Linda Rice, Michael R. Basso, and Brad Roper. 2016. Verbal fluency: Language or executive function measure? *Applied Neuropsychology: Adult* 23 (1): 29–34.

Williams, Angie, and Howard Giles. 1996. Intergenerational conversations: Young adults' retrospective accounts. *Human Communication Research* 23 (2): 220–250.

Williams, Kristine N., Ruth Herman, Byron Gajewski, and Kristel Wilson. 2009. Elderspeak communication: Impact on dementia care. *American Journal of Alzheimer's Disease and Other Dementias* 24 (1): 11–20.

Williams, Kristine, Frederick Holmes, Susan Kemper, and Janet Marquis. 2003. Written language clues to cognitive changes of aging: An analysis of the letters of King James VI/I. *Journals of Gerontology Series B: Psychological Sciences and Social Sciences* 58 (1): P42–P44.

Williams, Kristine N., and Susan Kemper. 2010. Interventions to reduce cognitive decline in aging. *Journal of Psychosocial Nursing and Mental Health Services* 48 (5): 42–51.

Williams, Kristine, Susan Kemper, and Mary L. Hummert. 2003. Improving nursing home communication: An intervention to reduce elderspeak. *Gerontologist* 43 (2): 242–247.

Wilson, Anna J., Stuart G. Andrewes, Helena Struthers, Victoria M. Rowe, Rajna Bogdanovic, and Karen E. Waldie. 2015. Dyscalculia and dyslexia in adults: Cognitive bases of comorbidity. *Learning and Individual Differences* 37:118–132.

Wilson, Timothy D. 2002. *Strangers to Ourselves: Discovering the Adaptive Unconscious*. Cambridge, MA: Belknap Press.

Wingfield, Arthur A., and Elizabeth A. L. Stine-Morrow. 2000. Language and speech. In *Handbook of Cognitive Aging*, 2nd ed., ed. Fergus I. M. Craik and Timothy A. Salthouse, 359–416. Mahwah, NJ: Erlbaum.

Wong, Paul T., and Lisa M. Watt. 1991. What types of reminiscence are associated with successful aging? *Psychology and Aging* 6 (2): 272–279.

Wray, Allison. 2002. *Formulaic Language and the Lexicon*. Cambridge: Cambridge University Press.

Zarrelli, Natalie. 2016. The neurologists who fought Alzheimer's by studying nuns' brains. *Atlas Obscura*, March 24, 2016. http://www.atlasobscura.com/articles/the-neurologists-who-fought-alzheimers-by-studying-nuns-brains.

Zec, Ronald F., Nicole R. Burkett, Stephen J. Markwell, and Deb L. Larsen. 2007. A cross-sectional study of the effects of age, education, and gender on the Boston Naming Test. *Clinical Neuropsychologist* 21 (4): 587–616.

Zechmeister, Eugene B., Andrea M. Chronis, William L. Cull, Catherine A. D'Anna, and Noreen A. Healy. 1995. Growth of a functionally important lexicon. *Journal of Reading Behavior* 27 (2): 201–212.

Zhan, Weihai, Karen J. Cruickshanks, Barbara E. K. Klein, Ronald Klein, Guan-Hua Huang, James S. Pankow, Ronald E. Gangnon, and Theodore S. Tweed. 2009. Generational differences in the prevalence of hearing impairment in older adults. *American Journal of Epidemiology* 171 (2): 260–266.

Zickuhr, Kathryn, Lee Rainie, Kristen Purcell, Mary Madden, and Joanna Brenner. 2012. Younger Americans' reading and library habits. *Pew Internet and American Life Project*, October 23, 2012. http://libraries.pewinternet .org/2012/10/23/younger-americans-reading-and-library-habits.

Ziegler, Johannes C., Conrad Perry, Anna Ma-Wyatt, Diana Ladner, and Gerd Schulte-Körne. 2013. Developmental dyslexia in different languages: Language-specific or universal? *Journal of Experimental Child Psychology* 86 (3): 169–193.

Zielinski, David, ed. 2013. *Master Presenter: Lessons from the World's Top Experts on Becoming a More Influential Speaker.* San Francisco: Wiley.

Index

Note: fictional characters are listed by first name.

About the Authors

Roger Kreuz has been a professor of psychology for thirty years. After studying psychology and linguistics at the University of Toledo, he earned his master's and doctoral degrees in experimental psychology at Princeton University and was a postdoctoral researcher in cognitive gerontology at Duke University. He has conducted research and published on diverse topics in the psychology of language, but primarily in the areas of text and discourse processing and figurative language. His research has been funded by the National Science Foundation and the Office of Naval Research. He has coedited two books: *Empirical Approaches to Literature and Aesthetics* and *Social and Cognitive Approaches to Interpersonal Communication*. He currently serves as an associate dean in the College of Arts and Sciences at the University of Memphis.

Richard Roberts's educational background spans the speech and hearing sciences, clinical psychology, and experimental psychology. After earning his doctorate at the University of Memphis, he was a postdoctoral researcher at the National Center for Health Statistics. He spent twelve years teaching psychology in Europe and Asia with the University of Maryland University College. Since 2006 he has been a US diplomat, serving at embassies in Niger, Japan, South Korea, and Mongolia. He has also studied French, Japanese, and Korean at the US Department of State's Foreign Service Institute. He is currently the public affairs officer for the US Consulate General in Naha, Okinawa, Japan.

Together, Roger and Richard have published research articles and book chapters on discourse processing and pragmatics. They are also the authors of *Becoming Fluent: How Cognitive Science Can Help Adults Learn a Foreign Language* (MIT Press, 2015) and *Getting Through: The Perils and Pleasures of Cross-Cultural Communication* (MIT Press, 2017).

About the Illustrator

Enkhtur Bayarsaikhan is a character designer and 3-D artist who resides in Ulaanbaatar, Mongolia. He is the illustrator for *Getting Through: The Perils and Pleasures of Cross-Cultural Communication* (MIT Press, 2017) and has also illustrated a book of Mongolian folktales and a book aimed at helping Mongolians learn English. His work has won several awards.